Eustasy: The Historical Ups and Downs of a Major Geological Concept

VIEW OF THE TEMPLE OF SERAPIS AT PUZZUOLI IN 1836.

See Vol. II. Chap. xxx.

Frontispiece. The Temple of Jupiter Serapis at Pozzuoli, Italy, one of the most celebrated evidences of relative changes of land and sea level that has occurred during recorded history. Together with evidence from Scandinavia, Serapis helped to focus 19th century attention upon the issue of eustatic versus tectonic causes of such changes. This drawing by Whitney Jocelyn Annin made in 1836 was reproduced by Charles Lyell as the Frontispiece for the later editions of *Principles of Geology*, a different view having been used for early editions. The clearly visible upper limit of holes drilled in the pillars by rock-boring bivalves records local sinking of the crust and submergence of the temple to a depth of 7 m during a span of approximately 1,400 yr. Two more periods of lesser subsidence and uplift have occurred since 1750. (From C. Lyell, 1872, *Principles of geology,* 11th edition: London, John Murray, v. 1, 671 p.)

Geological Society of America
Memoir 180

Eustasy: The Historical Ups and Downs of a Major Geological Concept

Edited by

Robert H. Dott, Jr.
Department of Geology and Geophysics
University of Wisconsin
Madison, Wisconsin 53706

1992

Published by The Geological Society of America, Inc.
3300 Penrose Place, P.O. Box 9140, Boulder, Colorado 80301

GSA Books Science Editor Richard A. Hoppin

Printed in U.S.A.

Library of Congress Cataloging-in-Publication Data
Eustasy : the historical ups and downs of a major geological concept /
   edited by Robert H. Dott, Jr.
        p.   cm. — (Memoir / Geological Society of America ; 180)
     Most papers from a symposium presented by the History Division of
the Geological Society of America at its 1990 annual meeting in
Dallas, Tex.
     Includes bibliographical references and index.
     ISBN 0-8137-1180-0
     1. Sea level—History—Congresses.   I. Dott, Robert H., 1929–
II. Series: Memoir (Geological Society of America) ; 180.
GC89.E87   1992
551.4'58—dc20   92-25961
                                                 CIP

10   9   8   7   6   5   4   3   2   1

Contents

Preface

This volume on the history of one of geology's most important concepts—the worldwide rise and fall of sea level—is the outgrowth of a symposium presented by the History Division of the Geological Society of America at its 1990 annual meeting in Dallas, Texas. One of the important roles of the History Division should be to remind the geological community of its historical roots so as to avoid, insofar as possible, having each generation reinvent the wheel and repeat many of its ancestors' mistakes. In these days of increasing numbers of ever-more-specialized earth scientists and a bewildering literature explosion, it is difficult to be aware of the history of our science except in the most superficial way. Therefore, the History Division can provide a service to the profession by organizing and publishing comprehensive historical reviews of major, timely topics, such as the concept of eustasy.

The current great interest in eustasy stems from two sources, the results of the Deep Sea Drilling Program and the growth of seismic stratigraphy during the 1960s and 1970s. The deep sea record has provided abundant evidence in support of the Croll-Milankovitch theory of orbital forcing of climate change, and seismic sequence stratigraphy has provided compelling evidence of the apparent synchroneity of major packages of strata on many, widely separated continental margins. Both results imply many worldwide sea-level changes, and this convergence of evidence from different fields has brought eustasy to the lips of very diverse specialists. That the topic continues to be timely is evidenced by the largest society for sedimentary geology, SEPM, choosing as the subject for its 1991 mid-year meeting in Portland, Oregon, "Continental Margins: Tectonics, Eustacy (sic) and Climate Change" (at which I presented a keynote address summarizing the Dallas eustasy symposium). In the wake of this recent surge of enthusiasm for many fluctuations of sea level, it is quite natural to assume that eustasy is a new intellectual product of the sixties and seventies. Nothing could be further from the truth, however, for this important concept has a long, complex history of ups and downs.

Besides wishing to minimize the repetition of the errors of the past, we may also hope to avoid the "conceptual impoverishment of a lack of historical perspective" (Rudwick, 1972, p. 266). Two anecdotes serve to illustrate such impoverishment. Allen Shaw confessed that as a student he had not heard of A. W. Grabau's prophetic ideas on stratigraphy until he made the "casual purchase" of a reprint of a classic Grabau paper (Shaw, 1964, p. ix). As for myself, I had not heard of continental drift or Alfred Wegener until fellow graduate student Digby McLaren—rather than a faculty member—introduced me to those heretical names; soon after, I made a "casual purchase" of Alex DuToit's inspiring book, *Our Wandering Continents.*

The symposium on the ups and downs of eustasy qualifies as internal history; that is, history written by scientists from a within-science perspective as opposed to history written by those external to a field, who may view the same subject from a broader sociological perspective. Although there is need for both perspectives of history, the chief goal of the present volume is to provide historical perspective for earth scientists of one of their more important concepts. It is assumed that the external historian also may find some things of value here.

The oral symposium in October 1990 at Dallas was a great success to judge from the large attendance. This success convinced the participants of the value of publishing their contributions for a wider audience. All but two of the papers presented orally are included in this volume, and an additional paper on neptunism by A. V. Carozzi is also presented for completeness. Following a general introductory chapter by myself and Carozzi's chapter, Anthony Hallam reviews the origin of the term "eustatic" and early 20th century European ideas about sea-level changes. This is followed by discussions of the early 20th century American ideas of T. C. Chamberlin by Dott and of A. W. Grabau by Markes Johnson. Two discussions follow of late Paleozoic cyclothems, which provide the strongest evidence for pre-Pleistocene eustatic changes. One by Nelson and Langenheim gives the Illinois history and another by Buchanan and Maples presents a Kansas viewpoint of cyclothems. Finally, two modern perspectives on eustasy are provided. First, Peter Vail gives a personal account of the development of seismic stratigraphy and the famous "Vail Curve" in Exxon; and, finally, Kendall, Moore, and Whittle ask if it is possible to distinguish an unambiguous eustatic signal from others reflected in the stratigraphic record.

I appreciate the splendid cooperation of all participants in the symposium and their encouragement to pursue publication of the results. Although Arthur L. Bloom and Clifford M. Nelson chose not to include manuscripts of their oral contributions for publication and Alexander Tollman (of the University of Vienna) was unable to participate because of infirmity, their encouragement and thoughtful critiques of manuscripts have been very helpful. Of the many others who have been especially supportive, I single out Markes E. Johnson, Laurence L. Sloss, and William M. Jordan for special thanks. Markes Johnson served as my principal advisor from the beginning of the planning of the symposium and as cochair for the oral session. He has my sincer-

est appreciation for his invaluable assistance. I also wish to thank Richard A. Hoppin, editor of memoirs and special papers, as well as Sharon Schwoch and her staff in the Society's publications department for their enthusiastic and efficient support in producing the volume.

R. H. Dott, Jr.
Madison, Wisconsin
May 1992

REFERENCES CITED

DuToit, A. L., 1937, Our wandering continents: Edinburgh, Oliver and Boyd, 361 p.

Rudwick, M.J.S., 1972, The meaning of fossils: London and New York, Macdonald-Elsevier, 287 p.

Shaw, A. B., 1964, Time in stratigraphy: New York, McGraw-Hill, 365 p.

Geological Society of America
Memoir 180
1992

Chapter 1

An introduction to the ups and downs of eustasy

Robert H. Dott, Jr.
Department of Geology and Geophysics, University of Wisconsin, Madison, Wisconsin 53706

ABSTRACT

Current interest in global sea level change was stimulated by the Deep Sea Drilling (DSDP) and CLIMAP programs and by the development of seismic sequence stratigraphy during the 1960s and 1970s. With *"eustatic"* now on the lips of climatologists, marine geophypsicists, tectonicists, and petroleum explorationists, as well as stratigraphers, there is a tendency to assume that eustasy is a new concept, whereas it has a long and complex history of ups and downs. This symposium volume presents much of that history.

Eustasy has ultimate roots in the flood myths of several ancient civilizations and in seventeenth century sacred theories, which sought geologic evidence of Noah's Flood. Then eighteenth century neptunism postulated a one-way eustatic fall to explain all rocks of the crust, while competing plutonism postulated uplift of land instead. It was Agassiz's 1840 glacial theory that nurtured our modern concept because of the implication of lowered sea level during an ice age, as first noted by MacLaren in 1842. Surprisingly, however, it was not until Daly's 1934 *Changing World of the Ice Age* that glacial eustasy became firmly established.

The term *eustatic* was coined by Suess (1888) for global changes of sea level, which he attributed to cyclic oceanic subsidence due to cooling and contraction of the earth. In 1898 and 1909, Chamberlin proposed a diastrophic (tectonic) control of sea level as a cause of periodic universal unconformities. Both eustasy and cyclicity then became so in vogue that by the 1930s and 1940s theories of global rhythms of everything were rampant. This era gave us Grabau's Pulsation theory, Haarman's oscillation theory, Stille's global orogenic cycles, Umbgrove's *Pulse of the Earth* and *Symphony of the Earth*, and Carboniferous cyclothems. In the 1950s, a reactionary continuist dogma arose, which retarded the acceptance of sequence stratigraphy first proposed by Sloss, Krumbein, and Dapples in 1948. It was the development of seismic stratigraphy by Vail and associates in the 1960s that firmly established sequence stratigraphy. Now, with rediscovery of Milankovitch cycles as a result of DSDP and CLIMAP, we have reinvented the wheel of global cyclicity, for which rhythmic eustatic change has provided the axle.

INTRODUCTION

Sea level is our most fundamental datum, being the boundary between land and sea as well as the ultimate reference for all elevations. Although on a day-to-day basis, sea level seems permanent, in reality it is constantly changing. During the twentieth century, it has been rising worldwide at 1 or 2 mm per year. During the Pleistocene ice ages, we know that sea level fluctuated on the order of 120 to 150 m as continental glaciers waxed and waned. Recent publicity about possible greenhouse warming predicts a farther rise of the order of 30 m due to the melting of the remaining Antarctic and Greenland ice caps. The resulting flood would impact at least half of the earth's human population, creating a potential calamity of great importance.

During the past 200 years, generations of geologists have recognized abundant evidence in the stratigraphic record of many

Dott, R. H., Jr., 1992, An introduction to the ups and downs of eustasy, *in* Dott, R. H., Jr., ed., Eustasy: The Historical Ups and Downs of a Major Geological Concept: Boulder, Colorado, Geological Society of America Memoir 180.

relative changes between the levels of land and sea. Each successive generation has concluded, however, that it is virtually impossible to prove whether, for any given case, it was the sea or the land—or both—that had moved up or down. The problem has always been that there is no fixed, absolute, datum of reference other than the inaccessible center of the earth. Only if a synchronous response could be demonstrated on two or more separate continents could a tentative case for eustatic change be made. In recent decades, we have come to realize that the problem of isolating an unambiguous eustatic signal is even more complex than prior generations could imagine (Vella, 1962; Sahagian and Watts, 1991). This is because there are so many complex feedbacks among glacial isostasy and glacial eustasy, hydro-isostasy affecting the entire world ocean through changing water volume, tectonic eustatic effects, erosional and sedimentational isostasy, compaction and decompaction of sediments, and even changing evaporative potential over the oceans.

The current interest in changes of sea level linked to changes of climate derives considerably from the great successes of the Deep Sea Drilling Program of the sixties and seventies, which provided compelling evidence to support the Croll-Milankovitch theory of orbital forcing as a major cause of glaciations and other climate changes (Croll, 1864; Milankovitch, 1920). Meanwhile, on another front during the sixties and seventies, the refinement of seismic profiling across continental margins led to breakthroughs in the analysis of global stratigraphy. The resulting seismic cross sections from widely separated continental margins provided evidence of the apparent synchroneity of major packages of strata defined by important unconformities, which implied many sea-level changes. By adapting Sloss' concept of sequence stratigraphy (Sloss and others, 1949; Sloss, 1963) to seismic profiles, Vail and co-workers at the Exxon Production Research Corporation concluded that the patterns were caused by eustatic changes. One result was the well-known "Vail Curve" (Vail and others, 1977; Haq and others, 1987).

The convergence on sea-level change by these two independent but simultaneous research efforts has brought eustasy to the lips of such diverse specialists as glacial geologists, climatologists, marine scientists, tectonicists, stratigraphers, and petroleum explorationists. Several recent book-length treatises and full journal issues have been devoted to sea-level change (e.g., Schlee, 1984; Wilgus and others, 1988; Revelle and others, 1990; Emery and Aubrey, 1991; Fischer and Bottjer, 1991; Macdonald, 1991; Sahagian and Watts, 1991; Johnson and Stright, 1992). With this explosion of interest, it is quite natural, especially for younger scientists, to assume that eustasy is a relatively new concept, which originated in the seventies either from DSDP or seismic stratigraphy. To the contrary, this important concept has had a long and complex history of ups and downs of both refinement and rejection. As science expands and accelerates, it becomes increasingly difficult to assimilate much of the contemporary literature and seemingly impossible to gain a grasp also of the earlier history of one's science. Thus there is a dangerous ten-

dency to assume that anything published more than ten years ago cannot be worth reading and citing. This is not a new problem.

I am only too painfully aware how increasingly difficult it is to keep pace with the ever-rising tide of geological literature. The science itself has so widened, and the avenues to publication have so prodigiously multiplied, that one is almost driven in despair to become a specialist, and confine one's reading to that portion of the literature which deals with one's own more particular branch of the science. But this narrowing of our range has a markedly prejudicial effect on the character of our work. (Archibald Geikie, 1901, p. 287)

It is as important now as 100 years ago to know something about the development of major concepts like eustasy, for "only by gaining an appreciation for the evolution of concepts can the young be protected from repeating the errors of past generations" (L. L. Sloss, written communication, 1991). Consider Allen Shaw's confession that he did not hear of A. W. Grabau as a student, but was introduced through the "casual purchase" of a reprint of one of Grabau's classic papers (Shaw, 1964, p. ix). Similarly, I did not hear of continental drift or Alfred Wegener until I was a graduate student in 1951. Significantly, it was not the faculty, but a fellow student, Digby McLaren, who first introduced us. That memorable encounter was reinforced a year or so later when I made a "casual purchase" of DuToit's *Our Wandering Continents* (1937).

Because the concept of eustatic change is so important to many branches of geology and climatology, the History Division of the Geological Society of America sponsored a symposium on the history of eustasy at its annual meeting in Dallas, Texas, in 1990. A large attendance at the session testified to the timeliness of the topic. This volume presents as a permanent record for a broader audience most of the results of that symposium plus an additional article on Maillet's neptunism by A. V. Carozzi. This introductory chapter provides an historical summary, which is intended to help link the other, more specialized contributions.

SUESS' DEFINITION OF EUSTATIC CHANGE

It was the great Austrian geologist, Eduard Suess, who coined "eustatic" in 1888 in Chapter xiv ("The Oceans") of Volume two of *Das Antlitz der Erde*. His definition is translated as follows:

We must commence by separating from the various other changes which affect the level of the strand, those which take place at an approximately equal height, whether in a positive or negative direction, over the whole globe; this group we will distinguish as *eustatic movements. The formation of the sea basins produces spasmodic negative eustaticc movements* (p. 538). . . .*The formation of sediments causes a continuous eustatic positive movement of the strand-line.* (p. 543; from the 1906 Sollas translation. All italics are original.)

It is clear enough that Suess meant to refer to worldwide changes of sea level, but he gave no hint of the etymology of his invention.

Given the emphasis upon classical languages in his day, it was probably unnecessary to do so. The word "eustatic" derives from the Greek. The prefix "eu" means good, well, true, or most typical. The familiar suffix "static" means stationary or at rest, but can also mean "balanced." Suess apparently meant "truly balanced or level," which Arthur Bloom suggests should be taken as "global level" (written communication, 1991).

Regardless of exact etymology, Suess' definitions of worldwide positive and negative eustatic movements of sea level have served geology well for a hundred years. There is another confusion, however, namely the spelling of the noun form, which Suess never used. Clearly *"eustasy"* is correct because of its similarity to words of common derivation such as isostasy and stasis (as in "homeostasis").

ROOTS OF THE IDEA OF SEA-LEVEL CHANGE

Deluges

The idea of important interchanges of sea and land is as old as human civilization, for several early peoples had some kind of flood myth (Huggett, 1989). The better known of these derived from the valleys and deltas of such great rivers as the Tigris-Euphrates, Indus, and Yellow. Although most of the myths probably were inspired by great, 500-year-type river floods, the ancient Greeks gave us their marine Deucalion flood, a precursor of the Hebraic Deluge of Noah. Medieval Judeo-Christian Europe attached much importance to that biblical eustatic event in forming the earth's surface. Phenomena such as mountains, marine shells far from the sea, erratic boulders, and boulder clay were all explained at various times in terms of the Deluge. Today, we still find holdovers of ancient "flood geology" in the modern Creationist movement.

The seventeenth century was highlighted by the Scientific Revolution wrought by Bacon, Galileo, Kepler, Newton, Boyle, and others. One consequence of the new science was the appearance of Natural Theology near the end of the century, especially in Britain. Several authors produced works that purported to present scientific explanations of the scriptures. All of these gave special prominence to the Deluge, but its significance was interpreted differently. In the most famous of these accounts, *The Sacred Theory of the Earth* (1681), Thomas Burnet postulated that heating by the sun caused the earth to crack and the waters of the deep to vaporize, then explode to the surface as "fountains of the abysse." The flood waters eventually drained back into the interior, leaving the surface a chaotic wreck with mountains as "the most spectacular ruins of a broken world." Burnet calculated that the eustatic rise necessary to overtop the highest mountains to a depth of 15 cubits, as specified in Genesis, would require eight times as much water as is contained in the present oceans. *Sacred Theory* was both enormously popular and controversial—in short, a best seller. Several competing theories were published (summarized by Dean, 1985). They focussed interest upon surface features and their histories, especially of interchanges between land and sea.

Important challenges to the delugers came especially from Italy, where active volcanoes and earthquakes fostered views of earth change different from those of geologically more tranquil northern Europe. Most important of the dissenters was Antonio Moro, who in 1740 downgraded the Deluge and argued that mountains, islands, and continents were all the products of the earth's fire. He cited the 1707 eruption of Santorini, which gave birth to a new island in the Aegean Sea, and the sudden formation 200 years earlier of a hill 152 m (500 ft) high by the eruption of Monte Nuovo at Pozzuoli near Naples. Fossils found in rocks had grown in the sea, and were later elevated to their present positions. Although Moro's book was widely circulated, his emphasis upon uplift of land rather than oscillations of sea level fell upon deaf ears. At the end of the century, James Hutton was only slightly more successful in arguing for uplift of land.

Neptunism

The eighteenth century, or Age of Reason, was dominated by the neptunian theory of a one-way eustatic fall of sea level, which is most familiarly linked with the teachings of Abraham Gottlob Werner, at Freiberg, Saxony. This influential idea predates Werner, being a descendent of Cartesian cosmogeny, and is epitomized by the *Telliamed* of Benoit de Maillet (1656–1738), circulated widely in manuscript from 1720 and first published in 1748. Maillet's curious speculations about the diminution of the sea are discussed in this volume by A. V. Carozzi, who has aptly characterized Maillet as the ultraneptunian.

The profound influence of neptunism upon late eighteenth century thought prompts one to wonder if there was some widely known empirical evidence of diminution or lowering of the sea other than the long-noted presence of marine fossils and salt deposits far from the present sea (and petrified logs interpreted by Maillet as masts of ancient ships stranded by marine retreat). Indeed, Wegmann (1969) and Ekman (1991) have documented a 1,000-year history of observations of shoreline retreat in the Gulf of Bothnia, the northern arm of the Baltic Sea, where rocks had emerged in navigable channels and reed beds had become meadows. The Vikings created laws for establishing ownership of new land as it emerged, and in 1694 Urban Hjarne circulated a questionnaire to inquire about the reality of alleged changes and to invite suggestions of their causes (e.g., falling sea level, rising land, or sedimentation; Wegmann, 1969). Some years later, both Celsius and Linnaeus gave much attention to the evidence for diminution of sea level along the Swedish coast. Celsius canvassed seal hunters about changing elevations of seal-resting stones (Fig. 1), and inferred a rate of diminution of about 1.2 m (4 ft) per century, which became known widely as the "Celsius value." In the spirit of experimentation, Celsius scratched water level marks on rocks along the coast in order to monitor future changes. These have been revisited by subsequent generations (Bergston, 1954).

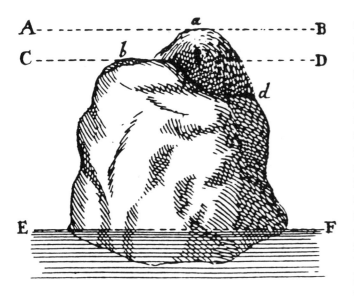

Rock in the Harbour of Löfgrund.

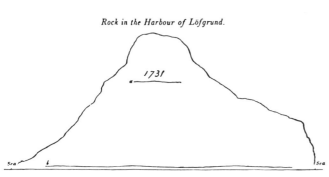

Figure 1. (Upper) Celsius' 1743 illustration of the seal rock at the island of Iggon, Sweden, used for his calculation of the "Celsius value" for the rate of decline of sea level. Local accounts indicated that about 200 years before (ca. 1530), sea level was at A–B in calm weather, and seals could be caught at "a." In A.D. 1563, sea level was at C–D, and seals lay at "b." In 1731, Celsius found sea level to be 2.4 m (8 ft) lower, at E–F, for a decline of 1.2 to 1.5 m (4 to 5 ft) in a century. (From Celsius, 1743.) (Lower) Lyell's sketch of the most famous seal rock, a mica-garnet schist at Löfgrund Harbor, Sweden, not far from Iggon. This rock was marked at mean water level and dated in 1731 (a) and at a lower level (b), which, though undated, was reported by locals to have been carved in 1820. In 1834, Lyell found the 1731 mark to have risen 76 cm (2.5 ft), and the 1820? mark about 10 cm (4 in) above mean water level, thus a little less than 91 cm (3 ft) per century. A photograph of the same rock published by Bergsten in 1954 (Fig. 10, p. 96) shows several later marks as well. (From Lyell, 1835, Fig. 10, p. 19.)

The Scandinavian paradox

Within Scandinavia, debate was lively. Hjarne had been puzzled by reports of advancing shorelines along the southern North Sea margin in contrast with the Baltic, but little was made of this seemingly obvious anomaly. In response to Celsius and Linnaeus, countervailing evidence of diminution of the Baltic sea level was cited. For example, on the Finnish coast at the southern

end of the Gulf of Bothnia, tree-ring counts for pine trees growing at the present shore indicated ages of 232 to 310 years (Wegmann, 1969). A simple extrapolation of the Celsius value suggested that these would have been growing below sea level for most of their lives. In Finland, Efraim Otto Runeburg, in his capacity as a tax official, had also amassed abundant data on the emergence of coastal land. He recognized for the first time that emergence was not uniform, for more land had been gained along the northern gulf. In 1765 he published an hypothesis that recognized a small local role for sedimentation, but a much greater role for differential warping of the land. He suggested that small movements along joints might explain such warping. He envisioned that displacements like those great ones associated with earthquakes, if of a much smaller scale, might raise the rocky foundation slightly without being accompanied by catastrophes. With the devastating Lisbon earthquake of 1755 still fresh in European minds, Runeberg's pioneering idea of slow uplift was rejected just as Moro's hypothesis of uplift by fire had been.

It was not until the early nineteenth century that the Scandinavian evidence for changing relative sea level attracted much outside attention. In 1806 to 1808 Werner's protégé, Leopold von Buch, observed much evidence in northern Finland of the withdrawal of the sea, and concluded that there was "no other way out of this than the conviction that the whole of Sweden is slowly rising" (von Buch, 1810, v. II, p. 503–504). He also suggested that Sweden may rise more than Norway, and more in the north than the south. In 1834 Charles Lyell visited Scandinavia to investigate the sea level controversy for himself. He reexamined some of Celsius' water level marks along the Gulf of Bothnia and added a few new ones (Fig. 1). He also examined elevated beaches in southern Sweden and assessed other clues. At Stockholm, Lyell reasoned from the position of mature trees that the relative sea level there could have changed no more than 25 cm (10 in) in a century, but acknowledged greater changes elsewhere. After 1835, Lyell devoted most of an entire chapter in *Principles of Geology* to the Scandinavian controversy. He accepted the view that the land around the Gulf of Bothnia had risen, but wondered if the change had remained constant either in rate or direction (Lyell, 1835, p. 32–33). Lyell cited evidence suggesting that, while some coastlines had risen, others had sunk, and also suggested that any given stretch of coast may have oscillated between elevation and subsidence. Lyell's prejudice for slow, vertical movements of land rather than sea was soon supported convincingly by the observations of a French survey in 1838 to 1839 on the Arctic coast of Finnmark in present northern Norway, where Auguste Bravais measured the elevations of two conspicuous raised beaches. In Altenfjord, which penetrates far inland, he discovered that the same beach lines were tilted, being higher near the head of the fjord than on the outer coast 90 km to the north (Bravais, 1840). Differential uplift of the land in Scandinavia now seemed an inescapable conclusion.

When Lyell went to Scandinavia, he was already conditioned to believe that land could rise or sink by observation of the celebrated ancient Temple of Jupiter Serapis at Pozzuoli near

Naples, which he made famous with the frontispiece for *Principles of Geology* (see Frontispiece for this volume). Although Lyell had visited Serapis in 1828, he relied mostly upon detailed descriptions by Babbage (1847). The temple housed a statue of Serapis, goddess of traders, reflecting the importance of Pozzuoli as a port for Roman trade with Egypt, where a similar temple stands at Alexandria. Pozzuoli, which derives its name from a Greek word for sulfur, lies within the Phlegrean Fields (a caldera) known for volcanic and solfatara activity, as well as for local emergence and submergence of the coastline (Fig. 2). Monte Nuevo, of which Moro wrote in 1740 (cited above), lies only 3 km to the northwest. The temple's three standing marble pillars first attracted attention in 1749. When excavated in 1750, the temple floor was just above sea level, but holes formed by the rock-boring bivalve *Lithodomus* were found extending 7 m above the base of each pillar. Clearly submergence of the area to a depth of 7 m had occurred sometime earlier. Historical records indicate that the area was submerged in the thirteenth century and that emergence begun in the sixteenth century continued until 1750. Submergence renewed thereafter, however, to cause shallow flooding of the floor of the temple during high tides at the time that Lyell and Babbage visited in 1828. Evidence of differential elevation and depression is abundant along the coast of the Pozzuoli-Naples region; Lyell mentioned elevated wave-cut cliffs encrusted with barnacles and beach terraces containing shells. There could be no doubt that here it was the unstable land that had moved differentially up and down. Modern analyses of the

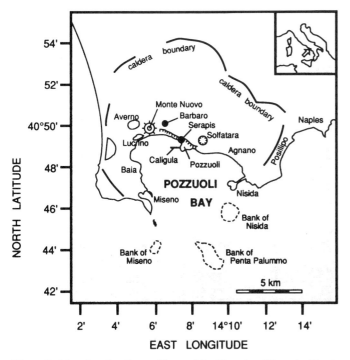

Figure 2. Map showing the positions of the Temple of Serapis, Monte Nuevo, and Pozzuoli Bay within the Campi Flegrei caldera. Naples is at the right edge. The inset shows the Pozzuoli area with respect to all of Italy. (From Dvorak and Mastrolorenzo, 1991, Fig. 5.)

Phlegrean caldera (Lirer and others, 1987; Dvorak and Mastrolorenzo, 1991) show that the temple area began subsiding about A.D. 200. During the 1538 eruption, it was uplifted to about 4 m above sea level, but then began subsiding again. By 1800 its floor was awash at high tide as when Lyell and Babbage visited. Subsidence continued at a rate of 14 to 15 mm per year until the late 1960s, when uplift recommenced (Vita-Finzi, 1986; Dvorak and Mastrolorenzo, 1991).

Diluvialism

Meanwhile, a geological role for the Deluge was still being claimed in some circles, even though there was growing uncertainty about both its importance and timing (Huggett, 1989). Rupke (1983) argues that the dramatic character of flood geology had great appeal to artists and literaries of the Romantic period. Especially significant was a growing belief that the scriptural account of history applies only to the Deluge itself and postdiluvian time, while geology gives an account of antediluvian history. This so-called "gap theory" represented an important abandonment of the long-reigning, biblically inspired dogma of a mere 6,000 years for all of history, and contributed to the development of diluvialism in the early nineteenth century. *Diluvium* was defined by famous English diluvialist, William Buckland, as

> those extensive and general deposits of superficial loam and gravel, which appear to have been produced by the last great convulsion that has affected our planet . . . I entirely coincide with the views of M. Cuvier, in considering them as bearing undeniable evidence of a recent and transient inundation. On these grounds I have felt myself fully justified in applying the epithet *diluvial*, to the results of this great convulsion; of *antediluvial*, to the state of things immediately preceding it; and *postdiluvial* or *alluvial*, to that which succeeded it, and has continued to the present time. (Buckland, 1823, p. 2)

The great French naturalist, Georges Cuvier, had formulated the influential new theory of multiple catastrophic floods to explain the stratigraphic and paleontologic records of the Paris basin, which revealed evidence of several alternations between marine and nonmarine conditions. Each flood was thought to have caused partial extinctions of existing biota. Cuvier postulated that each flood of the continent was caused by an inversion of the sea floor. What had been land before was converted to sea floor during a flood, and vice versa—a sea-floor inversion theory of eustasy.

Although Cuvier himself was not at pains to rationalize his theory with scriptures, others, such as Buckland, concluded that the last of the series was the Mosaic flood. Besides the diluvium spread widely over northern Europe, scattered caves and fissures containing masses of mammalian bones were widely known. The bones were thought to have been swept in violently by the Deluge until Buckland studied Kirkdale Cavern in eastern Yorkshire, which had been discovered in 1821. In his *Reliquiae diluvianae* (1823), Buckland showed that this celebrated cave had been a hyena den, which must have been occupied for a very long

Figure 3. Oxford Don William Buckland ecstatic with the disvovery of the paleontological riches of a hyena cave such as Kirkdale Cavern. Buckland's geologist-artist friend, Henry de la Beche, could not resist a liberal sprinkling of coprolites, which held a special interest for Buckland. (From McCartney, 1977, p. 49.)

time because it contained enormous numbers of gnawed bones of prey such as elephant and rhinoceras (Fig. 3). Rather than being the relics of the brief Deluge, here was the record of a long, mild, tropical antediluvial history. These findings limited the effect of the biblical Deluge to the mere deposition of a veneer of loose surficial material.

During the 1830s, so many questions and incongruities had arisen that the diluvial theory declined sharply, and by 1840, geology was ripe for an alternative explanation of changes of level between sea and land. In his lawyerlike fashion, Lyell offered a sly alternative, namely the substitution of drift geology for diluvial geology by using the same evidence that the diluvialists had cited. The conventional flood account for diluvium was too catastrophic for Lyell, so he argued for what he viewed as more uniformitarian marine processes to sculpture the land and deposit sediments during times of relatively high sea level. Valleys and escarpments were carved by marine currents and waves, while erratic boulders and other diluvium were "drifted in" by icebergs (Fig. 4), thus the term *drift* coined by Lyell in 1840 replaced diluvium. For the next three decades, Lyell was to be the principal advocate of marine erosion as the chief geomorphic agent (Davies, 1969). His favorite example was the Weald region of southeastern England, where Cretaceous strata occur in a large breached anticline. Cuestas formed by resistant strata were interpreted as wave-cut cliffs, and the valleys as eroded by marine currents.

In 1839, Lyell's friend, Charles Darwin, interpreted the celebrated Parallel Roads of Glen Roy in Scotland as high beach lines of a marine inundation. This interpretation was an extension of experiences in Patagonia, where Darwin had encountered clear evidence of such inundations, but it also must have reflected the influence of friend Lyell. Only one year later, in 1840, *Etudes sur Glaciers* appeared and its author, Louis Agassiz, toured Scotland with Buckland. In 1842, Agassiz published the favored glacial lake hypothesis for the roads. Today it seems self evident that glaciation offers the most satisfactory mechanism not only to impound temporary lakes, but also to deposit the boulder clay or glacial drift, erratic boulders, moraines, and the like. Nevertheless, it was to take more than two decades for glacial and fluvial processes to become fully accepted as the principal geomorphic agents responsible for the British landscape (Davies, 1969). Although Lyell was at first converted in 1840 by Agassiz and Buckland to a major role for glaciation, he soon reverted to his old preference for marine submergence as geomorphologically more important than glaciation. A nearly universal hostility toward the theory by members of the Geological Society of London was epitomized by Greenough's assessment that the glacial theory "is the climax of absurdity" (Davies, 1969, p. 287).

GLACIAL EUSTASY AND GLACIAL ISOSTASY

Although Agassiz' glacial theory paved the way for our modern concept of eustatic changes of sea level, it was a Scottish journalist who first saw the implication of huge ice caps for changing the volume of sea water. Charles MacLaren, a newspaper publisher with a strong interest in geology, wrote a 19-page review of Agassiz' glacial theory for the *American Journal of Science* in 1842. On the last page, MacLaren noted that

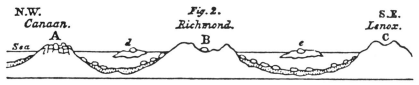

d, e Masses of floating ice carrying fragments of rock.

Figure 4. An illustration of Lyell's submergence theory and his proposed dispersal of erratic boulders by icebergs. This figure is from a paper about some well-known trains of erratic blocks in western Massachusetts, the Richmond erratics, which he had seen in the company of James Hall during his travels in America. (From Lyell, 1855, p. 92.)

there is a question arising out of the theory, which he has not touched upon. If we suppose the region from the 35th parallel to the north pole to be invested with a coat of ice thick enough to reach the summits of Jura, that is, about 5000 French feet, or one English mile in height, it is evident that the abstraction of such a quantity of water from the ocean would materially affect its depth . . . We find that the abstraction of the water necessary to form the said coat of ice would depress the ocean about 800 feet. Admitting further, that one-eighth of the fluid yet remains locked up in the existing polar ices, it follows that the dissolution of the portion which has disappeared would raise the ocean nearly 700 feet. The only very uncertain element here is the depth of the ice; but even if this should be reduced one-half, we would still have an agent capable of producing a change of 350 feet on the level of the sea. We are besides leaving out of view the southern polar region, which it is now known embraces a great extent of land. If this was also covered with ice, the change would be much greater than we have assumed. (MacLaren, 1842, p. 365)

In spite of the lucidity of Maclaren's argument, glacial eustasy was not taken very seriously for at least 20 more years. For example, a decade after Agassiz' theory appeared, the presidential address to the Geological Society of London was devoted largely (40 printed pages) to a detailed critique of the pros and cons of glaciation (Hopkins, 1852). In 1864, Scotsman James Croll made the first proposal of orbital forcing of glacial climate, but his brilliant theory was slow to receive serious recognition. In 1865 S. V. Wood in Britain (see Davies, 1969, p. 300) and in 1868 Charles Whittlesey in America both extended MacLaren's argument, but even they were not influential. Nor, apparently, was A. Tylor, who in 1872 suggested that "the great changes in the sea-level during the glacial period" might explain Darwin's Pacific coral reefs better than oceanic subsidence; he also ascribed an important influence of such sea level changes upon the world's river deltas.

Meanwhile, Scotsman Thomas F. Jamieson in 1865 suggested another glacially caused mechanism for changes of relative sea level, namely that the weight of huge ice caps must have depressed the continents; when the ice melted, the continents must have rebounded. Thus was born the important idea of glacial isostasy some 20 years before the general theory of isostasy. (Actually, in anticipating isostasy, John Herschel had earlier [1837] cited Scandinavian uplift in support of his argument for a pliable or yielding subcrust.) This new mechanism for sea-land changes offered a straightforward explanation for the long-

puzzling evidence in Scandinavia for differential apparent sea-level fall, but it, too, was largely ignored until 1888 when G. De Geer of Sweden proved Jamieson's hypothesis to be correct with the first isobase maps of Scandinavia and eastern North America (Fig. 5).

Glacial eustasy received little attention in part because of the widespread popularity of a postulated vertical movement of the crust. Lyell and Dana both advocated a major uplift of the continents prior to glaciation to cause climatic cooling. Small changes of sea level also may have occurred, but they were eclipsed in importance by the supposedly much greater movements of the crust (Meyer, 1986). Only when the evidence for multiple glaciation of the American Midwest and Scotland became insurmountable (ca. 1890) did this elevation hypothesis falter, several great upheavals being too incredulous. Glacially caused sea-level changes, however, remained in the background because Pleistocene glaciation was regarded by such authority figures as J. Barrell, W. M. Davis, and N. S. Shaler as only a minor perturbation in earth history—a mere "climatic accident."

In 1910, 30 years after Tylor's speculation, R. A. Daly published an argument for glacial-eustatic control of coral reefs as an alternative to the oceanic subsidence theory of Darwin and Dana. Daly called for substantial eustatic fluctuations with each Pleistocene glacial advance and retreat, which, he suggested, could account for the morphologies of tropical reefs and atolls located far from any glaciated region. Resistance continued, and leading books on geomorphology ignored glaciation as a significant cause of sea-level change (see Meyer, 1986).

In a 1922 book entitled *The Strandflat and Isostasy,* Fridtjof Nansen reviewed the status of glacial isostasy with respect to changes of sea level in Scandinavia and several Arctic regions. He speculated that deep crustal phase changes induced by loading and unloading by ice caps might explain isostatic movements. It was not until the 1930s that glacial eustasy finally achieved respectability and received serious attention by a wide spectrum of geologists. Daly's 1934 *The Changing World of the Ice Age* marked the turning point (after Davis' death). In it Daly emphasized for the first time that *both* eustatic and tectonic movements have occurred simultaneously, so that their effects must be sorted out from one another (Fig. 5). In 1935, H. Baulig popularized the terms *glacio-eustasy, tectono-eustasy,* and *sedimento-eustasy* for

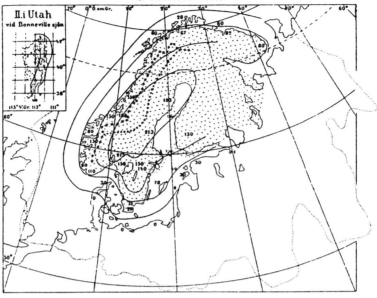

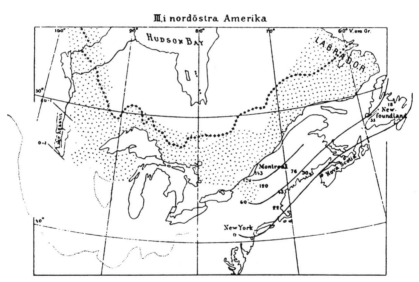

Figure 5. The first published maps of post-glacial uplift or rebound by Swedish geologist, Gerard DeGeer (1888). The contours (called isobases) show uplift in meters, and are based upon the displacement of maximum heights of ancient shorelines. DeGeer published companion maps of Scandinavia (upper) and eastern North America (lower). He also included an inset map (upper left) of isobases for Lake Bonneville, Utah, from G. K. Gilbert's work. (From DeGeer, 1888, Plates I, II, III.)

the three major causes of relative sea level change. In 1941, Beno Gutenburg published a detailed quantitative account, which firmly established the reality of glacial isostasy and highlighted its important implications for the physical behavior of the earth's interior; glacial isostasy provides the best evidence for the viscosity of the earth's mantle.

Newly discovered submarine canyons became the subject of intense debate during the 1920s and 1930s. At first, subaerial erosion during glacial eustatic falls was invoked, and in 1936, F. P. Shepard argued that Daly's estimate of sea-level falls of 300 m was much too small by a factor of 3 or 4; he soon abandoned this extreme view as implausible, however. Also during the 1920s and 1930s, elevated shore benches exposed on many Pacific islands received much attention for assessing eustasy (e.g., Wentworth and Palmer, 1925; Stearns, 1941). In 1939, Ph. H. Kuenen published quantitative estimates of eustatic movements. He concluded that major Phanerozoic transgressions and regressions required amplitudes of at least 40 m, and that the principal cause must be "some pulsatory, subcrustal influence" (p. 201). Disagreement over the magnitude of Pleistocene eustatic changes spilled over into anthropology, where argument raged about the Bering land bridge. Only after Daly's book appeared did the formation of that bridge by glacial-eustatic fall become orthodoxy. The new-found importance for eustasy is indicated by the presentation of a GSA-sponsored popular radio talk on "Shifting Ocean Levels" in 1939 as well as a 1941 Bicentennial Conference at the University of Pennsylvania on "Shiftings of Sea Floors and Coast Lines" (Bowen and others, 1941).

In 1961 Fairbridge presented a detailed review of the varied causes and magnitudes of eustasy. He concluded that the Pleistocene glacial eustatic variation was as much as 200 m. He showed how complex may be the multiplicity of factors that control sea level, including tides, glaciation, sedimentation, thermal expansion and contraction of water, and tectonics. In turn, tectonic processes include isostatic loading and unloading by ice, water, or sediments, epeirogenesis of either continents or ocean basins, orogenesis, and geoidal changes (Fig. 6). Today, sophisticated physical models that take account of such factors and their feedbacks are being developed and applied widely (e.g., Bloom and Yonekura, 1990; Matthews and Frohlich, 1991; Peltier and Tushingham, 1991). Tropical islands half-a-globe-away from any ice

sheet, large river, or appreciable tectonics have been regarded as ideal "dip sticks" for calibrating eustatic curves. Yet, even here, uncertainties arise because of necessary corrections for thermal subsidence and flexure of the lithosphere (Lincoln and Schlanger, 1991) and even from the small isostatic effect of the subtraction and addition of sea water during glacial-interglacial cycles (Clark, 1985). A tectonically rising coast (Fig. 7) may act in a manner analogous to "the operation of a natural strip chart" by recording glacio-eustatic oscillations as the coast rises (Mesolella and others, 1969, p. 271).

LYELL BY LAND—SUESS BY SEA

It is a curious fact that two of the most famous nineteenth century geologists held opposite opinions on the cause of relative changes of land and sea. We have seen that Lyell favored vertical movements of land as the dominant cause. Eduard Suess, however, staunchly maintained that apparent changes of land and sea levels of whatever age were overwhelmingly eustatic in origin. He acknowledged rare, local tectonic accidents as at "the temple of Serapis at Pozzuoli . . . produced by local movements within the crater of an expiring volcano (Suess, 1888, in Sollas translation, v. 2, p. 554) or the "true dislocations affecting the coast, as occurred in Cook Strait in New Zealand in 1856" (p. 555). But his preference is made clear in the following passage:

Eustatic Changes in Sea Level

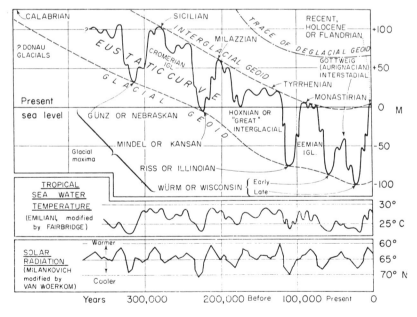

Figure 6. Diagrammatic portrayal of Quaternary sea-level changes published by R. W. Fairbridge in 1961, shortly before the Deep Sea Drilling Program. Note three geoidal curves for glacial, interglacial, and deglacial conditions as well as a eustatic curve. The author's caption reported that "absolute chronology establishes that the last major cycle [Würm or Wisconsin] is about 100,000 years, but earlier cycles can not be dated yet. . . ." (From Fairbridge, 1961, Fig. 2.)

R. H. Dott, Jr.

Figure 7. Air view of a flight of elevated marine, coral-reef terraces on the north coast of Huon Peninsula, near Sialum, Papua New Guinea. This spectacular succession has resulted from glacial eustatic oscillations superimposed upon a monotonic tectonic uplift of approximately 1 to 3 m per 1,000 years for at least 200,000 years. The broad terrace about 6 m above sea level (foreground) is Holocene. The middle set of well-defined terraces spans approximately 60,000 to 125,000 years ago, and the highest, more dissected terraces are probably 200,000 to 500,000 years old. (Courtesy of Arthur L. Bloom.)

Movements like those which present themselves as oscillations, and extend around all coasts and under every latitude in complete independence of the structure of the continents, cannot possibly be explained by elevation or subsidence of the land. Even as the transgressions of the ancient periods are much too extensive and uniform to have been produced by movements of the lithosphere, so too are the displacements of the strandline in the immediate past. (Suess, 1888, in Sollas translation, v. 2, p. 550)

Although Suess was responsible for focussing much attention upon orogenic belts and their island-arc counterparts, he did not believe that the lateral compressive tectonics responsible for them could change sea level significantly (Suess, 1888, in Sollas translation, v. 2, p. 552). Like American James D. Dana (1873), he believed in a cooling and contracting earth with practically all of the necessary accommodation of the lithosphere being confined to subsidence of the ocean basins. Thus, he argued, the sea floors sink spasmodically—but rhythmically—as the earth shrinks, and this causes the negative eustatic changes or regressions. *"The crust of the earth gives way and falls in; the sea follows it.* But while the subsidence of the [continental] crust are local events, the subsidence of the sea extends over the whole submerged surface of the planet. It brings about a general negative movement" (Suess, 1888, in Sollas translation, v. 2, p. 537–538; italics are in the original; bracket added here). "It is

in the history of the seas that we discover the history of the continent" (Suess, 1888, in Sollas translation, v. 2, p. 554). Resulting erosion of the emerged continents causes sedimentation at the ocean margins, which then raises sea level and produces more continuous transgressions (see Hallam, this volume).

Suess went to great lengths to deny a major role for vertical movements of the continents. For example, he followed Lyell and others to Scandinavia in 1885, but unlike Lyell, he was not disposed to accept evidence of movement of the land. In northern Norway, where Bravais in 1840 had reported tilted marine beaches, Suess pronounced that these same beach terraces are, in fact, horizontal, and that Bravais had miscorrelated among several shoreline terraces. Suess offered the alternate hypothesis that the many Norwegian terraces were not formed by the sea but by temporary lakes impounded in fjords by ice during glacial retreat (Suess, 1888, p. 361). He cited approvingly Robert Chambers' 1848 book, which had argued that marine shoreline terraces in northern Europe and North America were not the results of local vertical changes of the land, but required global changes of sea level. Chambers appealed to the Darwinian coral reef argument for subsidence of the Pacific Basin "causing the ocean waters to flow away from the poles" (1848, p. 320). Both Suess and Chambers noted that shore terraces were more numerous and extended to greater heights in the northern latitudes of Europe,

Greenland, and North America, but they concluded, nonetheless, that sea level was falling rather than the northern lands rising (Wegmann, 1969). For the Baltic, Suess asserted that

it is not, however, that Sweden is rising, but the enclosed Baltic sea, dependent on climatic influences, is gradually emptying, as it passes through a phase of increasing diminution; and it is from this cause that the strandline sinks lower and lower as it becomes increasingly remote from the Baltic entrance. (Suess, 1888, in Sollas translation, v. 2, p. 554)

THE TWENTIETH CENTURY PERIODICITY PARADIGM

In 1898 and 1909, T. C. Chamberlin published two short papers on the diastrophic control of stratigraphy by worldwide changes of sea level. His proposal for diastrophic control of universal unconformities was to have profound impact, especially in America. It is curious that, although his theory is almost identical with Suess' conception of eustatic changes, which had been stated clearly ten years earlier (Suess, 1888), Chamberlin never mentioned the Austrian nor did he use the term "eustatic." Like Suess, Chamberlin believed that subsidence of the ocean basins on a shrinking earth caused spasmodic worldwide regressions (they differed only in the mechanism of global shrinkage). Regressions were followed by synchronous, worldwide transgressions as sea water was gradually displaced by sedimentation on "circumcontinental submarine terraces," coupled with slow isostatic sinking of crustal blocks displaced by the prior spasm of oceanic subsidence. Because the displacements of sea level were global in scope, the resulting universal and synchronous base leveling should provide the best basis for subdivision of the stratigraphic column. The Chamberlin diastrophic control theory is discussed in Chapter 4 of this volume.

Among many Americans who were strongly influenced by Chamberlin, E. O. Ulrich stands out. After his appointment to the U.S. Geological Survey in 1897, Ulrich undertook a comprehensive study of Paleozoic stratigraphy and paleontology, which continued until his death in 1944. He adopted Chamberlin's concept of universal unconformities, and developed a controversial revision of the Paleozoic systems in the Mississippi Valley region. He coined two new lower Paleozoic systems, Ozarkian and Canadian, which he believed were necessitated by his discovery of major, widespread breaks (C. Nelson, 1976; Merk, 1985). Others, however, could not seem to find these same breaks, and much heated controversy developed around the dating and correlation of Upper Cambrian and Ordovician faunas in the region. In addition to his controversial stratigraphic revisions, Ulrich also adopted a singular view of faunal and depositional provinces. He never accepted the facies concept, but instead contended that differing lithologies must be separated by unconformities. Furthermore, differences between contemporary faunas were due to invasions of different seas rather than differences of adjacent environments.

Charles Schuchert, who also began as a Cincinnati amateur paleontologist, collaborated with Ulrich for a time at the survey before moving on to Yale. Together with Grabau and other American stratigraphers, Schuchert came to appreciate the importance of different, contemporaneous environments, while Ulrich remained rigidly frozen in his thinking. Schuchert was an early student of paleogeography, and developed an emergence-submergence curve for North America, which first appeared in 1909 (Schuchert, 1909, Plate 101).

In 1917, Joseph Barrell of Yale published a classic paper on geological rhythms. The opening lines reflect well the prevailing love affair with periodicity: "Nature vibrates with rhythms, climatic and diastrophic, those finding expression ranging in period from the rapid oscillation of surface waters, recorded in ripplemark, to those long-deferred stirrings of the deep titans which have divided earth history into periods and eras" (Barrell, 1917, p. 746). The last phrase clearly reflects Chamberlin's influence. Amadeus Grabau, a contemporary of Ulrich, Schuchert, and Barrell, was also an early student of changing sea level and paleogeography, as detailed in this volume by Johnson. At the 1933 International Geological Congress in Washington, he presented a Paleozoic sea level curve when he first stated his Pulsation Theory. Grabau postulated rhythmic advances and retreats of the seas caused by changes of the ocean basins produced by variations of radioactive heat loss from the interior. The resulting "Pulse Beat of the Earth" (Grabau, 1940, Chap. II) had a period of about 30 million years, and caused universal unconformities, which provided a basis for redividing the stratigraphic record (Johnson, this volume).

Meanwhile, in Europe, debate continued about the relative importance of tectonism and eustasy (see Hallam in this volume). Joly (1925) offered the novel speculation that terrestrial cyclic "revolutions" are caused by tides in the earth's "liquefied substratum" raised by peridic interaction with the moon. E. Haarmann (1930) proposed vertical oscillations of the land, but of particular importance was the work of Hans Stille, who compiled data that he interpreted to show global synchroneity of both epeirogenesis and orogenesis with resulting eustatic effects (Stille, 1924). By 1940 geologists everywhere were finding global synchroneity or cycles of all sorts—eustatic, orogenic, climatic, and even evolutionary ones.

Among pre-Pleistocene strata, evidence of apparently high-frequency repetitive changes of relative sea level are nowhere better displayed than in the late Paleozoic cyclothems of cratonic America. The repetition of coal-bearing packages of strata was first recognized by Udden (1912) in Illinois. Then in 1932, Wanless and Weller coined *cyclothem* for these repetitions. During the 1930s the investigation of Pennsylvanian cyclothems proceeded at a brisk pace from Illinois to Kansas and adjoining states (Fig. 8), and a lively debate developed over their cause—was it tectonic or climatic or eustatic? In 1935, by which time the writings of Daly and others had finally established the importance of Pleistocene eustatic changes, Wanless and Shepard proposed a glacial-eustatic cause for the Paleozoic cyclothems driven by wax-

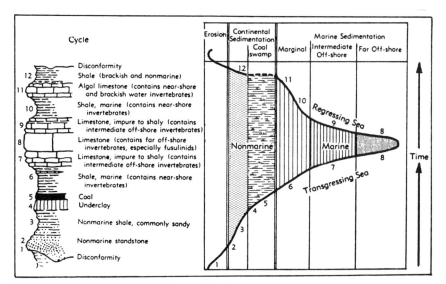

Figure 8. The ideal Kansas cyclothem of R. C. Moore based upon Upper Pennsylvanian (Virgilian) strata. This historic diagram was often published to show Moore's interpretation of sedimentary environments recorded in the cyclothems during one transgressive-regressive cycle. Buchanan and Maples (in this volume) report that Moore was not an enthusiastic advocate of eustasy as the principal cause of the cyclothems. (From Moore, 1949, Fig. 21.)

ings and wanings of Gondwana glaciers. Others accepted regular eustatic changes, but rejected a glacial cause. They invoked special conditions during late Paleozoic time of slow subsidence of sedimentary basins coupled with eustatic changes controlled, for example, by "the combination of the continuous effects of sedimentation and isostatic movements of the sea floor" (Wells, 1960, p. 389). Detailed accounts of the development of sometimes contentious ideas about cyclothems are presented in this volume by Nelson and Langenheim for Illinois, and by Buchanan and Maples for Kansas.

BACKLASH AGAINST PERIODIC EUSTASY

By the 1940s, the enthusiasm for global rhythms was overwhelming. There seemed adequate reason to suppose that Pleistocene glacial-eustatic changes were indeed periodic because glaciation was generally supposed to be controlled by some rhythmic climatic phenomena. And if Pleistocene changes were periodic, then why not also the late Paleozoic cyclothems, especially if also controlled by glacial-eustasy? It was mostly an article of faith that climatic phenomena were periodic, even though in 1920 Milankovitch had revived Croll's theory of orbital forcing of periodic climate change; students of pre-Quaternary geology remained largely oblivious of this theory until the 1970s. Most geologists were convinced that the major tectonic events of the earth also were periodic, as reflected in titles of major books like Grabau's *Pulsation Theory* (1940) and Umbgrove's *The Pulse of the Earth* (1947) and *The Symphony of the Earth* (1950).

Rare challenges to periodicity (e.g., Shepard, 1923; Berry, 1929) were voices in the wilderness, but it was inevitable that a reaction to rampant periodicity would occur eventually, and so it did after World War II. The continuist backlash is epitomized by James Gilluly's 1948 Presidential Address to the Geological Society of America (Gilluly, 1949). Gilluly was motivated to argue for continuous mountain building in reaction primarily to Stille's periodic and globally synchronous view of tectonics. Although the subject was specifically tectonic, the Gilluly paper represents a general turning away from periodicity. For example, Gilluly's address stimulated the Paleontological Society to initiate a symposium on the "Distribution of Evolutionary Explosions in Geologic Time," which was held at the Geological Society of America's annual meeting in 1949. The general conclusion was "devastating for the diastrophic theory" (Henbest, 1952, p. 299).

During the 1960s, the conventional eustatic cause for cyclothems was challenged by the suggestion of autogenic mechanisms, such as delta distributary switching, to explain the vertical repetition of facies (D. Moore, 1959; Duff and others, 1967; Ferm, 1970). Moreover, there was also a general decline of interest in stratigraphy accompanying the explosion of process and facies sedimentology. This resulted in declining interest in cyclothems and other regional stratigraphic phenomena. It was even difficult to find people who would admit to being stratigraphers—now they called themselves sedimentologists.

A NEW(?) PARADIGM FROM SEQUENCE STRATIGRAPHY AND DEEP SEA DRILLING

The latest chapter in the history of eustasy began at the same meeting as Gilluly's address. In a symposium on "Sedimentary Facies in Geologic History" (1949), Sloss, Krumbein, and Dapples first presented the concept of stratigraphic *sequences*. These were defined as large, lithostratigraphic units or "assemblages of strata and formations" bounded by prominent interregional unconformities (Sloss and others, 1949; Sloss, 1963). To distinguish sequences from European-based biostratigraphic and time stratigraphic divisions, they gave them formal Native American names. The original purpose of sequences was to serve as operational units for constructing pioneering interregional facies maps. Initial reaction was mostly negative. The sequence approach did not appeal to the stratigraphic community because the field was dominated by biostratigraphers, whereas the Gilluly school saw it as a dangerous reincarnation of Chamberlin-Stille style periodic diastrophism and universal unconformities. The fundamental stratigraphic significance of sequences dawned slowly outside Northwestern University (e.g., Clark and Stearn, 1960; Wheeler, 1964; Vail and Wilbur, 1966; Dott and Batten, 1971). It is a curious irony that contentious old Ulrich was vindicated for having correctly seen that the most important unconformities do not correspond with conventional system boundaries. Simultaneously, but quite separately, N. D. Newell reminded the profession that the paleontological record is, indeed, punctuated by conspicuous episodes of extinctions, which he attributed to severe environmental stresses, including especially eustatic falls (Newell, 1963).

The refinement of high-resolution seismic profiling in the petroleum industry during the 1960s and its application to several continental margins, stimulated a rapid refinement of sequence stratigraphy, especially at the Exxon Production Research Corporation and its Carter Oil Company predecessor (Vail and Wilbur, 1966; Vail and others, 1977, Parts 3 and 4; Haq and others, 1987). Vail discusses in this volume how seismic sequence stratigraphy evolved in Exxon, but it is beyond the scope of the volume to elaborate the details of the concept (e.g., supersequences, parasequences, multiple orders of cycles, accommodation space, maximum flooding, surfaces, toplaps, downlaps, systems tracts, and the like). When it appeared that North American sequence-bounding unconformities may be intercontinental and roughly synchronous, eustasy became the paradigm of sequence stratigraphy. The following statement seems to exemplify the Exxon thinking: "Major sequences are synchronous globally because of deposition during eustatic cycles" (Mitchum and others, 1976, p. 699). Many workers have remained skeptical of this circular, single-cause interpretation, as well they might in view of the stormy history of eustasy. Suggested alternatives include changing rates of sea-floor spreading (Pitman, 1978; Kominz, 1984; Gurnis, 1990), continental epeirogenic tectonism (Cloetingh, 1986; Sloss, 1991), orogenesis (Grasty, 1967; Klein and Willard, 1989), geoidal warping (Mörner, 1976), sedimentation and compaction (Reynolds and others, 1991), or combinations of such factors.

More or less simultaneous with the evolution of seismic stratigraphy, came detailed evidence from the Deep Sea Drilling and CLIMAP programs of climate change during the past few million years. The latter programs had been fostered by the pioneering documentation in the 1950s of Pleistocene marine temperature changes by D. B. Ericson using Foraminiferal morphology and C. Emiliani using oxygen isotopes (see Imbrie and Imbrie, 1979). The dating of such changes demonstrated close correspondence of glacial-interglacial events with the postulated Milankovitch orbital cycles. It was through this revelation and studies by A. G. Fischer (e.g., Fischer, 1981) of small-scale repetitive patterns in Cretaceous strata that most of the nonglacial geological community has been introduced to the venerable Croll-Milankovitch climatic theory.

CONCLUSIONS

There can be no doubt that seismic sequence stratigraphy and deep-sea drilling have revitalized stratigraphy and stimulated it with healthy multidisciplinary approaches. Vail ranks this renaissance of stratigraphy in importance with the plate-tectonics revolution. One of the consequences of that renaissance during the past two decades has been the rekindling of enthusiasm for eustasy and for cycles of several kinds. This has resulted in a fervent new orthodoxy, which Sloss (1991) has appropriately dubbed *neo-neptunism*. Not only is there a strong tendency to interpret every case of relative change of sea level as eustatic, but also to assume that such change must be periodic and then to seek one or more of the Milankovitch cycles to fit. The Milankovitch theory is very accommodating, for it provides a period to suit nearly every purpose—19,000, 23,000, 41,000, 100,000, and 400,000 years.

Although plate tectonics provides some basis for expecting more global synchrony than the Gilluly school realized, such synchrony by no means also requires periodicity. The new fixation upon periodic cycles is a throwback to pre–World War II thinking, yet few living geologists remember that era. Why should periodicity be such a powerful opiate for geologists? Obviously, periodicity comes naturally through the universal human experience of diurnal, tidal, and seasonal cycles. And it has ancient roots in the Aristotelian Greek world view of everything in nature being cyclic. The answer must lie more directly, however, in the innate psychological appeal of order and simplicity, both of which are provided by rhythmically repetitive patterns. For geologists, the instinctive appeal to periodicity constitutes a subtle extension of the uniformity principle, which is in turn a special geological case of simplicity or parsimony. We must be mindful, however, that much of the supposed geological periodicity may represent order imposed upon nature. I like to recall that reasonable facsimiles of Pennsylvanian cyclothems have been reproduced by using a telephone directory as a random-numbers table to generate synthetic vertical sections composed of three lithologic components (Zeller, 1964). Henbest expressed a similar reservation when he wrote for the Paleontological Society symposium noted above, "Without intending to deny that rhythm or vibration is a common characteristic of natural processes, it is evident that the theorizing on rhythm in nature has outrun the facts and possibly its actual importance" (Henbest, 1952, p. 318). After more than two centuries of geological study, we still do not know if the earth follows a *tempo giusto* (monotonic) beat or a *tempo rubato* (variable) beat.

Another manifestation of simplicity in the long history of the eustasy concept is the tendency to ascribe a single cause. In spite of full knowledge of a multiplicity of simultaneously acting factors that can affect sea level (e.g., glaciation, isostasy, sedimentation, compaction, orogenesis, etc.), even today workers tend to emphasize but one cause. Given the difficulty of isolating eustatic signals from the Quaternary record (summarized above), such practice for the older record is all the more suspect. For Quaternary time, the importance of a glacial-eustatic control of stratigraphy is amply demonstrated. For the Permo-Carboniferous, glacial eustasy is a plausible and appealing hypothesis, but the limitations of time resolution and lack of a detailed Gondwana glacial stratigraphy prevent adequate proof. The popular tendency to extrapolate glacial eustasy as the dominant factor also for much of the remainder of the Phanerozoic record taxes credulity, even though several more glacial episodes have been recognized over the past 20 years. How can we take it seriously for Mesozoic time, for example, for which we lack evidence of significant glaciation, but, instead, have the most compelling evidence of a "greenhouse" climate?

Only rarely can the hypotheses of eustasy and periodicity be demonstrated with the degree of certainty that is claimed in much recent literature. Moreover, the demonstration of eustasy is "ripe for circularity," as Sahagian and Watts observe (1991, p. 6585). Therefore, it is rather surprising that there have not been more published objections to the new orthodoxy. Notable examples include Sloss' "countervailing view" (1991) and Miall's vigorous challenge of the basis in seismic stratigraphy for the Vail sea-level curve (1986). Kendall and others in this volume present an additional challenge by reminding us that generations of geologists have concluded that it is virtually impossible to isolate an unambiguous cause for most cases of relative sea level change evidenced in the stratigraphic record. "Eustasy requires faith, for even if we see a eustatic signal, we can not discriminate its magnitude because of other complications" (Kendall, oral presentation at Dallas symposium, 1990). Although today the wealth of new types of data certainly provide better constraints, many of the fervent claims for periodic eustasy throughout Phanerozoic time are not well supported. Commonly the uncertainty of our data exceeds the refinement being sought. Thus different estimates for the average duration of a Carboniferous cyclothem vary from as little as 20,000 years to more than 1,000,000 years. Can we seriously believe it possible at this time to resolve the shorter Milankovitch periods in the Pre-Quaternary record?

The other chapters in this volume provide further insights into the long history of human ideas about relative changes of sea level. They show that eustasy is an old idea with a very complex genealogy. It is hoped that this symposium may help sort out what is really new about eustasy from what has been warmed over from the past—in short, to help present and future earth scientists to see that their "newest," exciting ideas have deep roots. Plus ça change, plus c'est la même chose!

ACKNOWLEDGMENTS

I greatly appreciate the continual encouragement and counsel of Markes E. Johnson throughout all stages of the organization and editing of the eustasy symposium. Johnson, Arthur L. Bloom, Laurence L. Sloss, and Clifford M. Nelson have provided valuable criticism of the manuscript for this introductory chapter. They have corrected several misconceptions and have directed me to relevant literature. All of the contributors to this volume, as well as William M. Jordan and other colleagues, have helped indirectly either in the preparation of this Introduction or in other ways. Richard A. Hoppin, Editor of Special Volumes for the Geological Society of America, has also been very supportive during the preparation of the manuscripts.

REFERENCES CITED

Agassiz, L., 1840, Etudes sur les glaciers: Neuchatel, privately published, 346 p., and a tray of plates.
—— , 1842, The glacial theory and its recent progress: Edinburgh New Philosophical Journal, v. 33, p. 271–283.
Babbage, C., 1847, Observations on the Temple of Serapis, at Pozzuoli, near Naples, with remarks on certain causes which may produce geological cycles of great extent: Quaterly Journal of the Geological Society of London, v. 30, p. 186–217.
Barrell, J., 1917, Rhythms and the measurements of geologic time: Geological Society of America Bulletin, v. 28, p. 745–904.
Baulig, H., 1935, The changing sea level: Institute of British Geographers Publication 3, 46 p.
Bergston, F., 1954, The land uplift in Sweden from the evidence of the old water marks: Geografiska Annaler, v. 36, p. 81–111.
Berry, E. W., 1929, Shall we return to cataclysmal geology?: American Journal of Science, 5th series, v. 17, p. 1–12.
Bloom, A. L., and Yonukura, N., 1990, Graphic analysis of dislocated Quaternary shorelines, *in* Studies in geophysics—Sea level change: Washington, D.C., National Research Council, National Academy Press, p. 83–103.
Bravais, A., 1840, Sur les lignes d'ancien niveau de la mer dans le Finmark: Compte Rendu Academie des Sciences de Paris, v. 10, 691 p.
Bowen, N. L., Cushman, J. A., and Dickerson, R., 1941, Shiftings of sea floors and coast lines: Philadelphia, University of Pennsylvania Bicentennial Conference Publication, 30 p.
Buch, L., von, 1810, Riese durch Norwegen und Lappland: Berlin, G. C. Nauck, v. 1, 406 p.; v. 2, 406 p.
Buckland, W., 1823, Reliquiae Diluvianae; or Observations on the organic remains contained in caves, fissures, and diluvial gravel, and on other geological phenomena attesting the action of a universal deluge: London, John Murray, 303 p.
Burnet, T., 1681, Telluris theoria sacra: London.
Celsius, A., 1743, Anmärkning om vatnets för minskande så i östersiön som vesterhafvet: Kongliga Swenska Wetensskaps Academiens Handlingar, v. 4.
Chamberlin, T. C., 1898, The ulterior basis of time divisions and the classification of geologic history: Journal of Geology, v. 6, p. 449–462.
—— , 1909, Diastrophism as the ultimate basis of correlation: Journal of Geology, v. 17, p. 685–693.
Chambers, R., 1848, Ancient sea margins as memorials of changes in the relative level of the sea and land: London, W. S. Orr, 335 p.
Clark, J. A., 1985, Forward and inverse models in sea-level studies, *in* Models in geomorphology: Winchester, Allen & Unwin, p. 119–138.
Clark, T. H., and Stearn, C. W., 1960, The geological evolution of North America—A regional approach to historical geology: New York, Ronald Press, 434 p.

Cloetingh, S., 1986, Intraplate stress: A new tectonic mechanism for fluctuations of relative sea level: Geology, v. 14, p. 617–620.

Croll, J., 1864, On the physical cause of the change of climate during geological epochs: Philosophical Magazine, v. 28, p. 435–436.

Daly, R. A., 1910, Pleistocene glaciation and the coral reef problem: American Journal of Science, 4th series, v. 30, p. 297–308.

—— , 1934, The changing world of the ice age: New Haven, Yale University, 271 p.

Dana, J. D., 1873, On some results of the earth's contraction from cooling, including a discussion of the origin of mountains and the nature of the earth's interior: American Journal of Science, 3rd series, v. 5, p. 423–443; v. 6, p. 6–14, 104–115, 161–172, 381–382.

Darwin, C., 1839, Observations on the Parallel Roads of Glen Roy, and of other parts of Lochaber, with an attempt to prove that they are of marine origin: Philosophical Transactions of the Royal Society, v. for 1839, p. 39–81.

Davies, G. L., 1969, Earth in decay—A history of British geomorphology: New York, American Elsevier, 390 p.

Dean, D. R., 1985, The rise and fall of the Deluge: Journal of Geological Education, v. 33, p. 84–93.

DeGeer, G., 1888, Om Skandinaviens nivåförändringar under qvartär-perioden: Geologiska Föreningens i Stockholm Förhandlingar, v. 10, p. 366–379.

Dott, R. H., Jr., and Batten, R. L., 1971, Evolution of the Earth (first edition): New York, McGraw-Hill, 649 p.

Duff, P.McL.D., Hallam, A., and Walton, E. K., 1967, Cyclic sedimentation: Amsterdam, Elsevier, 280 p.

DuToit, A. L., 1937, Our wandering continents: Edinburgh, Oliver and Boyd, 361 p.

Dvorak, J. J., and Mastrolorenzo, G., 1991, The mechanisms of recent vertical crustal movements in Campi Flegrei caldera, southern Italy: Geological Society of America Special Paper 263, 47 p.

Ekman, M., 1991, A concise history of postglacial land uplift research (from its beginning to 1950): Terra Nova, v. 3, p. 358–363.

Emery, K. O., and Aubrey, D. G., 1991, Sea levels, land levels, and tide gauges: Berlin, Springer-Verlag, 237 p.

Fairbridge, R. W., 1961, Eustatic changes in sea level, *in* Physics and chemistry of the earth: New York, Pergamon Press, v. 4, p. 99–185.

Ferm, J. C., 1970, Allegheny deltaic deposits, *in* Deltaic sedimentation, modern and ancient: Society of Economic Paleontologists and Mineralogists Special Publication 15, p. 246–255.

Fischer, A. G., 1981, Climatic oscillations in the biosphere, *in* Biotic crises in ecological and evolutionary time: New York, Academic Press, p. 103–131.

Fischer, A. G., and Bottjer, D. J., 1991, Orbital forcing and sedimentary sequences: Journal of Sedimentary Petrology, Special issue, v. 61, p. 1063–1252.

Geikie, A., 1901, The founders of geology: Baltimore, The Johns Hopkins University, 297 p.

Geological Society of America, 1939, Frontiers of geology: Ten papers originally prepared for fifteen-minute radio addresses by Fellows of the Society 1938–1939, 48 p.

Gilluly, J., 1949, Distribution of mountain building in geologic time: Geological Society of America Bulletin, v. 60, p. 561–590.

Grabau, A. W., 1940, The rhythm of the ages: Peking, Henri Vetch, 561 p.

Grasty, R., 1967, Orogeny, a cause of world-wide regression of the seas: Nature, v. 216, p. 779–780.

Gurnis, M., 1990, Ridge spreading, subduction, and sea level fluctuations: Science, v. 250, p. 970–972.

Gutenburg, B., 1941, Changes in sea level, postglacial uplift, and mobility of the earth's interior: Geological Society of America Bulletin, v. 52, p. 721–772.

Haarman, E., 1930, Die oszillationstheorie; eine erklarung der krustenbewegungen von erde und mond: Stuttgart, Ferdinand Enke Verlag, 260 p.

Haq, B. U., Hardenbol, J., and Vail, P. R., 1987, Chronology of fluctuating sea levels since the Triassic: Science, v. 235, p. 1156–1167.

Henbest, L. G., 1952, Significance of evolutionary explosions for diastrophic division of earth history—Introduction to the symposium on distribution of evolutionary explosions in geologic time: Journal of Paleontology, v. 26,

p. 299–318.

Herschel, J.F.W., 1837, A Fragment (Letters to C. Lyell), *in* The ninth Bridgewater treatise: London, John Murray, p. 207 and 216–217.

Hopkins, W., 1852, Anniversary address of the president: Quarterly Journal of the Geological Society of London, v. 8, p. xxiv–lxv.

Huggett, R., 1989, Cataclysms and earth history—The development of diluvialism: Oxford, Clarendon Press, 220 p.

Imbrie, J., and Imbrie, K. P., 1979, Ice ages—Solving the mysteries: Cambridge, Harvard University, 224 p.

Jamieson, T. E., 1865, On the history of the last geological changes in Scotland: Quarterly Journal of the Geological Society of London, v. 21, p. 161–203.

Johnson, L. L., and Stright, M., 1992, Paleoshorelines and prehistory: an investigation of method: Boca Raton, CRC Press, 243 p.

Joly, J., 1925, The surface history of the earth: Oxford, Clarendon, 192 p.

Klein, G. deV., and Willard, D. A., 1989, Origin of the Pennsylvanian coal-bearing cyclothems of North America: Geology, v. 17, p. 152–155.

Kominz, M., 1984, Oceanic ridge volumes and sea level changes—An error analysis: American Association of Petroleum Geologists Memoir 36, p. 10–127.

Kuenen, Ph. H., 1939, Quantitative estimations relating to eustatic movements: Geologie en Mijnbouw, v. 1, p. 194–201.

Lincoln, J. M., and Schlanger, S. O., 1991, Atoll stratigraphy as a record of sea level change: Problems and prospects: Journal of Geophysical Research, v. 96, p. 6727–6752.

Lirer, L., Luongo, G., and Scandone, R., 1987, On the volcanological evolution of Campi Flegrei: EOS, v. 68, p. 226–234.

Lyell, C., 1835, The Bakerian Lecture—On the proofs of a gradual rising of the land in certain parts of Sweden: Philosophical Transactions of the Royal Society of London, v. 125, p. 1–38.

—— , 1855, On certain trains of erratic blocks on the western borders of Massachusetts, United States: Royal Institution of Great Britain, Proceedings, v. 2, p. 86–97.

Macdonald, D.I.M., ed., 1991, Sedimentology, tectonics and eustasy—Sea-level changes at active margins: International Association of Sedimentologists Special Publication 12, 518 p.

MacLaren, C., 1842, Art. XVI—The glacial theory of Prof. Agassiz: Reprinted in American Journal of Science, v. 42, p. 346–365.

Maillet, B., de, 1748, Telliamed: ou entretiens d'un philosophe indien avec un missionnaire françois sur la diminution de la mer, la formation de la terre, l'origine de l'homme, & Mis en ordere sur les mémoires de feu M. de Maillet: par J.A.G.: Amsterdam, Chez L'Honoré & Fils, v. 1, 208 p; v. 2, 231 p.

Matthews, R. K., and Frohlich, C., 1991, Orbital forcing of low-frequency glacioeustasy: Journal of Geophysical Research, v. 96, p. 6797–6803.

McCartney, P. J., 1977, Henry de la Beche: Observations on an observer: Cardiff, Friends of the National Museum of Wales, 77 p.

Merk, G., 1985, E. O. Ulrich's impact on American stratigraphy, *in* Geologists and ideas: A history of North American geology: Geological Society of America Centennial Special Volume 1, p. 169–187.

Mesolella, K. J., Matthews, R. K., Broecker, W. S., and Thurber, D. L., 1969, The astronomical theory of climatic change: Barbados data: Journal of Geology, v. 77, p. 250–271.

Meyer, W. B., 1986, Delayed recognition of glacial eustasy in American science: Journal of Geological Education, v. 34, p. 21–25.

Miall, A. D., 1986, Eustatic sea level changes interpreted from seismic stratigraphy: A critique of the methodology with particular reference to the North Sea Jurassic record: American Association of Petroleum Geologists Bulletin, v. 70, p. 131–137.

Milankovitch, M., 1920, Théorie mathématique des phénomènes thermiques produits per la radiation solaire: Paris, Gauthier-Villars, 338 p.

Mitchum, R. M., Vail, P. R., Todd, R. G., and Sangree, J. B.,1976, Regional seismic interpretations using sequences and eustatic cycles [abs.]: American Association of Petroleum Geologists, v. 60, p. 699.

Moore, D., 1959, Role of deltas in the formation of some British Lower Carboniferous cyclothems: Journal of Geology, v. 67, p. 522–539.

Moore, R. C., 1949, Meaning of facies: Geological Society of America Memoir 39, p. 1–34.

Mörner, N.-A., 1976, Eustasy and geoid change: Journal of Geology, v. 84, p. 123–151.

Moro, L., 1740, De' Crostacei e degli altri marini corpi che si truovano su'monti: Venice, S. Monti, 426 p.

Nansen, F., 1922, The strandflat and isostasy: Vitenskapsselskapets skrifter, I. Matematisk-Naturvitenskapelig Klasse, 1921, No. 11: Kristiania, I. Kommission hos Jacob Dybwad, 313 p.

Nelson, C. M., 1976, Ulrich, Edward Oscar: Dictionary of Scientific Biography, v. 13, p. 531–534.

Newell, N. D., 1963, Crises in the history of life: Scientific American, v. 208, p. 1–16.

Peltier, W. R., and Tushingham, A. M., 1991, Influence of glacial isostatic adjustment on tide gauge measurements of secular sea level change: Journal of Geophysical Research, v. 96, p. 6779–6796.

Pitman, W. C., III, 1978, Relationship between eustasy and stratigraphic sequences of passive margins: Geological Society of America Bulletin, v. 89, p. 1389–1403.

Revelle, R., Chairman, 1990, Studies in geophysics: Sea-level change: Washington, D.C., National Research Council, Special report of the panel on sea level change, National Academy Press, 234 p.

Reynolds, D. J., Steckler, M. S., and Coakley, B. J., 1991, The role of the sedimentary load in sequence stratigraphy: The influence of flexural isostasy and compaction: Journal of Geophysical Research, v. 96, p. 6931–6949.

Rupke, N. A., 1983, The great chain of history: William Buckland and the English School of geology 1814–1849: Oxford, Clarendon Press, 322 p.

Sahagian, D. L., and Watts, A. B., 1991, Introduction to the special section on measurement, causes, and consequences of long-term sea level changes: Journal of Geophysical Research, v. 96, p. 6585–6589. (Complete special section, Proceedings of the 1989 Snowbird Conference on Sea Level Changes, p. 6583–6981.)

Schlee, J. S., ed., 1984, Interregional unconformities and hydrocarbon accumulation: American Association of Petroleum Geologists Memoir 36, 184 p.

Schuchert, C., 1909, Paleogeography of North America: Geological Society of America Bulletin, v. 20, p. 427–606 (printed in February 1910).

Shaw, A. B., 1964, Time in stratigraphy: New York, McGraw-Hill, 365 p.

Shepard, F. P., 1923, To question the theory of periodic diastrophism: Journal of Geology, v. 31, p. 599–613.

—— , 1936, The underlying causes of submarine canyons: Proceedings of the National Academy of Sciences, v. 22, p. 496–502.

Sloss, L. L., 1963, Sequences in the cratonic interior of North America: Geological Society of America Bulletin, v. 74, p. 93–114.

—— , 1991, The tectonic factor in sea level change: A countervailing view: Journal of Geophysical Research, v. 96, p. 6609–6617.

Sloss, L. L., Krumbein, W. C., and Dapples, E. C., 1949, Integrated facies analysis: Geological Society of America Memoir 39, p. 91–124.

Stearns, H. T., 1941, Shore benches on north Pacific islands: Geological Society of America Bulletin, v. 52, p. 773–780.

Stille, H., 1924, Grundfragen der vergleichenden Tektonik: Berlin, Borntraeger, 443 p.

Suess, E., 1885–1909, Das antlitz der erde: Vienna, F. Tempsky, v. 1, 1885, 778 p.; v. 2, 1888, 703 p.; v. 3, 1909, pt. 1, 508 p.; pt. 2, 789 p. English translation by Sollas, H.B.C., The face of the earth: Oxford, Clarendon, v. I, 1904, 604 p.; v. 2, 1906, 556 p.; v. 3, 1908, 400 p.; v. 4, 1909, 673 p.; v. 5, 1924, 170 p. (index and maps).

Tylor, A., 1872, On the formation of deltas and on the evidence and cause of the great changes in the sea-level during the glacial period: Geological Magazine, v. 9, pt. I, p. 392–399; pt. II, p. 485–501.

Udden, J. A., 1912, Geology and mineral resources of the Peoria Quadrangle: U.S. Geological Survey Bulletin 506, 103 p.

Umbgrove, J.H.F., 1947, The pulse of the earth: The Hague, M. Nijhoff, 358 p.

—— , 1950, Symphony of the earth: The Hague, M. Nijhoff, 220 p.

Vail, P. R.,and Wilbur, R. O., 1966, Onlap, key to worldwide unconformities and depositional cycles [abs.]: American Association of Petroleum Geologists Bulletin, v. 50, p. 638–639.

Vail, P. R., Mitchum, R. M., and Thompson, S., III, 1977, Part Three: Relative changes of sea level from coastal onlap; and Part Four: Global cycles of relative changes of sea level: American Association of Petroleum Geologists Memoir 26, pt. 3, p. 63–82; pt. 4, p. 83–98.

Vella, P., 1962, Terms for real and apparent height of sea level and of parts of the lithosphere: Transactions of the Royal Society of New Zealand, Geology, v. I, p. 101–109.

Vita-Finzi, C., 1986, Recent earth movements, an introduction to neotectonics: London, Academic Press, 226 p.

Wanless, H. R., and Shepard, F. P., 1935, Permo-Carboniferous coal series related to Southern Hemisphere glaciation: Science, v. 81, p. 521–522.

Wanless, H. R., and Weller, J. M., 1932, Correlation and extent of Pennsylvanian cyclothems: Geological Society of America Bulletin, v. 43, p. 1003–1016.

Wegmann, E., 1969, Changing ideas about moving shorelines, *in* Toward a history of geology: Cambridge, M.I.T. Press, p. 386–414.

Wells, A. J., 1960, Cyclical sedimentation: A review: Geological Magazine, v. 97, p. 389–403.

Wentworth, C. K., and Palmer, H. S., 1925, Eustatic bench of islands of the North Pacific: Geological Society of America Bulletin, v. 36, p. 521–544.

Wheeler, H. F., 1964, Baselevel, lithosphere surface, and time-stratigraphy: Geological Society of America Bulletin, v. 75, p. 599–610.

Whittlesey, C., 1868, Depression of the ocean during the ice period: Proceedings, American Association for the Advancement of Science, v. 16, p. 92–97.

Wilgus, C. K., Hastings, B. S., Kendall, C.G.St.C., Posamentier, H. W., Ross, C. A., and Van Waggoner, J. C., eds., 1988, Sea-level changes: An integrated approach: Society of Economic Paleontologists and Mineralogists Special Publication 42, 407 p.

Zeller, E. J., 1964, Cycles and psychology, *in* Symposium on cyclic sedimentation: Kansas Geological Survey Bulletin 169, v. II, p. 631–636.

MANUSCRIPT ACCEPTED BY THE SOCIETY JANUARY 14, 1992

Geological Society of America
Memoir 180
1992

Chapter 2

De Maillet's Telliamed (1748): The diminution of the sea or the fall portion of a complete cosmic eustatic cycle

Albert V. Carozzi
Department of Geology, University of Illinois, Urbana-Champaign, Urbana, Illinois 61801-2999

ABSTRACT

The diminution of the sea according to de Maillet represents the fall portion of an endlessly repeated complete and cosmic eustatic cycle during which water and ashes were exchanged between celestial bodies. This concept, concerning both the geological and biological sciences, is a remarkable achievement for an early eighteenth-century career diplomat and traveler. Furthermore, his ingenious approach to the history of the earth, according to which the sea—during thousands of millions of years of eustatic fall—was entirely responsible for all the physiographic, lithologic, and structural features of the earth's crust, made him an unusual forerunner of eustasy, generalized transformism, marine geology, and sedimentology.

INTRODUCTION

When Benoît de Maillet's *Telliamed, ou Entretiens d'un philosophe indien avec un missionnaire françois sur la diminution de la mer, la formation de la terre, ...*appeared in print in Amsterdam in 1748, the author (Fig. 1), a French diplomat and traveler, had already been dead ten years. Later editions were published (allegedly) in Basel (1749), the Hague-Paris (1755), and two English translations in London (1750) and Baltimore (1797). The Baltimore edition (Fig. 2) is in some respects a puzzle in American intellectual history because the persons and the reasons responsible for its publication remain unknown. Indeed, not many Americans of the time would have welcomed de Maillet's ideas, except perhaps the Englishman Thomas Cooper who immigrated to America in 1793 and could have brought along the English translation. He later taught chemistry and mineralogy, but is mainly remembered for his radical opinions.

All of de Maillet's editions were based on a rather thorough, but unsuccessful editing done by the Abbé Jean Baptiste le Mascrier in Paris in a futile attempt to reconcile the proposed system with the Dogma. Nevertheless, de Maillet's ideas—although presented through the subterfuge of an Indian philosopher bearing his name spelled backwards—remained strongly unorthodox and materialistic. Indeed, the concept of a personified God as a ruler and creator of everything was refuted and an eternal universe was assumed to undergo natural changes at random.

Although several copies of the original and unexpurgated manuscript circulated for almost 20 years, the reaction to the publication of de Maillet's new system of the world was in general violent. The orthodox were scandalized and wrote angry replies and refutations for almost a century. But because it was so well publicized by this opposition, *Telliamed* became a popular book, which affected the leading naturalists of its time, particularly Buffon whose history and theory of the earth (1749) clearly relied on many concepts by de Maillet, without ever quoting him. In modern times, *Telliamed* took an important place in many books dealing with the history of transformism and evolution.

The fundamental implications of de Maillet's contribution to geology, as well as a detailed analysis of his field observations, were established by Carozzi (1968, 1969) by means of the reconstitution of the original text based in particular on a new manuscript (ILL[1]), dated April 29, 1728, now in the library of the University of Illinois.

DE MAILLET'S LIFE

Little is known about Benoît de Maillet's youth, except that he was born at St. Mihiel (Meuse) on April 12, 1656, belonged to a noble family of Lorraine, and received an excellent education.

Carozzi, A. V., 1992, De Maillet's Telliamed (1748): The diminution of the sea or the fall portion of a complete cosmic eustatic cycle, *in* Dott, R. H., Jr., ed., Eustasy: The Historical Ups and Downs of a Major Geological Concept: Boulder, Colorado, Geological Society of America Memoir 180.

Figure 1. Benoît de Maillet (1656 to 1738) from a contemporary etching of Dutch origin in the author's collection.

TELLIAMED;
OR, THE
WORLD EXPLAIN'D:
CONTAINING
DISCOURSES
BETWEEN AN
𝕴𝖓𝖉𝖎𝖆𝖓 𝕻𝖍𝖎𝖑𝖔𝖘𝖔𝖕𝖍𝖊𝖗
AND A
MISSIONARY,
ON THE
DIMINUTION OF THE SEA—
THE
FORMATION OF THE EARTH—
THE
ORIGIN of MEN & ANIMALS
AND OTHER
SINGULAR SUBJECTS,
RELATING TO
Natural Hiſtory & Philoſophy.

◄◄◄◄◄◄◄◄◄◄◄◆❖❖►►►►►►►►►►►►
—A VERY CURIOUS WORK.—
◄◄◄◄◄◄◄◄◄◄◄◄◆❖❖►►►►►►►►►►►►

BALTIMORE:
PRINTED *by W. PECHIN, No. 15, Market-ſtreet—
for D. PORTER, at the* O**BSERVATORY**,
FEDERAL-HILL,
1797.

Figure 2. Title page of the English translation of *Telliamed* published in Baltimore (1797).

In February 1692, when he was only 35 years old, he was appointed—through the favors of his patron the Chancellor of Pontchartrain—General Consul of the king of France in Egypt. He occupied this position until 1708, and apparently conceived and wrote most of his system during the 16 years of his first foreign assignment. His diplomatic privileges allowed him to travel extensively throughout Egypt and the adjacent countries, thus undertaking long and expensive investigations, which only a man in his position could afford. Many of his friends made observations for him in places he could not reach. His perfect knowledge of the Arabic language gave him the opportunity to talk to scholars and to have access to private libraries containing the manuscripts of many ancient Arab authors not otherwise available to the public. While Consul in Leghorn (1708 to 1714), Inspector of French establishments in the Levant and on the Barbary Coast (1715 to 1720), and during a last trip to Egypt in 1718, he continued tirelessly to accumulate amazingly precise geological observations in favor of his idea of the diminution of the sea all along the coasts of the Mediterranean. He spent two years in Paris (1720 to 1721) during a severe epidemic of the plague at Marseille, and afterwards he retired to Marseille in 1721, where he remained until his death, January 30, 1738, at the

age of 82. As soon as de Maillet reached France, his valuable manuscript was recopied and, while he certainly retained the original draft, several copies circulated in literary and scientific circles, as was the custom at that time for controversial works. During this period, de Maillet made numerous additions and changes to his first draft based on additional reading; new personal observations around Marseille, in Provence, and in the Paris basin; and correspondence with contemporary naturalists (see Carozzi, 1968).

DE MAILLET'S COSMOGONIC SYSTEM

A study of de Maillet's cosmogonic system is necessary for a better understanding of his ideas concerning the geological evolution of the earth's crust. This system was based on the Cartesian theory of vortices and Fontenelle's concept of the plurality of inhabited worlds. It postulated that celestial bodies undergo an eternal cycle of dark and luminous phases, corresponding to a constant transmigration of matter within and between the various vortices. This cyclical evolution of the celestial bodies might be better understood with the use of arbitrary stages.

Stage 1. A vortex consisted both of a burning star (sun), which rotated on itself and a certain number of opaque bodies—arranged in order of radially decreasing density—that gravitated around the sun. Currents of subtle matter, corresponding to the sun's rays, were responsible for the rotation of the opaque bodies.

Stage 2. During its burning process, the sun gradually lost its matter in the form of ashes. These ashes were carried away radially by the sun's rays and they collected, on their path, additional dust and especially water from other globes. This association of ashes, dust, and water was transported toward the periphery of the vortex and deposited over light and porous opaque bodies (extinguished suns), which, because of their low density, were also located in the marginal parts of the vortex. By this process the extinguished suns regained the weight and humidity lost during their previous phase of burning and were covered by a thick layer of silty materials that settled at the bottom of an envelope of water formed at the same time.

Stage 3. After a gradual decrease of its intensity, when the sun was finally extinguished and became itself a light dark body, either one of two situations may have occurred: the sun was either carried to the periphery of its own vortex and its place was taken by the nearest planet that became inflamed, or the vortex was dispersed and the opaque bodies, including the former sun, wandered away at random—as comets—which were later incorporated into other vortices.

Stage 4. When an extinguished sun with its envelope of water was captured by another vortex and kept inside at a particular place, determined by the activity of the sun of that vortex, the water envelope either increased or decreased according to its distance from that sun. If the waters decreased by evaporation (as on earth at present, according to de Maillet), Primitive Mountains formed by currents on the floor of the universal ocean and eventually emerged (eustatic fall of sea level).

Life developed in the shallow waters surrounding these mountains and, through general transformism, eventually populated the continents. Secondary Mountains were formed by marine erosion and by reworking of the materials forming the Primitive Mountains to which numerous fossils were added. In short, all the materials forming the earth's crust, except the fossils, derived directly or indirectly from the various kinds of extraterrestrial ashes originally deposited at the bottom of the universal ocean. If an inhabited globe changed vortex and reached a new position in which its waters increased again, the former living organisms were destroyed and buried under new layers of silt. This is one of the processes by which life was destroyed on a globe (eustatic rise of sea level).

Stage 5. The other process occurred when the globe passed through the state of fire. While evaporation proceeded toward completion, combustible organic matters, corresponding to concentrations of fossils buried in the layers of the Secondary Mountains, began to burn, generating volcanoes. These gradually spread over the entire globe, destroying life and changing the opaque body into a new sun.

Stage 6. If the opaque body became a new sun before the sun regulating the vortex to which it belonged was extinguished, the new sun created a vortex of its own, taking away some of the planets of the previous vortex. This process brought the system back to the conditions in Stage 1, and the cycle started again.

Summary. The present-day diminution of the sea, as inferred by de Maillet, on the earth's surface is the sea-level fall episode of an eternally repeated cosmic and complete eustatic cycle produced by a complex interchange of water and ashes between celestial bodies within and between the various vortices. De Maillet did not explain the duration of a complete eustatic cycle because of its variants discussed above, but he assumed that a complete cycle of dark and luminous phases undergone by a celestial body may be considered to be about five billion years. This figure was based on his assumption—whether entirely gratuitous or gathered from uncited theories of his time—that the longest time during which the largest star could remain inflamed would be two billion years, and that the diminution of the sea on earth had been going on for at least two billion years.

THE DIMINUTION OF THE SEA OR
EUSTATIC FALL OF SEA LEVEL

The idea of a diminution of the sea on earth was introduced by de Maillet on the basis of several alleged observations made by the grandfather figure in *Telliamed*. This imaginary grandfather was of course de Maillet himself whose marine observations seem to have been fictitious only with respect to time. Indeed, by including his grandfather's research, de Maillet—actually his spokesman, the equally imaginary Indian philosopher—hoped to document observations of at least three generations on the diminution of the sea. Whether de Maillet actually sponsored the below-mentioned diving experiments himself or had merely heard about them is difficult to tell.

First, his grandfather observed during his lifetime a rock gradually emerging from the ocean on the coast of Egypt. Second, he confirmed the fact by recordings in wells connected with the sea. He calculated that the present diminution of the sea amounted to 7 cm (3 in) per century. He also drew plans for an oceanographic station inspired from the nilometer, or *Mikias,* a building containing an octogonal well with a central graduated

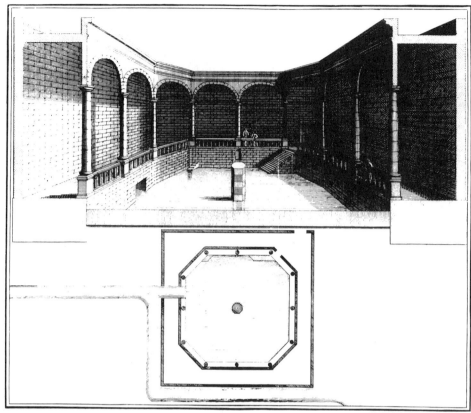

Figure 3. Nilometer (*Mikias*) of the island of Roda, south of Cairo, Egypt. Note the graduated pillar standing in the middle of the well communicating with the Nile (plate facing p. 66 of Le Mascrier's *Description de l'Egypte* . . .; 1735).

pillar used for measuring the rise and fall of the Nile during its periodical floods (Fig. 3).

In the belief that observations on the diminution of the sea showed the continuation of a more general process, de Maillet concluded that mountains had been formed in the sea in the past when its level was much higher. To understand the formation of mountains, he (his grandfather) decided to undertake an extensive oceanographical survey of the present-day shorelines and shallow waters with the clearly expressed uniformitarian statement that the present explained the past. In this section of *Telliamed,* erosional and depositional processes by waves and longshore currents along rocky coasts, beaches, and deltas are discussed in great detail. Similar descriptions of shallow-water processes were based on accounts from divers who allegedly remained several hours underwater. Each diver carried a compass and a sharp stick with a streamer, which, when stuck in the ooze, gave an idea of the direction and strength of bottom currents which could be mapped. For the exploration of greater marine depths inaccessible to divers, his grandfather invented and constructed an intricate diving apparatus which he fully described and called an "aquatic lantern" (Fig. 4). The descent was produced by means of a large stone ball acting as ballast, which was released for the ascent, completed by buoyancy of the machine

itself. Smaller stone balls at the sides kept the device in a vertical position. This device operated on the same principle as modern bathyscaphs (Monod, 1968). The pilot, standing upright in the middle of the lantern, observed the sea floor as far as 91 m (300 ft) around him through four glass windows. His breathing, for up to two hours, was provided by four other portholes closed by moveable leather membranes capable of extracting air from sea water. Several thin cables of known length connected the lantern to the surface and provided means to measure depth by breaking and activating a bell after having been fully stretched. The pilot had also a stop watch with which he could calculate the speed of descent. Observations from this aquatic lantern showed the important action of deep-water bottom currents which, in some places, accumulated muds into submarine mountains and in others actively eroded the substratum. On the basis of the data collected by the aquatic lantern, the topography of the deep sea floor was mapped and the strength and direction of bottom currents was determined by using a large streamer located at the top of the device in the same manner as individual divers had done in shallower waters. When data were unclearly reported, de Maillet's grandfather himself is supposed to have gone down inside the aquatic lantern.

De Maillet's extremely accurate observations of coastal and

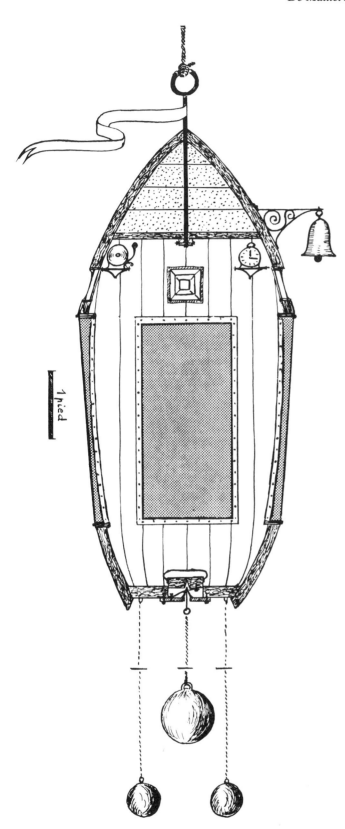

1 pied

Figure 4. Attempted reconstitution of de Maillet's "aquatic lantern" (from Monod, 1968).

deep-water processes and sediments imply a personal knowledge either of the author himself—in part represented by his mythical grandfather—or of some hired observer, or knowledge derived from the reading of some unidentified earlier (Arab?) author. Indeed, de Maillet mentioned as a forerunner of the concept of the diminution of the sea the famous Persian scholar Omar-al-Khayyam (1040 to 1123) who had written a very similar treatise on the subject supported by a comparison between older geographic maps and those of his time. He had also estimated the rate of diminution of the sea at 7 cm (3 in) per century. Unfortunately, this treatise was lost and de Maillet's account of Omar-al Khayyam may be the only one existing in a European language, so the circumstances of these early oceanographic studies remain clouded in mystery.

THE EVOLUTION OF THE EARTH'S CRUST

De Maillet's terminology of sedimentary rocks relied on the observation of recent marine coastal sediments and was mainly a classification based on grain size, with no reference to mineralogical compositions. All rocks consisted of angular blocks, cobbles, pebbles, sands, silts, and muds, and their induration was attributed to the crystallization of marine salt, an idea probably derived from the observation of the rapid induration of beachrock.

His ideas on the evolution of the earth's crust during the fall portion of the cosmic eustatic cycle can be summarized as follows. While the sea was surrounding the earth completely, its bottom currents circulated for countless ages, reworking and transporting ashlike materials consisting of sands, silts, and calcinated stones of extraterrestrial origin. On the floor of this deep ocean, the currents, by their combined depositional and erosional action, generated the so-called *Primitive or Primordial Mountains.* These, he said, are today, the highest on earth and consist of a simple and uniform substance, either massive or in beds of variable thickness and almost always horizontal. These rocks are devoid of fossils or contain a very small number of them because, at the time of their deposition, the ocean was too deep to allow any development of life (Fig. 5a).

This description applies to granite and metamorphic rocks, which commonly form the central and highest portions of many mountain ranges and are surrounded by marginal belts of lower mountains consisting of sedimentary rocks.

Because of his purely sedimentological approach, de Maillet interpreted all mountains and valleys—in other terms, the entire landscape—as the result of depositional and erosional actions of marine currents. In his mind, there was continuity in all respects between mountains exposed by the diminution of the sea and those still under water, in the process of being formed.

He explained the formation of mountains by considering them as equivalents of submarine bars generated by various patterns of currents on the sea floor or in front of deltas. He distinguished mountain types on the basis of their morphology. A simple, short, and elongate mountain resulted from the deposition of a bar at the meeting point of two currents flowing in opposite

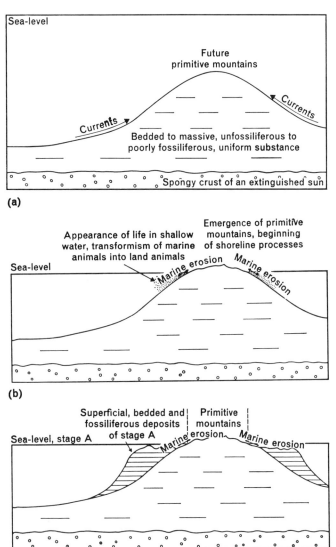

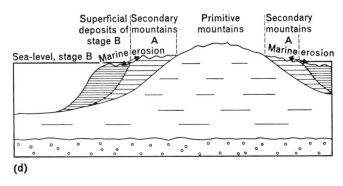

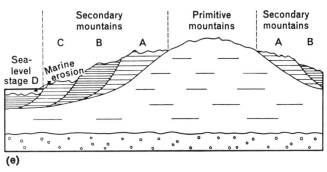

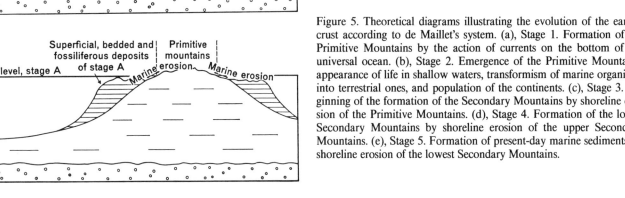

Figure 5. Theoretical diagrams illustrating the evolution of the earth's crust according to de Maillet's system. (a), Stage 1. Formation of the Primitive Mountains by the action of currents on the bottom of the universal ocean. (b), Stage 2. Emergence of the Primitive Mountains, appearance of life in shallow waters, transformism of marine organisms into terrestrial ones, and population of the continents. (c), Stage 3. Beginning of the formation of the Secondary Mountains by shoreline erosion of the Primitive Mountains. (d), Stage 4. Formation of the lower Secondary Mountains by shoreline erosion of the upper Secondary Mountains. (e), Stage 5. Formation of present-day marine sediments by shoreline erosion of the lowest Secondary Mountains.

direction or between a stream flow and an opposite marine current in front of a delta. A long chain of mountains was produced by two currents intersecting each other obliquely, causing the weakest current to deposit materials alongside the strongest. A similar type of mountain may have also been formed when two currents flowed parallel to each other but in opposite direction and formed a bar between each other. Two long chains of mountains separated by a longitudinal valley resulted from one powerful current cutting across two opposite ones, forming a double bar by eroding a channel through the original bar.

De Maillet considered the size of mountains a function of the importance of the generating current, of the amount of materials transported, and of the depth of the sea. All the valleys, with their steep slopes or cliffs, all passes, or any other interruptions between mountains were generated at the same time as the mountains themselves by truncation of the deposits by contemporane-

ous transverse currents. However, he interpreted gentle slopes as depositional in origin and produced by the normal termination of currents. In such a context, he considered the correlation of beds from one mountain to another, across a valley or a basin, a very logical procedure.

In summary, all morphological features of a given landscape were the results of erosional and depositional processes, mostly synchronous with the general marine sedimentation of soft materials. These were gradually indurated by crystallization of marine salt into a completed and "congealed" landscape that was to undergo only minor subsequent changes by weathering upon exposure to the atmosphere.

Although de Maillet understood fairly well the origin and properties of soils and the small-scale effects of weathering, and even described erosion, transportation, and deposition actions of streams, he took a contradictory position on a large scale by negating to rivers any major role in shaping the scenery. He clearly stated that stream valleys are preexisting channels carved by marine currents subsequently used after emergence by streams to concentrate and evacuate rain waters to the sea. Such channels were deepened, kept open, and extended downstream by tidal currents during the gradual retreat of the sea, as is the case today in estuaries.

After a certain amount of evaporation had taken place, the upper portions of the Primitive Mountains were finally exposed to the air. This emergence initiated the process of weathering, while life appeared in the shallow waters surrounding the newly emerged lands (Fig. 5b). According to de Maillet, the entire space of the universe is full of seeds of everything, sensitive or vegetative, able to live. These seeds are so minute as to be invisible and consequently cannot perish. They are more abundant around opaque globes, in thick airs, and in waters than in interplanetary spaces.

These seeds are available at all times to participate in the operations of nature that make the waters around globes at certain times proper for fecundity and for the creation of new species. On earth, such favorable conditions did not occur until the existence of shallow waters around the newly emerged Primitive Mountains. This situation provided a supply of food not available before and a good mixing between the agitated and shallow waters warmed by the sun and the air containing the seeds. Indeed, on the bottom deposits of retreating seas, particularly in the rich silts, the seeds found appropriate conditions for their initial stages of development. Thereafter, they went out into the waters searching for additional food to reach a final size characteristic of a given species.

De Maillet believed that because of the lowering of sea level and the continuously increasing continents, all forms of life underwent a generalized transformism to adapt themselves to the new environments. Marine plants slowly changed into land types; sea animals mastered flight and walking, giving rise to birds and land animals; mermen and mermaids abandoned their aquatic life to become terrestrial human beings.

While this spectacular transformism was taking place, the generation of the *Secondary Mountains,* daughters of the Primitive ones, began. They consisted of horizontally bedded sands and muds, deposited in shallow waters—no longer on the floor of the deep ocean—but derived from the erosion of the Primitive Mountains by wave action along shorelines. They typically contained abundant remains of marine organisms (Fig. 5c). These sedimentary rocks displayed all the features of the present coastal and shallow-water sediments described in de Maillet's oceanographical survey.

The formation of the Secondary Mountains was actually a generalized process of reworking of earlier coastal deposits by the sea (Fig. 5d). As the marine erosion of the Primitive Mountains provided the materials for the first set of Secondary Mountains, these, in turn, were the sources for the sediments of the second set of Secondary Mountains located at lower elevation. The process described by de Maillet as "higher mountains will give birth to lower ones" is consistent with his concept that excludes the action of streams. Indeed, during a lowering of sea level, these streams would have reworked all previous higher deposits mixed together, not only those located immediately above a given one. He wrote that this reworking process would continue as long as the sea existed to receive materials from its shoreline erosion (Fig. 5e).

With decreasing sea level, Secondary Mountains were younger and less elevated, but this age relationship does not contradict the fact that in a given geological section, beds are superposed from bottom to top following the law of superposition (Fig. 5). De Maillet was well aware of this fundamental principle when he stressed the idea that each horizontal layer is considered to have kept its original elevation when deposited on the bottom of the diminishing sea.

De Maillet's system was devoid of any orogenic mechanism that would uplift, tilt, or fold strata because his geological experience was limited to sedimentary rock areas with essentially horizontal or mildly deformed strata (Carozzi, 1968, 1969).

SIGNIFICANCE OF FOSSILS, ORIGIN OF HUMANKIND, AND "PETRIFIED SHIPS"

In his field descriptions, de Maillet recognized and demonstrated at great length the organic origin of fossils. At that time, the term "extraneous bodies" included everything dug out from the ground: that is, fossils of marine organisms, remains of continental vertebrates (interpreted as giant human beings), and the alleged products of their activity, such as ships, weapons, tools, and earthenware.

He noticed that fossils were frequently oriented parallel to bedding and concentrated in certain layers. Applying the same principle as for the enclosing beds, he said that fossils followed the law of superposition and were supposed to occur at the same elevation at which they originally lived and died on the sea floor during the diminution of the sea. Like other contemporary naturalists, de Maillet noticed that lower layers contained remains of animals and plants unknown along present coasts, whereas upper layers contained fossils comparable to modern coastal forms. He suggested three possible explanations: first, the faunas of the lower beds lived in deep water and faunas living at such depths are still poorly known; second, they became extinct when the basins in which they lived dried up as a consequence of the diminution of the sea (eustatic fall of sea level); third, when the sea was deeper and more extensive, long-distance flotation by marine currents could freely operate, bringing exotic forms into the lower layers of Europe from Asia or North America. Emerging lands gradually reduced and finally stopped the flotation, thus explaining the differences observed between older and modern faunas.

In the framework of his idea that the sea level had diminished for at least two billion years, de Maillet considered that mermaids and mermen came out of the sea as humans and populated continents many thousands of centuries after the emergence of the Primitive Mountains, probably when the earth reached half of its present age. According to him it took humankind the other half to develop navigation from a simple plank to those "fossilized" ships said to have been found in rocks on the tops of mountains. He furthermore postulated that cities and harbors already existed when sea level was 1,828 m (6,000 ft) above its present elevation. This statement, combined with the present rate of diminution of 7 cm (3 in) per century based on observations made by his grandfather in wells connected to the sea, would give to these harbors an age of 2.4 million years. Such a figure is actually in default, because de Maillet believed that the rate of the diminution of the sea increased with time as the sea became shallower, smaller, filled with additional sediments, and interspersed with more numerous and larger islands and continents.

In the context of such an early appearance of humankind, it is easy to understand why de Maillet interpreted Cenozoic vertebrate bones as human skeletons, fragments of red shales reworked in conglomerates as debris of earthenware, and particularly the spectacular silicified logs of fluviocontinental deposits of the Egyptian Desert as petrified ships, thus perpetuating the ancient legend of anchors and ships on mountain tops. This last subject is worth a short comment. Large outcrops of Oligocene vividly colored sands and gravels at Wadi-el-Faregh (formerly called Bahar-Balaama), south of Wadi Natrun, 70 km northwest of Cairo, display abundant silicified tree trunks, some of which reach 30 m in length and were remarkably aligned by stream currents during their final deposition. There is no doubt that the preferred orientation of the huge silicified logs associated with smaller debris suggested the appearance of ships with their broken masts and yards, confirming de Maillet's belief in the early appearance of humankind. A similar situation was recently described and illustrated (Albritton and others, 1990, p. 955, Fig. 3) in the Miocene Moghra Formation of the Qattara Depression in the Western Desert of Egypt.

De Maillet's discussion of the origin of humans integrated all living organisms into their geological framework, both resulting from the eustatic fall of sea level, a process by itself a fleeting phase of the endlessly repeated complete and cosmic eustatic cycles.

ACKNOWLEDGMENTS

The author is grateful to Robert H. Dott, Jr., Markes E. Johnson, and Kenneth L. Taylor for their critical review of the manuscript and constructive criticisms.

REFERENCES CITED

Albritton, C. C., Jr., Brooks, J. E., Issawi, B., and Swedan, A., 1990, Origin of the Qattara Depression, Egypt: Geological Society of America Bulletin, v. 102, p. 952–960.

Buffon, G.L.L., 1749, Histoire et théorie de la terre, *in* Histoire naturelle, générale et particulière, avec la description du cabinet du Roy: Paris, Imprimerie Royale, 612 p.

Carozzi, A. V., 1968, Telliamed or conversations between an Indian philosopher and a French missionary on the diminution of the sea by Benoît de Maillet, edited English translation: Urbana, University of Illinois Press, 465 p.

—— , 1969, De Maillet's Telliamed (1748): An ultra-neptunian theory of the earth, *in* Schneer, C. J., ed., Toward a history of geology: Cambridge, M.I.T. Press, p. 80–99.

Le Mascrier, J. B., 1735, Description de l'Egypte, contenant plusieurs remarques curieuses sur la géographie ancienne et moderne de ce païs, sur ses monumens anciens . . . composée sur les mémoires de M. de Maillet: Paris, Chez L. Genneau et J. Rolin, 570 p.

Maillet, B. de, 1748, Telliamed, ou Entretiens d'un philosophe indien avec un missionnaire françois sur la diminution de la mer, la formation de la terre, l'origine de l'homme, &. Mis en ordre sur les mémoires de feu M. de Maillet, par J.A.G. *** [i.e., Jean Antoine Guer]: Amsterdam, Chez L'Honoré & Fils, v. 1, 208 p.; v. 2, 231 p.

—— , 1797, Telliamed; or the world explain'd: Containing discourses between an Indian philosopher and a missionary, on the diminution of the sea, the formation of the earth, the origin of men & animals and other singular subjects relating to Natural History & Philosophy. A very curious work: Baltimore, printed by W. Pechin, No. 15, Marketstreet for D. Porter, at the Observatory, Federal-Hill, 268 p.

Monod, T., 1968, Un précurseur du bathyscaphe au XVIIIe siècle: la "lanterne aquatique" de Benoist de Maillet: Institut océanographique de Monaco, Bulletin, No. spécial 2, p. 25–33.

MANUSCRIPT ACCEPTED BY THE SOCIETY JANUARY 14, 1992

Geological Society of America
Memoir 180
1992

Chapter 3

Eduard Suess and European thought on Phanerozoic eustasy

A. Hallam
School of Earth Sciences, University of Birmingham, Birmingham B15 2TT, England

ABSTRACT

The Austrian geologist Suess was the person who introduced the concept of eustasy, distinguishing two types of movement, caused by different processes. Negative movements, involving lowering of sea level, were caused by spasmodic subsidence of the ocean floor as a consequence of global contraction. Positive movements, involving rise of sea level, were more continuous and caused by the displacement of seawater by ocean-floor sedimentation. Suess's eustatic interpretation was disputed by later scholars. Haug, thus, maintained that transgressions on the continents correlated with regressions in the geosynclines, and vice versa, and Haarmann argued for contemporary up and down movement of landmasses, with rises and falls of sea level a secondary consequence. However, the German geologist, Stille, was a confirmed eustasist, arguing that the major movements of the strandline had affected all the continents in much the same sense at the same time. Stille claimed that a series of relatively brief global "orogenic periods" increased the total continental area and caused general regression of the sea. Stille was the first to produce a eustatic curve for the Phanerozoic, but publication of this had to await a paper by Umbgrove shortly before the Second World War. Another Dutchman, Kuenen, was a pioneer in the use of the hypsographic curve to attempt a crude estimate of the amount of sea-level change resulting from a given change in area of land flooded by epicontinental seas. He rejected Suess's explanations of positive and negative eustasy, preferring with Umbgrove an underlying mechanism bound up with mantle processes.

After the Second World War a reaction set in against Stille's geotectonic ideas, but eustatic studies were given support by oceanographic studies that suggested a plausible mechanism for long-term eustatic changes, and more detailed stratigraphic work across the world, which supported the reality of eustasy. Modern work concentrates on applying the concepts of sequence stratigraphy.

INTRODUCTION

Near the end of the last century the Austrian geologist Eduard Suess published his great synthesis *Das Antlitz der Erde* (1888), which achieved a wider readership once it had been translated by Sollas as *The Face of the Earth* (Suess, 1906). He was the first person to take up the idea of global sea-level changes as a general working theory, and introduced the term "eustatic" for such changes. While studying Tertiary deposits in Europe, he was impressed by the way that successive marine transgressions seemed to correlate across wide regions, notably in the Paris Basin, the Rhone Valley, Italy, the Pannonian and Vienna Basins, Galicia, and the Black Sea area. While local tectonic movements had disturbed the simple picture, the eustatic "signal," to use modern jargon in information theory, was clearly discernible from such local tectonic "noise," and he used such terms as First and Second Mediterranean Invasions. Suess was also struck by the wide distribution over the continents of the Late Cretaceous chalk and stratigraphically equivalent marine deposits, which he related to the "Cenomanian Transgression."

The original definition of eustatic movements is to be found in Suess (1888, p. 680):

Hallam, A., 1992, Eduard Suess and European thought on Phanerozoic eustasy, *in* Dott, R. H., Jr., ed., Eustasy: The Historical Ups and Downs of a Major Geological Concept: Boulder, Colorado, Geological Society of America Memoir 180.

Figure 1. Portrait of Eduard Suess (1831 to 1914). (Frontispiece of the French translation of *Das Antlitz der Erde*; Suess, 1918).

Veränderungen . . . welche annähernd in gleicher Hohe, in positivem oder in negativem Sinne über die ganze Erde sich äussern, und bezeichnen diese Gruppe von Bewegungen als eustatische Bewegungen.

This passage was translated by Sollas (Suess, 1906, p. 538) thus:

changes . . . which take place at an approximately equal height, whether in a positive or negative direction, over the whole globe; this group we will distinguish as *eustatic movements*. (Italics in the original.)

Suess recognized a difference between the positive and negative movements. "We are acquainted with two kinds of eustatic movements; one, produced by subsidence of the earth's crust, is spasmodic and negative; the other, caused by the growth of massive deposits, is continuous and positive" (Suess, 1906, p. 544). One can add parenthetically here that it is perhaps a pity that Suess did not give the noun corresponding to the adjective eustatic, because many people continue to misspell eustasy as eustacy, forgetting the spelling of such words as isostasy and ecstasy.

It is clear from the above quotation that Suess envisaged eustatic movements as asymmetric in character, the falls being more temporally irregular, and perhaps more rapid, than the rises,

and related to different phenomena. The falls were the result of subsidence of the ocean floor as a consequence of Earth contraction, while the rises were due to the upward displacement of sea water by sedimentation on the ocean bottom. Like Dana in North America, Suess believed in a thermally cooling and contracting earth, with sea-floor subsidence causing eustatic falls, while the continents remained virtually rigid and unchanging in level. It is perhaps curious that, in spite of his extensive, pioneering discussions of orogenic belts and island arcs, he regarded lateral orogenic compression as having insignificant effects upon sea level.

AFTER SUESS

In the early part of this century, it had become conclusively established that large parts of North America and Eurasia had been covered by ice caps in the geologically recent past, and that sea level had risen subsequently as the ice caps melted. The alternation of glacial and interglacial deposits indicated that the sea-level changes resulting from successive melting and freezing of polar ice caps had been a repeating phenomenon in the Quaternary. Thus glacioeustasy has been universally accepted throughout this century as an important phenomenon by Quaternary geologists, with dispute being centered only on the details. However longer-term Phanerozoic changes, involving tectonoeustasy, have proved more controversial. Haug (1900), for example, argued that transgressions and regressions in geosynclines were not simultaneous with those of the continents, that in fact transgressions on the continents correlated with regressions in the geosynclines, and vice versa. His "orogenic" movements in the geosynclines occurred in an opposite direction to epeirogenic movements on the continents. Haarmann's (1930) oscillation theory postulated contemporary up and down movement of land masses as the primary phenomenon of tectogenesis, with rises and falls of sea level a secondary consequence.

On the other hand, Haarmann's German compatriot Stille (1924) concluded that the major movements of the strandline, positive and negative, had affected all the continents in much the same sense at the same time; that is, the movements were genuinely eustatic. Very long periods of geological time were characterized by relative tectonic quiet, by the so-called "epeirogenic processes." These alternated with relatively brief "orogenic periods" during which there was widespread deformation of the crust, of which 30 were recognized and given names such as Taconic and Sudetic. These orogenic episodes, accompanied by accentuated uplift of regions outside the fold belts, increased the total continental area and caused general regression of the sea (Fig. 2).

The Haarmann interpretation was challenged by Grabau (1936), who propounded instead a theory of rhythmic pulsation involving rise and fall of sea level as the primary controlling factor, with land movements effecting secondary modifications. Positive pulsations brought about transgressions and negative pulsations caused regressons, with formation of continental deposits and extensive erosion. Supporting examples were drawn from the

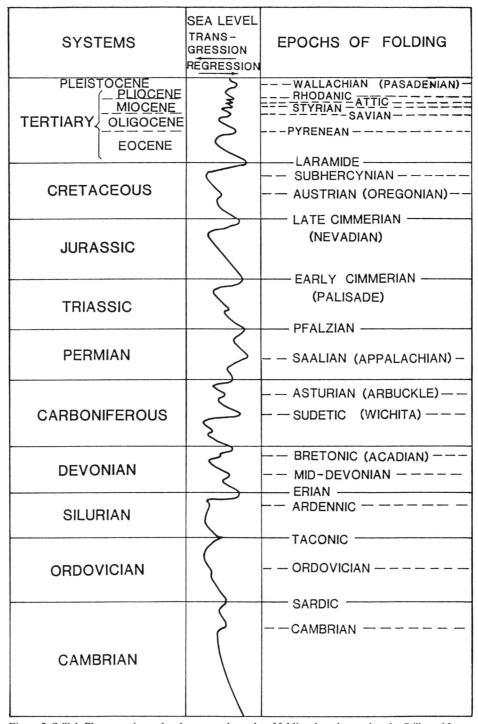

Figure 2. Stille's Phanerozoic sea-level curve and epochs of folding, based on a chart by Stille and Lotze exhibited in Berlin University. (Simplified from Umbgrove, 1939, Fig. 1.)

Palaeozoic of Europe, North America, and China. The Dutch geologist Umbgrove (1939) was stimulated by Grabau into proposing that eustatic movements were a major rhythmic phenomenon throughout Phanerozoic time, with both these as well as movements of the continents being caused by unspecified pulsatory processes in the mantle. He was the first to publish a eustatic curve for the whole Phanerozoic, based on a chart by Stille and Lotze exhibited in Berlin University (Fig. 2).

Umbgrove invited his more numerate colleague Kuenen to investigate quantitative relationships associated with eustasy, and to him indeed goes the credit of being the first person to present tentative figures on the possible extent of eustatic change and associated areal spread of epicontinental seas, based on use of the hypsographic curve (Kuenen, 1939). According to Kuenen, at most periods in Earth history a relative sea-level rise of 100 m would have caused a transgression of approximately half the continental area, and 50 m about a quarter. He thought it safe to conclude that most eustatic changes have been between 25 and 100 m. Many Umbgrove-type rhythms occurred at times when there were no ice ages and involved movements about three orders of magnitude slower than glacioeustatic events. Consequently these longer-term movements must be attributed to changes in the cubic capacity of the ocean basins, presumably bound up with subcrustal phenomena. Kuenen challenged Suess's eustatic interpretation. Earth contraction was rejected as a phenomenon to cause regressions, and sedimentation rates on the ocean floor were by the 1930s known to be too low to have had more than a negligible effect on transgressions.

In the years following the Second World War, a reaction set in against Stille's geotectonic ideas, especially in North America (e.g., Gilluly, 1949), and there was an associated scepticism concerning the related phenomenon of tectonoeustasy. In particular the reality of Stille's brief, globally embracing orogenic episodes was called into question, and stratigraphic work, while becoming increasingly detailed, tended to focus on limited regions. Matters began to change in the 1960s as a consequence of two developments. Oceanographic studies had revealed the existence of a mid-oceanic ridge system, and the growth and decline of such ridges provided a ready mechanism for changing the cubic capacity of the ocean basins and hence a means of causing long-term changes of sea level (Hallam, 1963). In addition, increasing amounts of thorough biostratigraphic work, both on the continents and under the oceans, was tending to confirm in detail what had long been suspected by the older eustasists, namely that transgressions and regressions on the continents, and corresponding events in the fully marine record, could be traced very extensively and sometimes globally. This could be true even on a fine scale. Thus it was concluded that, whereas most sedimentary "cycles" probably had a local or regional cause associated with variations in tectonic uplift and subsidence, and associated sedimentation patterns, there was a significant minority of "cycles" that were likely to have had a eustatic control (Duff and others, 1967).

In 1956 the Hungarian geophysicist Egyed put forward a model of slow Earth expansion since the Precambrian that is related to phase transformation of the core to material with a lower density, with a consequent increase in mantle volume. He supported his model by reference to paleogeographic maps indicating the degree of flooding of the continents at different times in the Phanerozoic. Egyed's argument was that, disregarding shorter-term oscillations, if the Earth has been expanding through the Phanerozoic, there should have been a gradual withdrawal of sea from the continents.

Egyed's claim appeared to be supported by paleogeographic

maps produced by the Russian N. M. Strakhov (1948) and the French couple H. and G. Termier (1952). Although independent analysis of both these and other paleogeographic maps supports the notion that, for example, Paleozoic seas were more extensive than subsequently (Hallam, 1977), and, although Egyed's idea was enthusiastically supported by the great British geologist Arthur Holmes (1965), there is a more conservative explanation of this phenomenon. If the ocean volume has changed negligibly during the Phanerozoic but the average thickness of the continents has increased slightly, then the secular withdrawal of epicontinental seas, superimposed on a pattern of oscillations, can be accounted for without invoking a change of Earth radius that leads to geophysical difficulties (Hallam, 1971).

Short-term eustatic changes have remained more controversial than long-term ones, and it has been argued by the Swedish geologist Mörner (1976) that, because of geoid changes, the very concept of eustasy must be modified to be confined to merely regional events. Mörner's interpretation is challengeable on theoretical grounds (Steckler, 1984) and can also be tested empirically. If geoidal variations significantly affect sea level, then transgressions in one part of the Earth should correlate with regressions elsewhere. There appears in fact to be abundant evidence that many important transgressions can be correlated both within extensive regions of the same continent and between different continents.

CONCLUSIONS

It is difficult at present to perceive a consensual European view about eustasy. Currently an increasing number of European workers are studying regional sea-level changes using the methods of sequence stratigraphy developed by Exxon geologists in North America, but this does not necessarily mean that they accept a global as opposed to a regional tectonic explanation. On grounds of stratigraphic correlation, however, a reasonable number are sympathetic to eustatic explanations of the stratigraphic record (Hallam, 1984). As regards short-term changes, a majority are probably happy with the end-Ordovician regression, late Tertiary events, and Carboniferous cyclothems being bound up with glacioeustasy, but short-term changes at times of apparent global equability pose more of a problem. While most geologists are sceptical of invoking glacioeustasy for the Jurassic and Cretaceous, for instance, a few are, however, prepared to speculate along these lines (e.g., Brandt 1986; Weissert and Lini, 1991).

ACKNOWLEDGMENTS

I thank R. H. Dott, Jr., for the invitation to participate in the symposium on the History of Eustasy in 1990 and to contribute a manuscript for publication in this volume. I also appreciate helpful reviews of the manuscript by William M. Jordan (Millersville State University) and Alexander Tollman (University of Vienna).

REFERENCES CITED

Brandt, K., 1986, Glacioeustatic cycles in the Early Jurassic? Neues Jahrbuch für Geologie und Paläontologie Monatshefte, p. 257–274.

Duff, P.McL.D., Hallam, A., and Walton, E. K., 1967, Cyclic Sedimentation: Amsterdam, Elsevier, 280 p.

Egyed, L., 1956, The change of the Earth's dimensions determined from paleogeographic data: Geofisica Pura Applicata, v. 33, p. 42–48.

Gilluly, J., 1949, Distribution of mountain-building in geologic time: Geological Society of America Bulletin 60, p. 561–590.

Grabau, A. W., 1936, Oscillation or pulsation?: International Geolgical Congress Report of the 16th Session, United States of America 1933, v. 1, p. 539–552.

Haarmann, E., 1930, Die Oszillationstheorie, eine Erklärung der Krustenbewegungen von Erde und Mond: Stuttgart, Ferdinand Enke Verlag, 260 p.

Hallam, A., 1963, Major epeirogenic and eustatic changes since the Cretaceous and their possible relationship to crustal structure: American Journal of Science 261, p. 397–423.

—— , 1971, Re-evaluation of the palaeogeographic argument for an expanding Earth: Nature, v. 232, p. 180–182.

—— , 1977, Secular changes in marine inundation of USSR and North America through the Phanerozoic: Nature, v. 2698, p. 769–772.

—— , 1984, Pre-Quaternary sea-level changes, Annual Review of Earth and Planetary Sciences 12, p. 205–243.

Haug, E., 1900, Les géosynclinaux et les aires continentales: Bulletin de la Société Géologique de France, ser 3, v. 28, p. 617–711.

Holmes, A., 1965, Principles of Physical Geology (second edition): London and Edinburgh, Nelson, p. 1288.

Kuenen, P. H., 1939, Quantitative estimates relating to eustatic movements: Geologie en Mijnbouw, no. 8, p. 194–201.

Mörner, N. -A., 1976, Eustasy and geoid changes: Journal of Geology, v. 84, p. 123–151.

Steckler, M., 1984, Changes in sea level, in Holland, H. D., and Trendall, A. F., eds., Patterns of change in Earth evolution: Berlin, Springer-Verlag, p. 103–121.

Stille, H., 1924, Grundfragen der vergleichenden Tektonik: Berlin, Bornstraeger, p. 526.

Strakhov, N. M., 1948, Outlines of historical geology: Moscow, Government Printing Office, p. 373.

Suess, E., 1888, Das Antlitz der Erde: Prague, Vienna, Leipzig, Tempsky-Freytag, v. 2, 703 p.

—— , 1906, The Face of the Earth, translated by Sollas, W. J., Oxford, Clarendon, v. 2, 556 p.

—— , 1918, La face de la terre, translated by E. de Margerie: Paris, Colin, partie 4, 258 p.

Termier, H., and Termier, G., 1952, Histoire géologique de la Biosphère: Paris, Masson, p. 152.

Umbgrove, J.H.F., 1939, On rhythms in the history of the Earth: Geological Magazine, v. 76, p. 116–129.

Weissert, H., and Lini, A., 1991; Ice age interludes during the time of Cretaceous greenhuse climate, in Muller, D. W., McKenzie, J. A., and Weissert, H., eds., Controversies in modern geology: London, Academic Press, 1973–191.

MANUSCRIPT ACCEPTED BY THE SOCIETY JANUARY 14, 1992

Geological Society of America
Memoir 180
1992

Chapter 4

T. C. Chamberlin's hypothesis of diastrophic control of worldwide changes of sea level: A precursor of sequence stratigraphy

Robert H. Dott, Jr.
Department of Geology and Geophysics, University of Wisconsin, Madison, Wisconsin 53706

ABSTRACT

T. C. Chamberlin's 1898 diastrophic (tectonic) control paper was a short editorial-like response to a questionnaire about geologic time divisions; the more famous and even shorter 1909 paper restated the primacy of diastrophic control of worldwide unconformities as a basis for correlation. This hypothesis derived from Chamberlin's beloved planetesimal theory, which postulated a gravitationally shrinking globe. The earth was considered entirely solid with isostatic equilibration being effected by periodic vertical adjustments between deep, wedge-shaped blocks. During early planetesimal accretion, minor heterogeneities augmented by weathering processes led to denser, lower oceanic and lighter, higher continental wedges. Shrinkage-induced global stress caused spasmodic sinking of the oceanic wedges, which produced elevation (or lesser subsidence) of continental ones, thus regression. During subsequent, longer diastrophic quiescence, erosion reduced continents and extended the "circumcontinental submarine terrace" (shelf) by sedimentation. Areas elevated above their isostatic equilibrium level would slowly settle back to equilibrium. This crustal sinking, coupled with sedimentation-induced displacement of sea water, now caused transgression. The oscillations of sea level would also dramatically affect organic evolution and produce important climatic effects as well. During continental emergence, weathering would consume CO_2, causing cooling, but during transgressions, CO_2 would accumulate in the atmosphere to cause greenhouse warming. Such climatic changes should accentuate the effects of global diastrophism as the "ulterior basis of time divisions."

Although Chamberlin did not employ the term *eustasy*, he presented an appealing and influential mechanism, which showed striking resemblances to Eduard Suess' concepts of global contraction and periodic eustatic changes published ten years earlier. Chamberlin's hypothesis of repetitive, synchronous worldwide changes of sea level with resulting universal unconformities punctuating the global stratigraphic record—"correlated pulsations"—was to have a profound effect upon many subsequent workers, especially in North America, and was an important precursor of modern sequence stratigraphy.

INTRODUCTION

T. C. Chamberlin's hypothesis of universal unconformities resulting from worldwide sea-level changes caused by synchronous global diastrophism contained clear premonitions of modern sequence stratigraphy. Thus, "correlation by unconformities" (Chamberlin, 1909, p. 691) and "periodic development [progra-

dation] and emergence of circumcontinental terraces" (Chamberlin, 1898, p. 462) have a disarmingly modern ring. The only thing lacking was the use of Eduard Suess' term "eustatic" to identify the postulated successive drownings and emergences of continental terraces. When we consider the profound impact of Chamberlin's "diastrophic control" upon American stratigraphic thinking up to World War II, it is apparent that any historical analysis

Dott, R. H., Jr., 1992, T. C. Chamberlin's hypothesis of diastrophic control of worldwide changes of sea level: A precursor of sequence stratigraphy, *in* Dott, R. H., Jr., ed., Eustasy: The Historical Ups and Downs of a Major Geological Concept: Boulder, Colorado, Geological Society of America Memoir 180.

of the concept of eustasy and of sequence stratigraphy must take account of Chamberlin. In attempting such an analysis, this paper draws upon other Chamberlin writings to amplify the development of his thinking, for diastrophism was a theme to which he returned again and again (e.g., Chamberlin, 1918, 1920, 1921a, b).

As founder and Czar of the *Journal of Geology,* T. C. Chamberlin (Fig. 1) commonly used the pages of his journal to highlight major contemporary issues, chiefly through the mechanisms of invited commentaries by experts and extended editorial discourses by himself (Schultz, 1976). An example of the former technique appeared in the 1898 May-June issue of the *Journal* under the title "A Symposium on the Classification and Nomenclature of Geologic Time-Divisions" (Anonymous, 1898, p. 333–355; author not identified). This 22-page article presented the responses by six distinguished American geologists to a questionnaire prepared by co-editor Roland Salisbury. Fourteen questions were posed, which dealt with various aspects of stratigraphic classification that might lead to an acceptable, uniform geologic time scale. Make-up of the questionnaire reflects the fact that there were many conflicting usages of age terms and many diverse opinions about the best scheme to use. Should the European standard classification be imposed upon American rocks, or should there be a separate classification "better adapted to North America"? Should there be formal nouns to distinguish time from formations? Should the sub-Carboniferous (Devonian) and Permian be separated from the Carboniferous? Should the Cretaceous be formally subdivided into two divisions (Upper and Lower or Comanche)? Reading these questions today gives one an eery feeling of prescience for the modern Stratigraphic Code.

Publication of the "Symposium" involved a two-page preamble, which explained the motivation for the questionnaire. "We appear to have been receding from uniformity, rather than approaching it, for the past two decades" (Anonymous, 1898, p. 334). This, in spite of the fact that "The importance of a more systematic classification of time-divisions and rock-series has been recognized by the international congresses of the last two decades" (Anonymous, 1898, p. 333). Next, the statement of the 14 questions asked of the respondents spanned 2.5 pages. Finally, widely varying responses by Joseph L. Leconte, G. K. Gilbert, Wm. Bullock Clark, S. W. Williston, Bailey Willis, C. R. Keyes, and Samuel Calvin were published without any further summary or commentary.

Chamberlin's second tactic for comment on contemporary issues through editorials and editorial-like articles is exemplified in the very next issue of the *Journal* for July to August of 1898. Here, in response to his own symposium, he presented for the first time his opinion of what should be the proper basis for subdivision and correlation of the stratigraphic record under the title "The Ulterior Basis of Time Divisions and The Classification of Geologic History" (Chamberlin, 1898, p. 449–462). Chamberlin began by claiming that the introduction to the symposium had "intimated" that "the ulterior basis of classification and nomenclature must be dependent on the existence or absence of natural

Figure 1. Portrait of Thomas Chrowder Chamberlin (1843–1928) during his Madison, Wisconsin, years before going to the University of Chicago in 1892 and before his hair turned white as it appears in most published photos. (From University of Wisconsin archives.)

divisions resulting from simultaneous phases of action of worldwide extent" (Chamberlin, 1898, p. 449). (This claim could not be substantiated; even the most careful rereading of the "Symposium" revealed to me no hint of such "intimation".) Chamberlin went on to say in the first paragraph:

If there have been such universal phases and if they can be detected, they must ultimately be accepted not only as the true basis of division, classification and nomenclature, but their exposition must constitute the major work of research and of instruction. The most vital problem before the general geologist today is the question whether the earth's history is naturally divided into periodic phases of worldwide prevalence, or whether it is but an aggregation of local events dependent upon local conditions uncontrolled by overmastering agencies of universal dominance. (Chamberlin, 1898, p. 449).

Why would T. C. Chamberlin, who was not known to be strongly oriented toward stratigraphy, bother to writer this paper *and* a second, better-known one on the same theme in 1909? The later paper, "Diastrophism as the Ultimate Basis of Correlation," was republished verbatim in 1910 as the last chapter of a volume of 16 papers presented at the 1908 meeting of the American Association for the Advancement of Science. That volume dealt with correlation of formations of various ages and included a series of eight paleogeographic maps of North America prepared by symposium organizer, Bailey Willis. (A similar set of maps had been published in 1909 by Schuchert.) Clearly, the subdivision of geologic time was an important contemporary issue appropriate for his journal to address. Perusal of the contents of the first six volumes of the *Journal* indicates several titles dealing with stratigraphic classification. Moreover, this timely subject provided a nice vehicle for Chamberlin to pontificate about his new ideas of global tectonics, which were soon to appear in a more fully developed form as part of the "Planetesimal Hypothesis" (Chamberlin, 1905).

The great impact that the two papers on "diastrophic control" were to have is curious, for each was uncharacteristically short for their normally verbose author (14 and 9 pages, respectively, with only three small figures in the first paper). Moreover, their stratigraphic theme was tangential to his principal interests. Chamberlin's research began in glacial geology, then expanded logically from that to the controls of climate, and then into the sweeping, new planetesimal hypothesis. One wonders if Chamberlin himself was not a bit surprised at the attention given to "diastrophic control." *Diastrophism,* which was Chamberlin's favorite collective term for all kinds and scales of structural disturbances, was becoming an important preoccupation because of its prominence within the planetesimal theory. Moreover, Chamberlin was always a consummate generalist, who took a holistic overview of everything that he studied. Therefore, it was both in character and farsighted for him to extrapolate to stratigraphy the implications of sea-level changes caused by global isostatic adjustments as he was coming to envision these within his new theory.

DIASTROPHISM AND THE PLANETESIMAL THEORY

Chamberlin's two papers on "diastrophic control" can best be understood by remembering that the long-standing assumption of contraction of the earth due to cooling from a molten origin had been largely rejected by the end of the nineteenth century. This was primarily because calculations suggested that global shrinkage could not account for the magnitude of lateral shortening implied by the deformations seen in mountain ranges. Chamberlin and Salisbury (1906, v. I, p. 548–551) estimated a maximum of 51 km (32 mi) of Phanerozoic circumferential shortening by thermal contraction alone versus a total approaching 322 km (200 mi) of shortening indicated by compression in Phanerozoic mountain ranges. The global tectonic implications of radioactive heating were slow to be appreciated, and had no impact until after both of Chamberlin's papers had appeared (see Reade, 1906; Joly, 1909; Holmes, 1913; Chamberlin, 1916). So what mechanism was to replace thermal contraction as the domi-

nant driving force for deformation of the earth? The theory of isostasy had emerged, but was by no means generally accepted as a complete alternative to contraction. In turn, these changes of thought were focussing increasing attention upon the need to understand the physical nature of the earth's interior. Chamberlin was very concious of these important shifts in thinking, and his own planetesimal theory, with its reliance upon gravity as the primary diastrophic force in the planet, was dependent upon one version of isostasy. Greene (1982) has argued that Chamberlin rescued contraction with the gravitational mechanism central to his theory. Indeed, he was coming to view *all* major global structural changes as due ultimately to vertical gravitational adjustments in the solid earth, and because such adjustments must affect sea level on a global scale, "diastrophic control" seemed inevitable (Fig. 2).

The relevant aspects of the planetesimal theory can be summarized as follows: (1) accession or accretion of cold planetesimals; (2) gravitational shrinkage and heating of the embryonic planet; (3) early differential settling of oceanic and continental sectors with wedgelike cross sections extending to the earth's center; (4) continents made lighter by preferential removal of more basic constituents through weathering; (5) denser sea-floor wedges sink more and periodically squeeze continental wedges upward; (6) crowding was concentrated at continental-oceanic wedge margins, causing the compression seen in mountains; and (7) stresses among wedges accumulate slowly, but are relieved quickly and periodically.

Chamberlin first presented the planetesimal hypothesis orally at the University of Wisconsin in 1900, then at the A.A.A.S. meeting in Denver in 1901, at the Geological Society of

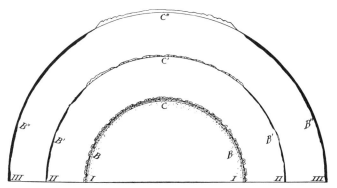

FIG. 32*a.*—Diagram intended to illustrate the evolution of the ocean basins under the planetesimal hypothesis. *I* represents an early stage in the evolution of the hydrosphere when it was largely subterranean, being held in the porous zone and only appearing at the surface in the volcanic pits developed by explosive vulcanism of the supposed lunar type. These are somewhat more abundant in the regions of *B B* than in that of *C*. *II* represents a more advanced stage in which the crater lakes of the regions *B, B* had become largely confluent, giving the interrupted water areas *B', B'*, while the region *C* had become the more protuberant area *C'*, which was chiefly land. *III* shows the further progress of the aggregation of the water, the relatively greater depression of the oceanic basins, *B'', B''*, and the protrusion of the continent, *C''*.

Figure 2. Chamberlin's conception of the evolution of the ocean basins by differential contractional subsidence. The different sizes of the three stages are shown concentrically for illustrative compactness; they do *not* imply an expansion of the earth. (From Chamberlin and Salisbury, 1906, v. 1, p. 109.)

America meetings in 1903 and 1904, and at both Harvard and the Washington Geological Society also in 1904 (Schultz, 1976). The first fully developed written version was published in the Carnegie Institution of Washington's Yearbook for 1904 (Chamberlin, 1905), where it was presented as "a valuable working hypothesis." It was also published in 1906 in the Chamberlin and Salisbury textbook of geology. There were many subsequent publications as the hypothesis was refined by Chamberlin and his University of Chicago astronomer collaborator, Forest R. Moulton. One of the more accessible treatments was a little book by Chamberlin entitled *Origin of the Earth* published in 1916.

Around the turn of the century, it was universally assumed that continents and ocean basins were permanent, fixed features of very ancient origin. Given the venerable contracting-earth paradigm, vertical or radial tectonics was emphasized, with the evidence of lateral deformation in mountain ranges being interpreted as a secondary consequence of vertical adjustments. The gradual acceptance of isostasy at the turn of the century reinforced the idea of persistent, high-standing continents and low-standing ocean basins. Moreover, it was both parsimonious and appealingly orderly to envision a broadly unified global history highlighted by more or less synchronous, worldwide events (see the Introduction to this volume for a fuller discussion of periodicity).

The nature of the earth's interior obviously was critical to understanding the behaviour of continents, oceans, and mountains. Therefore we should ask what was the conventional wisdom at the turn of the century? It had long been recognized both from gravity and the earth's angular momentum as determined from the precession of equinoxes that the average density of the interior must be at least double that of surficial rocks. Moreoever, an iron-rich, metallic internal composition had been inferred from terrestrial magnetism and the meteorite analogy. The transmission of seismic waves through the earth implied an internal "rigidity said to be equal to steel" (Powell, 1898, p. 2), but the oblateness of the earth, together with the rise of Scandinavia and the former Lake Bonneville basin in Utah, suggested some degree of pliability. Thus the possibility had been recognized of a visco-elastic interior experiencing creep. That geologists were striving to understand the behavior of rocks at elevated temperatures and pressures in terms of fundamental physics and physical chemistry is evidenced by major articles published in the decade in which Chamberlin's 1898 paper appeared (e.g., Becker, 1892; Van Hise, 1898a, b).

Zonation of the interior was postulated even before seismic evidence had demonstrated discrete discontinuities. In the first paper of the 1898 volume of the *Journal of Geology,* John Wesley Powell envisioned a rocky crust of *lithosphere* and a metallic nucleus or *centrosphere* with a density of 5.6. For the nucleus he suggested (Powell, 1898, p. 2) "the trans-solid state, as the metals are found to flow under pressure" (visco-elastic in modern terminology). He noted also that molten material brought to the surface is never metallic, therefore "It may be that there is [another] zone of matter beneath the structural rock [crust] and overlying the metallic nucleus. . . ." (Powell, 1898, p. 2). By the time of Chamberlin's second "Diastrophic Control" paper in 1909, Weichert (1897; cited by Suess) had deduced mathematically a rocky mantle with density 3.0 to 3.4 and a sharply bounded iron nucleus of density 7.8. Then in 1906, Oldham recognized the seismic shadow zone and inferred from it the core boundary, but although he also recognized the near absence of records for "second phase" [shear] seismic waves that had passed through the core, he refused "to offer any opinion as to whether this centrall core is composed of iron, surrounded by a stony shell, or whether it is the central gaseous nucleus of others" (Oldham, 1906, p. 472). A supplemental paper the next year demonstrated "differences in the constitution of the substance beneath [continents and oceans] which extend inwards to a distance of about one-quarter of the radius" (Oldham, 1907, p. 347). The Mohorovicic discontinuity was discovered in 1909 (Mohorovičić, 1910), the same year that Chamberlin published his second paper. Also in 1909, Suess proposed a more explicit scheme of three compositional zones, the thin, rocky crust composed of *Sal* (Si-Al; later spelled Sial), an intermediate zone of *Sima* (Si-Mg), and the nucleus of *Nife* (Ni-Fe) (Suess, 1909, in Sollas translation, 1909, v. 4, p. 543).

Chamberlin disbelieved the long-popular view that the earth had once been entirely molten and had differentiated enough to become internally zoned. Indeed, the most novel feature of his planetesimal hypothesis was a cold origin with subsequent heating by self-gravitation as the planet grew. Citing colleague and friend Van Hise as authority (Chamberlin and Salisbury, 1906, v. 1, p. 127; v. 2, p. 555, 570, 589), he recognized phase changes from less to more dense mineral forms as well as failure by fracture at shallow depths but by flow at greater depths (e.g., Van Hise, 1898a, b). It is then puzzling that, although Chamberlin appealed to isostasy for vertical adjustments between his solid wedges (Fig. 3), he denied a significant role for plastic flow. The pervasive, steeply inclined foliations in Archean rocks of the shields were taken to be remnants of past vertical adjustments now exposed by deep erosion. The following statement clarifies Chamberlin's special view of isostasy in a "solid, elastico-rigid earth":

In strict consistency with such an earth isostatic readjustments are assumed to take place by wedging and not by undertow beneath a floating crust. This type of isostatic adjustment is analogous to the familiar balancing of weight against weight on a pair of scales and is clearly distinguishable in mode, though not in principle, from the more common concept of flotation which has for its analogue the hydrometer. (Chamberlin, 1918, p. 194)

Besides rejecting internal pliability, Chamberlin also opposed the idea of internal zonation; rather he believed in a heterogeneous interior inherited from random accretion of planetesimals with incomplete "recombination" (chemical and physical differentiation). The first indication that he begrudgingly acknowledged any internal zonation was in a 1921 paper (Chamberlin, 1921b, Fig. 4), but even then he remained very skeptical.

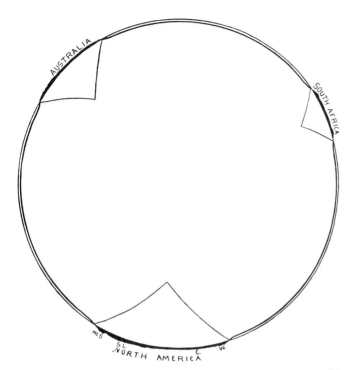

Fig. 1.—The continental wedges. Section through Washington, Chicago, Salt Lake, Mt. Shasta, Australia, and South Africa. Surface relief exaggerated and diagrammatic. Drawn in 1910.

Figure 3. The only published diagram that could be found of Chamberlin's conception of continental wedges. "The vaster and heavier oceanic segments take the lead in descending and as they do so, the continents . . . are wedged upward. . . .A thinner shell along the borders of a continent, yielding more readily and suffering much greater shortening, may be folded and faulted into a mountain system" (Chamberlin and Chamberlin, 1921, p. 424). In early statements of the planetesimal hypothesis, the wedges were said to extend to the earth's center, but this illustration of the "wedge theory" was influenced by the growing popularity of the strain ellipsoid with its theoretical 45° angle between planes of no strain. (From R. T. Chamberlin, *in* Chamberlin and Chamberlin, 1921, p. 420.)

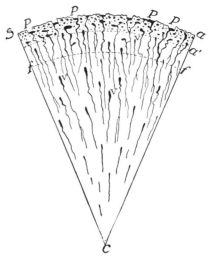

Fig. 32.—Ideal section of a portion of the early earth, illustrating its assigned modes of vulcanism. *C*, center; *S*, surface; *a–a'*, fragmental zone; *a'–f*, zone of continuous rock below surface melting temperature; *ff–c*, interior portion whose temperatures rise from the surface melting-point at *f–f* to a maximum at *C*; *V, V*, threads or tongues of molten rock rising from the interior to various levels, many of these lodging within the fragmental zone as tongues, batholiths, etc.; *PPP*, explosion pits formed by volcanic gases derived from tongues of lava below.

Figure 4. A radial segment of the early earth during its "great volcanic stage" and illustrating Chamberlin's idea of "recombination" within a heterogeneous planetesimal earth. Partial melting and the rise of "tongues" of magma produced limited chemical-physical differentiation and carried heat upward so that the deeper interior could remain perpetually solid. (From Chamberlin and Salisbury, 1906, v. 1, p. 105.)

As the planet grew and contracted during its *first or accession stage,* increasing pressure would elevate the fusion temperature for most materials, keeping them in the solid state. A solid interior would preclude both convection and complete differentiation. Because thermal conductivity of rock is very slow, contraction would occur throughout the earth. "Selective liquefaction" (partial melting) of silicate materials with relatively lower fusion temperatures would produce limited "recombination." As contraction proceeded, temperature would increase outward, causing successively shallower zones to approach their fusion temperatures. High-frequency, "rhythmic kneading" by earth tides presumably facilitated local liquefaction, and the resulting "liquid threads" would rise and carry heat upward (Fig. 4). This ingenious process would help keep the deeper interior below its fusion temperature and therefore keep it solid. Such "recombination" was thought to have dominated a *second or great volcanic stage* (presumably early Archean), which was followed by a *third or hydro-atmospheric eon,* which represents most of earth history (Chamberlin and Salisbury, 1906, v. I, p. 102–106, 122–132).

In view of Chamberlin's well-connected position in his profession and the fact that he was one of the co-founders of the Carnegie Institution of Washington in 1902 and its Geophysical Laboratory in 1906, it is surprising that he could have ignored (or torturously rationalized) much of the rapidly growing evidence about the nature of the earth's interior. For example, two close associates in the founding of the Geophysical Laboratory, C. R. Van Hise and G. F. Becker, had published important papers on rock behavior at depth (cited above) before Chamberlin's 1898 paper on diastrophic control. And before his second paper appeared in 1909, each of them had published second papers assessing fundamental questions about the applications of physics and chemistry to the earth (Becker, 1904; Van Hise, 1904). These had been presented in a symposium on "Present Problems in Science" at the 1904 International Congress of Arts and Sciences held during the St. Louis World's Fair—a meeting in which Chamberlin also participated. Another associate, Bailey Willis, in 1907 postulated "deep seated suboceanic spread" (i.e., creep or flow) as the mechanism for tangential compression to form mountains at continental margins. Evidence for internal zonation was also accumulating rapidly, and the geological implications of radioactivity both for dating and for thermal energy were being publicized. But Chamberlin's numerous papers on diastrophism from 1898 to his death in 1928 reveal a great love affair with his planetesimal theory characterized by elaborate, rhetorical pirouetting with old and new evidence. Seemingly, in this way he blinded himself to most of the evidence for a very warm, zoned, viscous, earth. As Schultz (1976) has argued, Chamberlin did not practice all that he had preached about the virtues of the principle of multiple working hypotheses. Apparently Thomas Chrowder Chamberlin was human after all.

THE 1898 PAPER: "THE ULTERIOR BASIS OF TIME DIVISIONS"

Chamberlin emphasized at the outset his rejection of catastrophism. "The old doctrine of physical cataclysms attended by universal destruction of life has passed beyond serious consideration. . . . If, therefore, we seek for *absolute* divisions we doubtless seek in vain. But this does not dismiss the question whether this continuity of physical and vital action proceeded by heterogeneous impulses or by correlated pulsations" (Chamberlin, 1898, p. 449–450). Having stated the two options of *complete continuity* versus *correlated pulsations* in good multiple working hypothesis tradition, he let there be no doubt of his preference for a periodically punctuated earth history. He then stated three "general grounds" for such a view, which can be paraphrased as follows:

1. The presumption that great earth movements affect all quarters of the globe;

2. Belief in a fundamental periodicity in terrestrial progress is founded upon the conviction that the major movements of the earth's surface have consisted of the sinking of the ocean bottoms and the withdrawal of waters into the basins; and

3. An assumed fluctuation in the constitution of the atmosphere due to the alternating enlargement and shrinkage of land area, which would cause variations of atmospheric carbon dioxide due to variations in its contribution through the weathering of exposed rocks.

Chamberlin then elaborated each of these items as background for his hypothesis of a global diastrophic control of sea level. Under the first ground, he argued that major stresses in one part of the globe must affect stresses elsewhere. "Any massive earth movement must change the gravitative stresses of all parts of the globe (Chamberlin, 1898, p. 450). . . . A downward movement in one region is correlated with an upward movement in

some other region" (p. 451). From this he concluded that if these opposite phases with ocean basins becoming progressively deeper as mountains become higher are "habitual" movements, then herein lies a basis for the natural division of geologic events.

In developing his argument, Chamberlin noted two postulates "which are almost universally assumed by geologists" (1898, p. 452). These were that the earth began as a nearly perfect spheroid and that great movements of the earth's crust have resulted in shrinkage. "Probably no serious geologist maintains that the earth has enlarged. . . ." (Chamberlin, 1898, p. 452). He then asserted that the radial shrinkage of the ocean bottoms has exceeded that of the continental platforms by an average of 3,000 to 3,660 m (10,000 to 12,000 ft). And because the ocean basins are about four times larger than the continents, the deepening of the oceans by shrinkage must have been the dominant change on earth. It was debatable how much absolute uplift the continents have experienced, it being probable, thought he, that they, too, have mostly sunk, but to a lesser relative degree than the ocean basins (Fig. 2). Not only had ocean basins deepened, their capacity also had increased from nearly zero originally to their present volume capable of holding practically all of the globe's water. But, while these internal structural adjustments generally increase the capacity of the ocean basins, "External readjustments work to precisely opposite ends, the degration of the land and the filling of the basins" (Chamberlin, 1898, p. 453).

Chamberlin next addressed the consequences of the partial filling of the ocean basins by sediment eroded from land. He noted that "Every continent which stands in a given position with reference to the sea for any prolonged period develops a submarine terrace about its borders . . . formed from the debris of the land . . . [and] as it develops it becomes a broad submerged platform with a steep face dropping away to the abysmal depths of the ocean" (Chamberlin, 1898, p. 454; see Fig. 5 of this chapter). He alluded to John Wesley Powell's relatively new concept of *baseleveling,* and noted that the upper surface of the terrace is a function of how long the level of the crust remains fixed and the intensity of erosion. Any sea cliffs retreat inland and valleys develop "base plains," which are the correlatives of (i.e., graded to) the terrace plain as it grows seaward (Fig. 5, upper). The limit of these processes is "when the continent has been baseleveled" (Fig. 5, middle).

Another key element of Chamberlin's argument followed from the development of the continental terraces, namely the displacement of sea water by sedimentation. This was stated as follows:

1. The transfer of debris from the land to the sea displaces an equivalent amount of water, and raises the sea level proportionately, and causes an advance upon the land. The effects are volumetrically small compared with the great body of the ocean, but a slight rise in the surface as the baselevel stages of the continent are attained is peculiarly effective. This cooperates with the cutting back of the sea cliff, and, combined, they become effective in advancing the edge of the sea upon the border of the land (Chamberlin, 1898, p. 455).

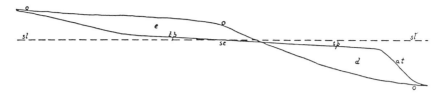

FIG. 1.—*o-o* Original surface. *s l* Sea level. *e* Land carried away by erosion. *d* Detritus built into circumcontinental terrace. *t p* Terrace plain. *a t* Abysmal terrace face. *b p* Base-plain developing landward.

FIG. 2.—*b p* Continental base-plain. *s l* Sea level. *t p* Submerged terrace plain. *a t* Abysmal terrace face.

FIG. 3.—*a* Former sea level. *b* Succeeding sea level. *c* Former ample shallow-water tract. *d* Succeeding constricted shallow-water tract.

Figure 5. The three diagrams from Chamberlins's first (1898) paper on diastrophism, unconformities, and geologic time divisions. His captions are self explanatory. Neither these nor any other figures were reproduced in the 1909 paper.

In addition to upward displacement of water by sedimentation, the author postulated that the slow, isostatic sinking of structurally elevated blocks of the continental crust to or below base level would enhance the transgression. This point was stated as follows:

2. There are both theoretical and observational grounds for the belief that in the process of periodic readjustment of the earth to its internal stresses, portions of the crust are thrust up to heights notably above the plane of isostatic equilibrium, and that these portions gradually settle back toward equilibrium by virtue of the fluency or quasi-fluency of the rocks. (Chamberlin, 1898, p. 455)

Chamberlin concluded that there seemed to be "sufficient data to warrant entertaining tentatively the doctrine that in periods following crustal upheavals which pass beyond the plane of equilibrium the lifted portions slowly settle back toward equilibrium. If so, this retrocession would cooperate with the filling of the basins in causing an advance of the sea upon the land" (Chamberlin, 1898, p. 456).

Revealing his characteristic holistic tendency, Chamberlin went on to discuss the implications for marine life of alternating advances and retreats of the sea. The "submerged seashelf" was seen as a "critical geologic zone" because it is the habitat of shallow-marine life, which is most important in the geologic record. When earth movements caused deepening of the ocean basins, water would withdraw from the submerged shelves of all continents (i.e., a eustatic fall). The "ample fauna" that had "peopled" the shallow shelf seas would be "forced into the constricted zone and brought under the direst stress of competition and scant room" (Chamberlin, 1898, p. 457; see Fig. 5, lower). If a long period of structural quiescence followed, baseleveling of lands would cause the formation of new marine terraces (i.e., a eustatic rise) and thus "an ample zone for the evolution of a new shallow water fauna . . ." (Chamberlin, p. 458). Slow settling of highly elevated land areas to achieve isostatic equilibrium would cause the sea to make an even greater incursion "as it did in Cretaceous times." Chamberlin concluded this discussion by stating that the "sinking sea bottom induces that form of evolution in which stress is the dominant factor," and structural "quiescence induces that form of evolution in which new ground and rich opportunities constitute the dominant condition (Chamberlin, 1898, p. 458). . . . Such a succession of shallow sea incursions and withdrawals reciprocating with crustal movements and quiescence seem to me to be well indicated as the master features of geologic progress from the beginning of the Palaeozoic era to the present time. To these features I look for the primary terms of a natural and permanent system of classification and nomenclature" (Chamberlin, 1898, p. 458–459).

The final section of the paper, which deals with Chamberlin's third "general ground" (see above), seems like an appendix to the main theme. It reflects the author's long-standing interest in linkages between atmosphere and climate (e.g., Chamberlin, 1897) by postulating fluctuations of atmospheric CO_2 due to changing areas of land versus sea. When large areas of crystalline rocks were exposed following sinking of the sea floors, weathering processes involving carbonic acid would consume CO_2. Conversely, when continental areas were reduced by incursion of the ocean, less carbonic acid would be consumed by weathering, therefore atmospheric CO_2 would increase, causing greenhouse warming. "The carbon dioxide is critical because of that peculiar thermal capacity by virtue of which it retains the heat of the sun to a relatively extraordinary degree, a capacity which is shared with water vapor . . . (Chamberlin, 1898, p. 460). If these considerations are valid, the history of the earth has been marked by periods of relative cold and aridity resulting from stages of rapid rock disintegration, alternating with periods of warmth and moisture corelated with periods of limited rock disintegration and of carbonic acid accumulation" (Chamberlin, 1898, p. 461). Chamberlin concluded that "We have, therefore, the conjoint action of topographic agencies with atmospheric constitution in producing alternations of cold and aridity with warmth and moisture." Because "these atmospheric influences are strictly simultaneous for all parts of the globe . . . . . . they furnish an additional basis for the strict correlation of transoceanic action and for the division of geological history into its natural epochs" (Chamberlin, 1898, p. 461).

THE 1909 PAPER: "THE ULTIMATE BASIS OF CORRELATION"

Although shorter and lacking any illustrations, the 1909 paper (republished in 1910) is the more famous. As suggested by the title, it is slightly more explicit about "correlation by unconformities," but why was it written and why does it not contain any reference to *his own* nearly identical 1898 article? A slightly polemical tone of the first two pages hints that Chamberlin may have been responding to skepticism by restating his thesis nine years later, but one would think that reference to the earlier paper would have strengthened his case. Equally surprising is the fact that he takes no note whatsoever of the leap in thought about the earth's interior between 1898 and 1909, some of which derived from work by close associates (see above).

A defensive posture is suggested by a series of disclaimers to the effect that "We do not have to agree completely about this-or-that." Then, with a characteristically authoritarian note, he states on the second page, "Let us agree to deal only with factors of the larger order and to neglect incidentals;" (Chamberlin, 1909, p. 686). A few lines farther on, he suggests that for two proposi-

tions "if we can not all agree respecting them, we must agree to differ . . ." (Chamberlin, 1909, p. 686).

Next, Chamberlin states two contesting propositions about global diastrophism. Either (1) deformations have been indifferent to their predecessors, so are asynchronous and without temporal pattern; or (2) deformations have followed one another in "dynamical kinship" so that "ocean basins and continental elevations tended toward self-perpetuation" (Chamberlin, 1909, p. 687). Of course Chamberlin accepted the second view with much confidence—and just a hint of dogma. He then reemphasized his 1898 position that "each great diastrophic movement tended toward the rejuvenation of the continents and toward the firmer establishment of the great basins" (Chamberlin, 1909, p. 687). Continuing, "The base-leveling processes have shown that they are able to lower the continents approximately to the sea-level in a fraction of geologic time. The continents would therefore have long since disappeared, if they had not been rejuvenated by renewed relative elevation or the withdrawal of the sea. I am able to find no evidence of lost continents" (Chamberlin, 1909, p. 687–688). And then we find the following rather paternalistic passages: "I trust that many of you will agree that, in general the relatively upward movements of diastrophism have been located continuously in the continents, and the broad downward movements continuously in the ocean basins, and that, setting aside incidental features, the dominant effect of the successive diastrophic movements has been to restore the capacity of the ocean basins and to rejuvenate the continents" (Chamberlin, 1909, p. 688). And on the following page we find these assertions. "It is important that we should agree or agree to disagree on one further point. Have diastrophic movements been in progress constantly, or at intervals only, with quiescent periods between? Are they perpetual or periodic? The latter view prevails, I think, among American geologists" (Chamberlin, 1909, p. 689).

Chamberlin presses his argument by stating that "base-leveling of the land means contemporaneous filling of the sea basins by transferred matter, and hence a slowly advancing sea-edge that is thus brought into active function as a base-leveling agent. This water movement is essentially contemporaneous the world over, and is thus a basis for correlation. *The base-leveling process implies a homologous series of deposits the world over*" (Chamberlin, 1909, p. 690; italics his). He also states that "correlation by base-levels (i.e., unconformities) is one of the triumphs of American geology. . . ." (Chamberlin, 1909, p. 690), but offers a shrewd qualifying caution about the precision of *correlation by unconformities* because "the different parts of the same unconformity vary much in time" (p. 691). Chamberlin then sums up as follows:

Correlation by general diastrophic movements takes cognizance of four stages: (1) the stages of climacteric base-leveling and sea-transgression, (2) the stages of retreat which are the first stages of diastrophic movement after the quiescent period, (3) the stages of climacteric diastrophism and of greatest sea-retreat, and (4) the stages of early quiescence, progressive degradation, and sea-advance. (Chamberlin, 1909, p. 691)

The author concludes the paper by stating that stratigraphy and paleontology go hand in hand, but

> diastrophism lies back of both and furnishes the conditions on which they depend . . . (p. 692). It seems clear that diastrophism is fundamental to deposition, and is a condition prerequisite to epicontinental and circum-continental stratigraphy. . . . It therefore seems to be the ultimate basis of correlation. (Chamberlin, 1909, p. 693)

ORIGINALITY

T. C. Chamberlin's diastrophic control hypothesis, as a component of the more inclusive planetesimal theory, has some clear commonalities with other, late nineteenth century theories of earth evolution, especially those of Dana and Suess. Chamberlin's "structure lines" (Fig. 6) are reminiscent of Dana's earlier northeast- and northwest-trending global "cleavage structure" (Dana, 1856). All three men affirmed the primacy of subsiding ocean basins crowding against the continents as in Dana's geosyncline-geanticline couplet (Dana, 1873), Suess' outward thrusting by continents to form foredeeps and island arcs (Suess, 1885–1909), and Chamberlin's jostling continental and oceanic wedges (Fig. 3). Most important, Suess and Chamberlin both assigned a major role to the ocean basins in controlling sea level. For example, Suess wrote (translated from Suess, 1888, v. 2), "The earth yields, the ocean follows (p. 680), and "the history of the continents results from that of the seas" (p. 700). There are also striking similarities between the Chamberlin and Suess views of sedimentation and sea level. Suess anticipated Chamberlin's postulate of shallow-marine sedimentation as an important mechanism for raising sea level when in 1888 he wrote "*the formation of sediments causes a continuous, eustatic positive movement of the strand-line* (Suess, 1888, in Sollas translation, 1906, v. 2, p. 543, italics his). And "every grain of sand which sinks to the bottom of the sea expels, to however trifling a degree, the ocean from its bed" (Suess, 1888, in Sollas translation, 1906, p. 555). Obviously both authors overestimated the displacement of sea water by sedimentation and, seemingly, were unaware of isostatic subsidence due to sedimentation. They also had in common a strong devotion to periodic cyclicity in the oscillations between land and sea.

The similarities of the Suess and Chamberlin theories of global sea level change are so striking as to raise the question of originality. It is inconceivable that a man of Chamberlin's synthetic mind and his role as founder of an international journal could have been unaware of the great Austrian's treatise, the relevant second volume of which was published ten years before Chamberlins' first diastrophic paper. From its beginning in 1893, the *Journal of Geology* numbered among its associate editors German-speaking H. Rosenbusch and Albrecht Penck. Moreover, early volumes of the journal even carried occasional articles in German. Chamberlin and Salisbury's 1906 book contains specific references to Suess' treatise, and, finally, the Sollas' translation of volume 3 of *Das Antlitz der Erde,* which appeared in 1908, lists on the title page "T. C. Chamberlin" as one of nine

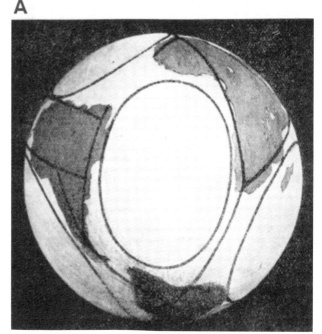

Fɪɢ. 31.—South Atlantic view of the globe, showing also the South American and South African bifurcations and angulations of the main structure lines and yield-tracts, indicated by the straight lines which outline the quadrilaterals inclosing the oceans.

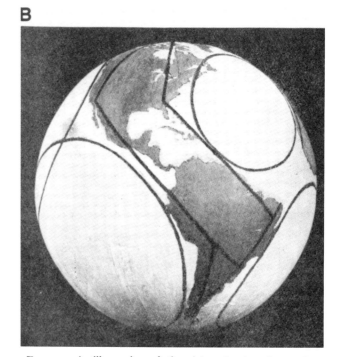

Fɪɢ. 32.—Antillean view of the globe, showing the northwest-southeast trend lines and their angulations with the meridional trends in the high latitudes of both hemispheres.

Figure 6. Two views of the earth showing the "main structure lines," which Chamberlin envisioned as delineating the continents and ocean basins. The "bifurcations and angulations" shown here are reminiscent of Dana's global "cleavage structure" and of similar, earlier ideas of fundamental trends in Europe (see Greene, 1982). (From Chamberlin, 1916.)

advisory editors. Thus it is certain that Chamberlin was well aware of Suess' great synthesis before he published his second paper, and it seems inescapable that this was also true before he wrote the 1898 one. Even so, Chamberlin's planetesimal theory and the idea of gravitational contraction of a largely and ever-solid earth was entirely original. At the turn of the century, conventions for literature citation were not so rigorous as today. Moreover, because in 1909 Chamberlin neglected to cite his own 1898 paper, perhaps we should not be surprised that he failed to mention Suess.

CONCLUSIONS

Whatever the connections between the ideas of Suess and Chamberlin, the impact of diastrophic control upon subsequent workers is clear and profound, especially in America. In subdividing the Paleozoic strata east of the Mississippi River, E. O. Ulrich (1911) was perhaps the first to invoke the hypothesis. He argued for a stratigraphy riddled with universal unconformities, and wrangled vehemently with those, such as Charles Schuchert and A. W. Grabau, who invoked lateral facies changes instead of unconformities to explain many stratigraphic changes. Joseph Barrell's 1917 classic on sedimentary rhythms shows Chamberlin's influence in the following passage: "[diastrophic] stirrings . . . which have divided earth history into periods and eras" (Barrell, 1917, p. 746). As detailed by Johnson in this volume, Grabau was also influenced by Chamberlin. He postulated rhythmic advances and retreats of the seas controlled by a kind of continental drift (really crustal shift), and in his 1930s pulsation theory, Grabau subdivided the stratigraphic record in a novel way—and with new systemic names—based upon inferred universal unconformities (Grabau, 1940). These then provided the basis for a detailed Phanerozoic sea-level curve. In Germany, Hans Stille had already begun to construct sea-level curves linked to orogenies, which he assumed were globally synchronous (see Hallam, this volume). Perhaps the ultimate in repetitive stratigraphy accompanied by widespread unconformities, however, came in the 1930s with the concept of Carboniferous cyclothems, which, in the view of some, required high-frequency eustatic oscillations similar to those of the great ice age (see Nelson and Langenheim, this volume).

There are two important legacies from Chamberlin's diastrophic theory, namely (1) eustatically controlled unconformities, and (2) the implication of both global synchrony and periodicity. By World War II, the latter notion had become rampant—cycles of many kinds were seen everywhere! There had been a few eloquent protests against periodic diastrophism, notably by Shepard (1923) and Berry (1929). Berry presented a vigorous attack directed at Chamberlin and Salisbury, which is epitomized by the following colorful passage:

So much nonsense has been written on various so-called ultimate criteria for correlation that many have the faith or the wish to believe that the interior soul of our earth governs its surface history with a periodicity like that of the clock of doom, and that when the fated hour strikes strata are folded and raised into mountains, epicontinental seas retreat, and the continents slide about, the denizens of the land and sea become dead and buried, and a new era is inaugurated. This picture has an epic quality which is very alluring and it makes historical geology *so very understandable,* but is it a true picture? (Berry, 1929, p. 2; italics his)

Berry saw "diastrophism" simply as a substitute for "cataclysm," and thus a throwback to Cuvieran catastrophism (note the title of his article, "Shall we return to cataclysmal geology?"). He challenged not only synchrony and periodicity of diastrophism, but also felt sure (in good Lyellian tradition) "that life has always developed in an orderly way; that physical conditions have always changed slowly; and that the slowly shifting geographic pattern, through its influence on climate, was a more general and more potent factor in evolution than orogenesis" (Berry, 1929, p. 12).

It was not until 1948 that the periodicity stampede was slowed. That year James Gilluly vigorously denounced both synchronous and periodic tectonism in his presidential address to the Geological Society of America (Gilluly, 1949). He drew aim especially at Stille, but sent ricochets toward other workers as well. The impact of Gilluly's anti-synchrony probably retarded the spread of the brand new idea of sequence stratigraphy first proposed by Sloss, Krumbein, and Dapples (1949) in the same year and even at the same meeting as Gilluly's address. H. E. Wheeler (1958) and especially L. L. Sloss (1963) pressed this new version of an unconformity-defined, physical stratigraphy, but it did not really catch on until the later 1960s, when its applicability in the petroleum industry was demonstrated by Vail and others (1977).

And so we have come full circle. Today we see not only the new paradigm of sequence stratigraphy with its emphasis upon widespread, broadly synchronous unconformities, but also an emphasis upon eustasy as the principal explanation advocated by many, but not all, of its practitioners (see Sloss, 1991, for a "countervailing view"). How ironic that universal unconformities, so controversial in mid-century, are now ardently endorsed as orthodoxy. Moreover, with the advent of plate tectonics, we also have seen a return to favor of global synchrony and cyclicity, which are carried to the extreme in the current rush to discover expressions of Milankovitch climatic cycles everywhere. Thomas Chrowder Chamberlin surely would have approved!

ACKNOWLEDGMENTS

First, I thank Clifford Nelson and Mary Babbitt for an invitation to participate in a 1989 symposium sponsored by the History Division of the Geological Society of America on "Geology and Geophysics Since 1904." That experience deepened my interest in the turn-of-the-century state of knowledge of tectonics and earth physics and convinced me of the exceptional importance of that period during which such notable events as the creation of the Geophysical Laboratory occurred. Therefore, when I conceived of the History of Eustasy as the topic for the

1990 History Division symposium, it was obvious that I should investigate further another product of the same era—T. C. Chamberlin's ideas about the diastrophic control of sea level. I am indebted to L. L. Sloss and C. W. Byers for constructive criticisms of the manuscript. I also have profited from stimulating discussions with other colleagues, especially Herbert Wang.

REFERENCES CITED

Anonymous (probably R. T. Salisbury), 1898, A symposium on the classification and nomenclature of geologic time-divisions: Journal of Geology, v. 6, p. 333–335.

Barrell, J. 1917, Rhythms and the measurements of geologic time: Geolgcial Society of America Bulletin, v. 28, p. 745–904.

Becker, G. F., 1892, Finite homogeneous strain, flow and rupture of rocks: Geological Society of America Bulletin, v. 4, p. 12–90.

——, 1904, Present problems of geophysics: Science, v. 20, p. 545–556.

Berry, E. W., 1929, Shall we return to cataclysmal geology?: American Journal of Science, Fifth Series, v. 17, p. 1–12.

Chamberlin T. C., 1897, A group of hypotheses bearing on climatic changes: Journal of Geology, v. 5, p. 653–683.

——, 1898, The ulterior basis of time divisions and the classification of geologic history: Journal of Geology, v. 6, p. 449–462.

——, 1905, Fundamental problems of geology: Carnegie Institution Yearbook for 1904, no. 3, p. 117–118, 195–258.

——, 1909, Diastrophism as the ultimate basis of correlation: Journal of Geology, v. 17, p. 685–693.

——, 1910, Diastrophism as the ultimate basis of correlation, *in* Willis, B. and Salisbury, R. D., eds., Outlines of geologic history with especial reference to North America: Chicago, The University of Chicago, p. 298–306.

——, 1916, The origin of the Earth: Chicago, The University of Chicago, 271 p.

——, 1918, Diastrophism and the formative processes IX—A specific mode of self-promotion of periodic diastrophism: Journal of Geology, v. 26, p. 193–197.

——, 1920, Diastrophism and the formative processes X—The order of magnitude of the shrinkage of the Earth deduced from Mars, Venus, and the Moon: Journal of Geology, v. 28, p. 1–17.

——, 1921a, Groundwork of the earth's diastrophism: Geological Society of America Bulletin, v. 32, p. 197–210.

——, 1921b, The greater earth: Geological Society of America Bulletin, v. 32, p. 211–226.

Chamberlin, T. C., and Chamberlin, R. T., 1921, Diastrophism and the formative processes XIV—Groundwork for the study of megadiastrophism: Journal of Geology, v. 29, p. 391–425.

Chamberlin, T. C., and Salisbury, R. D., 1906, Geology: New York, Holt, v. 1, 684 p.; v. 2, 692 p.

Dana, J. D., 1856, On the plan of development in geologic history of North America: American Journal of Science, 2nd ser., v. 22, p. 305–335.

——, 1873, On some results of the earth's contraction from cooling, including a discussion of the origin of mountains, and the nature of the earth's interior: American Journal of Science, 3rd ser., v. 5, p. 423–475; v. 6, p. 6–382.

Gilluly, J., 1949, Distribution of mountain building in geologic time: Geological Society of America Bulletin, v. 60, p. 561–590.

Grabau, A. W., 1940, The rhythm of the ages: Peking, Henri Vetch, 561 p.

Greene, M. T., 1982, Geology in the nineteenth century—changing views of a changing world: Ithaca, Cornell University Press, 324 p.

Holmes, A., 1913, The age of the Earth: London, Harper & Brothers, 196 p.

Joly, J., 1909, Radioactivity and geology: London, Constable, 287 p.

Mohorovičić, A., 1910, Potres od 8 × 1909, Godishje Izvjesce Zagrebackog Meteoroloskog Opservatorija za godinu 1909: Zagreb, 56 p.

Powell, J. W., 1898, An hypothesis to account for the movement in the crust of the earth: Journal of Geology, v. 6, p. 1–9.

Reade, T. M., 1906, Radium and the radial shrinkage of the earth: Geological Magazine, v. 3, p. 79–80.

Oldham, R. D., 1906, The constitution of the interior of the earth, as revealed by earthquakes: Quarterly Journal of the Geological Society of London, v. 62, p. 456–457.

——, 1907, The constitution of the interior of the earth, as revealed by earthquakes: (second communication) Some new light on the origin of the oceans: Quarterly Journal of the Geological Society of London, v. 63, p. 344–350.

Schuchert, C., 1909, Paleogeography of North America: Geological Society of America Bulletin, v. 20, p. 427–606 (printed in February 1910).

Schultz, S. F., 1976, Thomas C. Chamberlin—An intellectual biography of a geologist and educator [Ph.D. thesis]: Madison, University of Wisconsin, 448 p.

Shepard, F. P., 1923, To question the theory of periodic diastrophism: Journal of Geology, v. 31, p. 599–613.

Sloss, L. L., 1963, Sequences in the cratonic interior of North America: Geological Society of America Bulletin, v. 74, p. 93–114.

——, 1991, The tectonic factor in sea level change: A countervailing view: Journal of Geophysical Research, v. 96, p. 6609–6617.

Sloss, L. L., Krumbein, W. C., and Dapples, E. C., 1949, Integrated facies analysis, *in* Longwell, C., chairman, Sedimentary facies in geologic history: Geological Society of America Memoir 39, p. 91–123.

Suess, E., 1885–1909, Das antlitz der erde: Vienna, F. Tempsky, v. 1, 1885, 778 p.; v. 2, 1888, 703 p.; v. 3, 1909, pt. 1, 508 p.; pt. 2, 789 p. English translation by Sollas, H.B.C., The face of the earth: Oxford, Clarendon, v. 1, 1904, 604 p.; v. 2, 1906, 556 p.; v. 3, 1908, 400 p.; v. 4, 1909, 673 p.; v. 5, 1924, 170 p. (index and maps).

Ulrich, E. O., 1911, Revision of the Paleozoic systems: Geological Society of America Bulletin, v. 22, p. 281–680.

Vail, P. R., and 7 others, 1977, Seismic stratigraphy and global changes of sea level, *in* Payton, C. E., ed., Seismic stratigraphy-Applications to hydrocarbon exploration: American Association of Petroleum Geologists Memoir 26, p. 49–205.

Van Hise, C. R., 1898a, Metamorphism of rocks and rock flowage: Geological Society of America Bulletin, v. 9, p. 269–328.

——, 1898b, Earth movements: Transactions of Wisconsin Academy of Sciences, Arts, and Letters, v. 40, p. 465–516.

——, 1904, The problems of geology: Journal of Geology, v. 12, p. 489–616.

Wheeler, H. E., 1958, Time-stratigraphy: American Association of Petroleum Geologists Bulletin, v. 42, p. 1047–1063.

Wiechert, E., 1897, Massenvertheilung im Innern der Erde: Nachrichten Gesellschaft Wissenschaften Gottingen, p. 221–243.

Willis, B., 1907, A theory of continental structure applied to North America: Geological Society of America Bulletin, v. 18, p. 389–412.

MANUSCRIPT ACCEPTED BY THE SOCIETY JANUARY 14, 1992

NOTE ADDED IN PROOF

After type had been set, a clear 1898 reference to Suess by Chamberlin was discovered. This proves beyond doubt that the latter was indeed well informed of Suess' prior theory of the dominant control of sea level by global shrinkage with resulting adjustments of the ocean floors. In this reference, published only one month after his own first diastrophic control paper, Chamberlin wrote ". . . the dominant fact in the bodily history of the earth is the shrinkage of its outer parts as has been so signally urged by Suess" (Chamberlin, T. C., 1898, A systematic source of evolution of provincial faunas: Journal of Geology, v. 6, p. 597–608).

Geological Society of America
Memoir 180
1992

Chapter 5

A. W. Grabau's embryonic sequence stratigraphy and eustatic curve

Markes E. Johnson
Department of Geology, Williams College, Williamstown, Massachusetts 01267

ABSTRACT

One of the most knowledgeable stratigraphers during the first half of the twentieth century was Amadeus William Grabau (1870 to 1946), whose prolific career included wide experience in North America, Europe, and Asia. He was both a proficient field geologist capable of generating his own original data and a brilliant synthesizer with an encyclopedic grasp of received data from the stratigraphic community at large. His Pulsation Theory was introduced in 1933 at the 16th International Geological Congress in Washington, D.C., and it was greatly expanded in 1940 with publication of his book *The Rhythm of the Ages*. This remarkable book contains the first detailed representation of Phanerozoic sea-level fluctuations related to unconformity-bound units on a global scale.

The origin and gradual development of Grabau's views on the interrelationship between what is now called sequence stratigraphy and eustasy are traced in this review. An attempt is made to test the accuracy of Grabau's intercontinental correlations, drawing on a comparative sample of the Silurian System as understood by Grabau and as subsequently refined during the more than 50 years since publication of *The Rhythm of the Ages*.

INTRODUCTION

Eustasy, or the notion that worldwide fluctuations in sea level are recorded in the geologic record, has a long history of appeal to those who would find order in nature. All defenders of this concept have been burdened by three fundamental requirements. They must demonstrate a method to decode reliable information on sea-level changes from the actual rock record. They must have the perseverance to develop a global data base with the capability to date and correlate events from one place to another. Most elusive of all, they must relate their observations and correlations to some explanatory model. The historical pathway on the quest for eustasy is littered by fallen champions who failed to satisfy fully these conditions.

De Maillet (1748, translation in 1968), in one of the earliest treatments of eustasy, associated former highstands in sea level with step-like amphitheaters eroded into mountain sides. His confidence in decoding relevant information from the rock record was heightened by important observations of fossil marine en-

crusters and borers preserved on what surely were exhumed rocky shores (de Maillet, 1748; translation in 1968, p. 70). The best de Maillet could do in terms of a global data base, however, was to recommend a universal gauging system to monitor a predicted continuous drop in sea level through historical time.

One hundred years later, Chambers (1848) attempted to fix the former position of ancient sea levels to a uniform series of elevations attributed to marine terraces traceable throughout the British Isles and abroad. His basic thesis on the diminution of sea level through time was not unlike de Maillet's, but he tried to improve on it by providing a more substantial global data base. Unhappily for Chambers, the celebrated Quaternary terraces painstakingly surveyed under his direction in the Lochaber of Scotland owe their formation to glacial lakes (as later proven by Jamieson, 1863) and not marine erosion in fiord settings (as suggested by Darwin, 1839). At some localities, such as Covesea on Moray Firth or Craigmillar Castle, more credible evidence of sea caves and "sea-worn" cliffs was cited by Chambers (1848, p. 71, 144).

Johnson, M. E., 1992, A. W. Grabau's embryonic sequence stratigraphy and eustatic curve, *in* Dott, R. H., Jr., ed., Eustasy: The Historical Ups and Downs of a Major Geological Concept: Boulder, Colorado, Geological Society of America Memoir 180.

Nearly another century later, the publication in 1940 of *The Rhythm of the Ages* by Amadeus William Grabau (1870 to 1946), marked the achievement of the first well-balanced attempt to illustrate the effects of eustasy during the passage of deep geological time. Although there were many rough edges to his work, Grabau satisfied as no one else before him had, the main requirements in testing eustasy. It is the origin and gradual development of Grabau's thoughts on what he came to call his Pulsation Theory, which I trace in this contribution. Grabau never used the terms eustasy or sequence stratigraphy, but he clearly thought in terms of unconformity-bound units related to global sea-level fluctuations. The gross similarity between his approach and the currently fashionable practice of seismic stratigraphy is unmistakable.

Geological theories are only as good as the field data upon which they rest. Grabau was very proud, if not somewhat defensive about the massive edifice of stratigraphic detail upon which his Pulsation Theory was built. It is not within the scope of this paper to check all the Phanerozoic correlations proposed by Grabau but I do have a pesonal motive for undertaking a limited review of Grabau's work on eustasy. I have visited many of the same Silurian outcrops in North America, Europe, and Asia described by Grabau in support of his global sea-level curve and I do have opinions on the accuracy of Grabau's correlations, based on a sampling of the Silurian System as perceived now more than 50 years after his interpretations were published in *The Rhythm of the Ages*. Perhaps one needs no other motive in looking back through the history of geology, than a simple curiosity about a fellow traveler whose pioneering trail one stumbles across repeatedly.

This is not intended to be a remembrance dealing with Grabau's life history, his personal problems, or his character. His peers covered some of that ground, reflecting on his life before and after he left Columbia University in 1920 for China (Shimer, 1947; Sun, 1947; Kay, 1972). The tremendous respect earned by Grabau in China as a highly influential educator also has been reviewed recently (Johnson, 1985; Zhang and Faul, 1988). It is the fascinating paper trail of ideas on sea-level changes expressed in Grabau's writings to which I confine myself here.

WHAT'S SO SPECIAL ABOUT AN OLD BOOK?

Published in Peking in 1940 under difficult war-time conditions, Grabau's *Rhythm of the Ages* is a rather rare book. Only 800 copies were printed. The book later received wider distribution through a 1978 reprinting in the United States. At first glance, the book appears to be a general textbook on historical geology, but at least two significant features place it well apart from any other contemporary text book.

The most immediately striking of these is a set of colored paleogeographic maps appended to the back of the book in twelve foldouts and nine other single plates. The maps depict evolving continental assemblies based on the notion of continen-

tal drift. Grabau clearly was inspired by the work of Alfred Wegener (1924), whose book *The Origin of Continents and Oceans* is cited in the bibliography. In 1940, it was already ten years since the death of Wegener in Greenland and few geologists continued to support his theory. Grabau (1940, p. 9) mentions F. B. Taylor only briefly and although he does not reference Taylor (1910), he subscribes to a concept of "Polar Control Theory" not unlike Taylor's polar-spin mechanism of continental drift. In the preface to *The Rhythm of the Ages,* Grabau (1940, p. vii) writes:

The second significant concept is that of periodic shifting of the earth's crust or sial-sphere, through the impetus given by the rotation of the earth on an axis of essential constancy of position, and therefore under permanency of poles and climatic zones. . . . This shifting brings diverse parts of the sial-crust into polar position, and in the movement develops geosynclinal depressions on the side of pressure of the moving sial against the resistant sima, in which it is largely sunk. On the opposite side of the moving mass, drag produces tension which may result in rupture and in volcanism. Translation of the polar site through shifting of the crust is accompanied by the geographic migration of the polar ice-caps at each end of the axis, and of the equatorial and intermediate climate belts, and eliminates the necessity of assuming universal refrigeration to account for continental glaciation in regions now tropical, or a sufficient rise in temperature all over the earth to account for tropical conditions in regions now within the arctic.

The polar-spin mechanism of continental drift already was outdated in 1940, a fact not fully lost on Grabau. Until a more suitable explanation could be found, he asserted that drift should be treated as a working hypothesis to be tested by "all observable and deducible facts" (Grabau, 1940, p. 13). What is fascinating is that Grabau's maps show flourishes of prophetic detail that continue to be substantiated on the ground to this day. His maps of Ordovician and Silurian Pangaea (Grabau, 1940, Plates V and VI), for example, illustrate polar ice caps covering large parts of present-day North Africa and Arabia. Paleopingos and glacially striated pavements in the Upper Ordovician of Saudi Arabia were described most recently by Vaslet (1990) and similar features in North Africa have been well known since the early 1970s.

At the heart of Grabau's book, however, is his entirely original "Pulsation Theory," according to which the "pulse beat" of the earth could be measured in terms of global transgressions and regressions preserved in the stratigraphic record. The pattern of these pulsations represented, for him, the most important feature of historical geology—"the rhythm of the ages." Again, from the preface, Grabau (1940, p. vii) writes:

The first [concept of importance] is the rhythmic movement or pulsation of the sea, which, unlike tidal phenomena, is of simultaneous occurrence in all the oceans of the earth. This is shown by the record of transgressions and regressions everywhere in the strata of all continents, and I have embodied it in the law of slow pulsatory rise and fall of the sea-level in each geological period . . . Each positive pulse-beat sends the marine waters in slow transgression into all the geosynclines as the sea-level rises, and each negative pulse-beat causes their withdrawal as the sea-level sinks.

From this perspective, the unique feature of *The Rhythm of the Ages* is its tabulation of global transgressive-regressive cycles, or "pulsation systems." Thirteen such cycles, separated by 14 interpulsation periods, are listed for the Paleozoic (Grabau, 1940, p. 27), and subsequently discussed in detail, chapter-by-chapter. Figure 1 is a reproduction of Grabau's (1940, p. 208) Figure 66 from the chapter on the "Siluronian Pulsation Period." The diagram summarizes development of the Appalachian geosyncline in North America, inclusive of Upper Ordovician to Lower Devonian strata (two pulsation and two interpulsation cycles). Other tabulations (Grabau, 1940, p. 379, p. 434–435, and p. 446–447) summarize transgressive-regressive cycles for the Mesozoic and Cenozoic.

Typically, Grabau (1940) provided extensive stratigraphic details and correlations on his pulsation cycles from North America, Europe, and Asia. Taken altogether, the tabulations of pulsation cycles outlined in *The Rhythm of the Ages* constitute the first comprehensive survey of Phanerozoic sea-level fluctuations related to unconformity-bound units on something approaching a global scale. This is the main significance of the book. Unlike the direct connection of Grabau's paleogeographic maps to the influence of Alfred Wegener, the source of inspiration for his "Pulsation Theory" is much less obvious. Something may be learned by consulting the book's bibliography, where an incomplete listing of Grabau's previous papers is given. The titles of three out of 68 citations use the key word "pulsation" and the oldest of these references dates from 1933. Clearly, Grabau was thinking about his "Pulsation Theory" throughout much of the 1930s.

More obscure, another clue buried in the *Rhythm of the Ages* is significant in tracing Grabau's chain of thought relative to pulsations. Figure 2 is a reproduction of Grabau's Figure 13 (1940, p. 50) from the chapter on "Orogeny." In the related text, Grabau introduces the term "shantung" for a monadnock, or residual peak of erosion, which has been drowned by sediments. The name is derived from the "rocky eminence of Shantung province in the line of the Huangho geosyncline of China" or the plain of the Yellow River near its confluence with the ocean. Grabau (1940, p. 50) makes the following associations with other structures in North America and the British Isles:

Such buried *shantungs,* are sometimes met with in older geosynclines, or on their marginal platforms. Barraboo ridge of Wisconsin is an example of a "shantung," which has now been partly re-exhumed, and Caradoc Mountain of Shropshire appears to represent another.

The Baraboo Quartzite and the sandstones of the Longmynd both formed resistant rocky shores during the Cambrian and Silurian, respectively. They represent unconformity surfaces with major topographic relief. This theme was a formative element of Grabau's earlier work in North America, necessary as an entry to the concept of facies migration.

Grabau devoted comparatively little space to an analysis of how his global transgressive-regressive cycles may have been emplaced, but he believed their "ultimate cause must probably be sought in the periodicity of the processes of heating and expansion, followed by cooling and contraction, of the sima-shell of the ocean floor" (Grabau, 1940, p. 25). In his longest statement on the topic (Grabau, 1940, p. 15), he wrote:

The rocks of the earth's crust are all radioactive. The radioactive elements generate heat by the energy of their radiations. Periodic increase of heat is followed by loss of heat through conductivity to the cold ocean-floor. Expansion is followed by contraction, and the ocean rises and falls with the changes in its floor; transgression is followed by regression, and a pulsation period is completed. Joly estimates that perhaps thirty million years are required for each of the two processes of such a pulsation, perhaps more. After the cooling and the sinking of the ocean-floor, accompanied by retreat in the geosynclines, another thirty million years or more, are required for the accumulation and conservation of the necessary heat to start the process over again. That interval of rest, I have called the interpulsation period.

The individual cited by Grabau is John Joly, whose 1924 book on *Radioactivity and the Surface History of the Earth* is listed in his bibliography.

INFLUENCES FROM GRABAU'S PRE-CHINA PERIOD

From the start of his professional career, Grabau was a field man. One of his earliest papers dealt with the nature of the Silurian-Devonian transition in western New York State (Grabau, 1900). Another classic is his study on the Silurian geology of Niagara Falls (Grabau, 1901). Early on, he also demonstrated great potential for encyclopedic organization. In partnership with H. W. Shimer, Grabau published the groundbreaking *North American Index Fossils* (1909–1910). When he attended the 11th Geological Congress of 1910 in Stockholm, he took with him a report summarizing the Ordovician-Silurian of North America (Grabau, 1912). Significantly, it may be observed that Grabau delivered his presentation in German. During that visit, Grabau availed himself of a Congress field trip to the Island of Gotland where he studied the celebrated Silurian succession at first hand. His massive textbook *Principles of Stratigraphy* appeared soon afterward (Grabau, 1913).

One kind of talent is required for good field work and another kind of talent is involved with the drive to organize data on a massive scale. In Grabau's case, these talents were reinforced by his ability to theorize. The key to Grabau's "Pulsation Theory," and the connecting link with his definiton of a "shantung" given in *The Rhythm of the Ages,* rest on the foundation of his paper on sedimentary overlap (Grabau, 1906). Figure 3 is reproduced from Figures 7 and 8 of Grabau (1906, p. 616). The pair illustrate the expected diachronistic pattern of facies deposition resulting from a marine regression and transgression, and show how the events may be separated in time by a widening hiatus. Recurrent cycles would define a series of unconformity-bound units and it was just such units that Grabau later tried to identify and correlate on a global basis.

The basic theory expounded by Grabau's (1906) diagrams derives from Johannes Walther's law of the correlation of facies

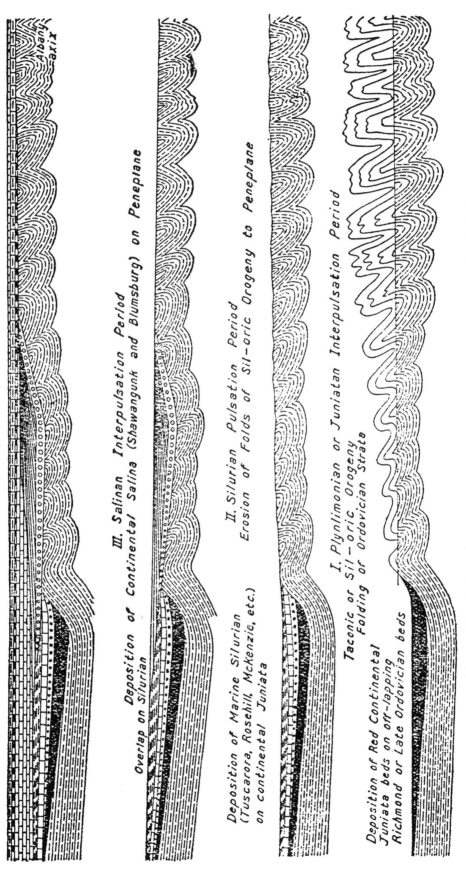

Figure 1. Reproduction of Figure 66 from *The Rhythm of the Ages* (1940), illustrating Grabau's interpretation of eustatic events in the eastern United States during Late Ordovician and Early Silurian time.

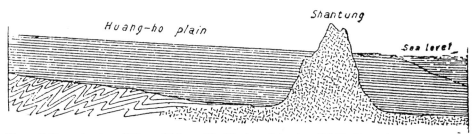

Figure 2. Reproduction of Figure 13 from *The Rhythm of the Ages* (1940), illustrating Grabau's term, shantung, for a monadnock buried by regressive or transgressive deposits. In this particular case, the sediments are essentially Recent.

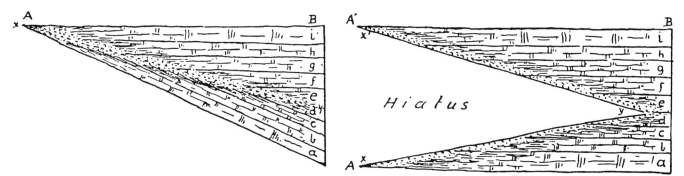

Figure 3. Reproduction of Figures 7 and 8 from Grabau's (1906) paper on sedimentary overlap, illustrating the concept of unconformity-bound stratigraphic units.

(see Middleton, 1973). Walther's own great textbook, *Introduction to Geology as Historical Science* (1893–1894, p. 979) gives us the dictum that "only those facies and facies-areas can be superimposed primarily which can be observed beside each other at the present time." Grabau read Walther (1893–1894) in the original German and was inspired to seek out examples of facies migration in the geology of North America. Figure 4 is reproduced from Grabau's (1906, p. 572) Figure 2, illustrating the progressive burial of a Cambrian rocky shore consisting of Precambrian gneiss in Newfoundland. The use of the "Smith Point Limestone" as a marker bed in this example, indicates that the surface of transgression entailed significant topographic relief. Several other examples from the Cambrian of North America are described by Grabau (1906), all of which would fit under his later definition (1940) of a "shantung."

During his American years, Grabau's application of the facies concept stirred up controversy in the American geological community. In particular, E. O. Ulrich at the U. S. Geological Survey fought hard to suppress the notion of diachronous rock units. His opposition may be summarized fairly by the following quotation on biofacies (Ulrich, 1911, p. 295):

The idea of "shifting of faunas"—that is, tangential transgression of faunas in migration—is of course true theoretically and in fact. The passage between two points requires some, however infinitesimal, lapse of time. But, speaking geologically, the proposition is, in my opinion, purely theoretical. Its practical application in the correlation of geological formations seems impossible and can be assumed only in entire disregard of the general coarseness of geological time units.

By no means did Ulrich disregard the importance of unconformities. Intstead of a prolonged transgression over a surface of major topographic relief as often envisioned by Grabau, Ulrich called for the relatively rapid diastrophic tilting of unconformity surfaces which brought about geologically instantaneous flooding (oscillations).

GRABAU'S WORK IN THE 1920s AND 1930s

Ultimately, the dispute between Ulrich and Grabau boiled down to what was more dominant in the fabric of stratigraphy: local to regional diastrophism or global events involving eustasy. Grabau was in no position to settle this issue prior to his departure for China in 1920. Some might argue that we are still strug-

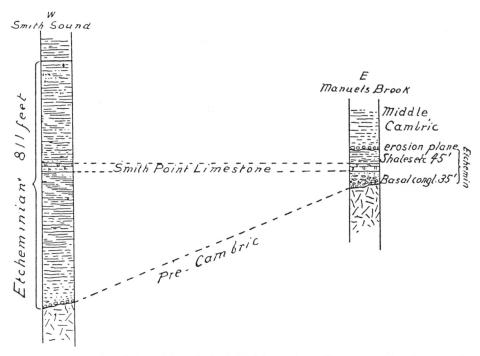

Figure 4. Reproduction of Figure 2 from Grabau's (1906) paper on sedimentary overlap, demonstrating the nature of topographic relief on a rocky shore transgressed by Cambrian sediments in Newfoundland.

gling with this question today and that it can never be resolved. For Grabau, in any case, the debate over facies relationships was at an intellectual dead end. What was needed for progress to be made was a more global data base. At best, Grabau's reasons were mixed for giving up his post at Columbia University and permanently leaving the United States (Johnson, 1985). It is far from clear what research goals he had in mind, if anything beyond normal stratigraphic and paleontologic work in China.

The 1920s were for Grabau a crucial turning point in his career. It was during this decade that he mastered the stratigraphy of China. One of Grabau's former students (Wang Yu, personal communication, 1983) revealed that the only field work ever conducted by Grabau in China was shortly after his arrival when he studied the Ordovician of Hubei Province. This resulted in a monograph on the Orodovician fossils of North China (Grabau, 1922). Afterwards, Grabau became increasingly arthritic; he no longer went into the field but his students conducted extensive field work under his direction. For example, his students Hsieh and Chao (1925) worked on the Silurian section in the Yichang (=I Chang) District. They collected the fossils for Grabau's (1925) study of the Sintan Shale. Although physically restricted himself, Grabau remained an active researcher on the basic stratigraphy of China. It was during this critical decade Grabau convinced himself that cyclic transgressions and regressions in China were coeval with cycles he was already familiar with in North America and Europe. His work in China gave to

Grabau a third leg upon which to establish his global system of eustatic events.

The key concept and correlative data central to his "Pulsation Theory" were well established by Grabau already in the early 1930s. Between 1933 and 1938, Grabau was absorbed in publishing over 3,000 pages of documentation on the global extent of Cambrian to Ordovician sea-level cycles. Projected to cover the entire Paleozoic, three volumes of his tome on *Palaeozoic Formations in the Light of the Pulsation Theory* (Grabau, 1933–1938) were published by the Peking University Press, but the fourth volume was taken over by Henri Vetch, publisher of *Rhythm of the Ages*. These volumes, plus two other references to papers published in the *Bulletin of the Geological Society of China* (Grabau, 1936a, 1938) are cited in *The Rhythm of the Ages*. It is overwhelmingly clear from these that Grabau took special care to incorporate new data from the stratigraphy of China.

Grabau also took the opportunity to introduce personally his theory at the 16th International Geological Congress held in Washington, D.C., in 1933. It was to be his first and only return visit to the United States since his departure for China in 1920. His paper entitled "Oscillation or pulsation" was published in the proceedings of the congress a few years later. Figure 5 is a reproduction of the only illustration used in this paper (Grabau, 1936b, p. 551). It is perhaps the best known, single most important figure from Grabau's work, as it represents a unified eustatic curve for

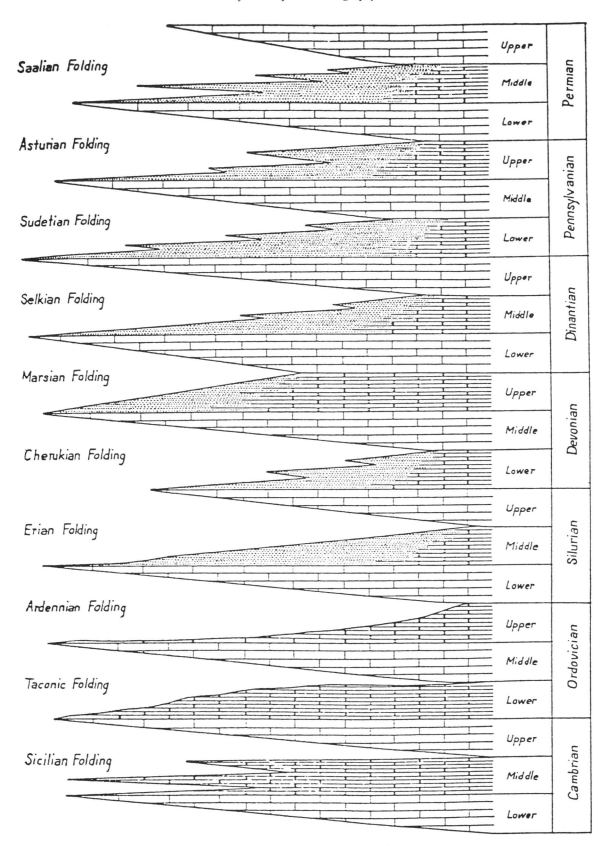

Figure 5. Reproduction of Figure 1 from Grabau's (1936b) presentation on his Pulsation Theory at the 1933 Geological Congress in Washington, D.C., illustrating a eustatic curve for the Paleozoic.

the entire Paleozoic. The listing of orogenic events equated with maximum regressions (Fig. 5) makes it tempting to suppose that Grabau considered mountain-building events a causal agent of regression. Indeed, this was the unambiguous position taken by Umbgrove (1939, p. 128) in his subsequent presentation of a Phanerozoic sea-level curve based primarily on Grabau's stratigraphic data. Grabau's own thinking on this question is made clear by the recorded response to a statement by Hans Stille at the Washington Congress (Grabau, 1936b, p. 553).

It is a pleasure to receive Dr. Stille's strong confirmation of the succession of pulsations which I have proposed. I have welcomed Dr. Stille's succession of tectonic disturbances and have entered them in my diagrammatic table of pulsations for the Paleozoic era. But I question the probability that a tectonic disturbance, as recorded in a continent, would affect the entire world at the same time, so as to cause pulsations. Rather I should expect such tectonic effects to be local, though of profound importance in the regions where they occur. Worldwide, simultaneous pulsations of marine advance and retreat must be caused by changes within the ocean basins.

In fact, the term "oscillation" in the title of Grabau's paper was meant for purposes of contrast to represent the alternative view of sea-level change influenced by non-eustatic diastrophism, as promoted by Ulrich. It is in the short closing lines of Grabau's congress report (1936b, p. 552) that he first mentioned the possible causal role of radioactive heating cycles in the earth's oceanic crust. Although stimulated by John Joly, it must be pointed out that Grabau's views on this topic reflect a selective point of view on Joly's theory. Joly believed that major vertical movements of the continents were coordinated by the slow build-up and comparatively rapid drain of radioactive heat, which periodically escaped from beneath the continents to the ocean crust. Part of his theory recognized that "The ocean floor undoutedly takes up the greater part of the areal extension of the earth's surface and has to accommodate an increase of area which in the long period of crustal expansion must add up to several hundreds of thousands of square miles" (Joly, 1930, p. 95). For Joly, the earth's eustatic cycles were regulated first and foremost by the synchronous rise and fall of continents relative to sea level. Grabau, on the other hand, looked to the eustatic displacement of sea water onto static continental shelves as due exclusively to cyclic crustal expansion in the ocean basins.

The same year that Grabau's congress report was published, a longer, unillustrated presentation of his Pulsation Theory was published in *The Pan-American Geologist* (Grabau, 1936c). Grabau must have realized that he would never be able to complete the detailed documentation of his theory in the style inaugurated by his stratigraphic tomes in 1933. Writing *The Rhythm of the Ages* was a means not only to summarize his earlier work on the Paleozoic, but to sketch out his views on the rest of the Phanerozoic.

Another recorded exchange, which took place following the delivery of Grabau's (1936a) paper before the Geological Society of China, is very revealing about the evolution of Grabau's ideas

on eustasy. Hans Becker is said to have favored Grabau's "bold attempt in the coordination of major geological events by the creation of the pulsation theory but . . . doubted the wisdom of applying an untested theory to the whole world" (Grabau, 1936a, p. 44). Becker indicated that the proper approach would be to "begin such an attempt in one continent and check the results with the facts gathered in other parts of the earth." To this point, Grabau (1936a, p. 48) made the following reply:

The criticism of Dr. Becker regarding the wisdom of applying an untested theory to the whole world, would be well taken if the premises were correct. As a matter of fact, it is not a question of coining a plausible theory of world evolution and then attempting to apply it superficially to the history of all continents. The theory is rather a summation of the critical study of stratigraphic and paleontological facts from all parts of the world assembled by me during a period of more than 30 years.

Becker's analysis of how science is done probably reflects the way most of us really do science. If we accept Grabau at his own word, however, his career experience on three continents led him gradually to a belief in eustasy. His was not a theory in search of data, but rather a set of data somewhat reluctantly entrusted to a theory of murky crustal mechanisms. Given the fact that no mention of global events appear in Grabau's writings until well after his arrival in China, the evolution of his thoughts on this subject seem to have been truly gradual. The data accumulated until it reached a critical global mass. As a result, Grabau was not merely the German-American spokesman for Walther and his law of correlation of facies. Grabau greatly expanded the facies concept into an original theory of eustasy.

RECEPTION OF GRABAU'S IDEAS IN AMERICA

Although he was recognized by his immediate peers, Grabau the expatriot, found essentially no following in the next generation of American geologists. Less than a decade after the publication of *The Rhythm of the Ages,* two important symposia on topics relevant to Grabau's experience were organized under the umbrella of the Geological Society of America. Chester Longwell chaired a symposium on "Sedimentary facies in geologic history" at the November 1948 meeting of the society in New York City and Winifred Goldring and others chaired a symposim on "Distribution of evolutionary explosions in geologic time" at the November 1949 meeting of the society in El Paso, Texas. The Texas symposium was specifically called to "examine the foundation in paleontology for the principle that diastrophism is the ultimate basis for dividing geologic history" (Henbest, 1952, p. 299). It is surprising to note that the published papers and discussions among the participants from both these symposia bear no reference to Grabau's work or influence (Longwell, 1949; Goldring and others, 1952). One reason for this may have been that the 1940 printing of *The Rhythm of the Ages* was small, and from a publishing house very far away during awkward war-time conditions. Such an explanation does not account for the fact that Grabau's earlier books and journal articles on facies relationships were easily available in the United States. There are other possibile explanations, but the one which makes the most sense is simply that Grabau had no American graduate students to send into the profession and carry on his tradition in the West. He did, of course, have many advanced Chinese students who carried on his tradition in the East (Johnson, 1985). It may be argued that Grabau could never have fully developed his ideas on eustasy without going to China, but in so doing he cut himself off from a direct American line of intellectual descendants. Later generations of Americans have managed to rediscover Grabau and his work.

THE ACCURACY OF GRABAU'S CORRELATIONS

It is one thing to establish a local record of sea-level change, but it is another thing altogether to correlate local records from one region to another or from one continent to another. Grabau understood perfectly well the difference between transgressive and regressive facies. None of his peers, not even E. O. Ulrich, would have disagreed with him much regarding the differentiation of sea-level events interpreted from any one stratigraphic section. Grabau was as well equipped a biostratigrapher as anyone else from his generation. He had behind him a great encyclopedic work on the *North American Index Fossils* (Grabau and Shimer, 1909–1910) and he had continued to do paleontological research in China. How accurate were his intercontinental correlations, wed as they were to eustasy? The following short appraisal is derived from the Silurian System, as a representative sample.

Summaries of Silurian eustasy based on research published 50 years or more after *The Rhythm of the Ages* include those by Johnson and others (1991) and Johnson and McKerrow (1991). Figure 6 is a general sea-level curve for the Silurian, modified from Johnson and McKerrow (1991). This curve incorporates data collected from the Silurian continents of Laurentia (North America), Baltica (northern Europe), Siberia, South China, the Australian sector of Gondwana, and the microcontinent of Avalonia (including parts of the British Isles). Marked on this curve by arrows (Fig. 6) are the stratigraphic positions representing Silurian low stands in sea level as determined by Grabau.

Grabau (1940, Chapter 15, p. 155–162) identified the transition from the Ordovician to the Silurian systems as one of his interpulsation periods. He called it the "Plynlimonian" after the region of Mount Plynlimon in Cardiganshire, Wales. He likened the massive progradations of river sediments from the end of the Ordovician Period in Wales and England, Pennsylvania and New York (Fig. 1), and Bohemia to the formation of the flood plains of the Yellow River in China. His interpretation remains basically correct in terms of recent analysis, although Berry and Boucot (1973) invoked the mechanism of a glacio-eustatic draw-down in sea level. Indeed, there are very few localities in the world where continuous sedimentation across the Ordovician-Silurian boundary may be observed. The large arrow at the base of the Silurian column (Fig. 6) shows agreement with Grabau's interpretation.

Grabau had more difficulty in establishing the timing of the next interpulstion period, which he called "Salinan" in reference to the great Upper Silurian salt deposits of North America. In South China, he argued that "the Silurian transgression is represented by the Sintan Shales series, while the evidence of regression is furnished by the terminal sandstone into which these beds merge" (Grabau, 1936a, p. 34). This sandstone would be the Shamao Formation, as represented near Yichang and its position in the Silurian column is indicated by small arrow number 1 (Fig. 6). From his experience on the Swedish island of Gotland, Grabau (1936b) identified two places where the interpulsation phase might be observed. One locality well known as the Galgenberget (= gallows hill) on the north side of Visby exposes the oncolite-bearing Tofta Beds, marking a sharp regression from the underlying reefs of the Hogklint Beds. The other locality toward the south end of the island was characterized by Grabau as exposing a pure quartz sandstone with eolian cross-bedding. This locality could only have been at the Burgsvik Beds. The positions of these regressive beds in the Silurian column are indicated by the small arrows numbered 2 and 3 (Fig. 6). Finally, at least some of the North American salt beds referred to the Salina are considered to be even younger in Silurian age (Fig. 6, small arrow number 4). All of Grabau's units demonstrate regressive characteristics but they are not coeval in time with one another.

The general trend in recent research on the Silurian has been to delineate a more sinuous sea-level curve (Fig. 6). Most of Grabau's points still are considered to mark eustatic regressions, but not the same protracted "interpulsation period" of 30 million years. The periodicity of Silurian eustasy suggested by more recent work is on the order of one to two million years. Work by other stratigraphers on the Devonian (House, 1983; Johnson and others, 1985) and Carboniferous-Permian (Heckel, 1986; Ross and Ross, 1988) suggest equal to much shorter cycles of eustasy.

CONCLUSIONS

Amadeus William Grabau was a geologist with many talents. He was a competent field geologist with a firm understanding of field relationships in stratigraphy. He was also a brilliant encyclopedist, who had a capacity to collate the work of other geologists into a greater coherence. These abilities are well demonstrated by his books *Principles of Stratigraphy* (Grabau, 1913) and *North American Index Fossils* (Grabau and Shimer, 1909–1910). He was, in addition, a remarkable theorist able to focus his field and library talents on the larger canvas of earth history. Nowhere are his full talents more brilliantly combined than in his book *The Rhythm of the Ages.* Therein is developed the first comprehensive treatment of Phanerozoic sea-level fluctuations related to unconformity-bound units based on data of global reach.

Much influenced by Johannes Walther and his concept of shifting facies, Grabau succeeded in taking a theory with interest-

M. E. Johnson

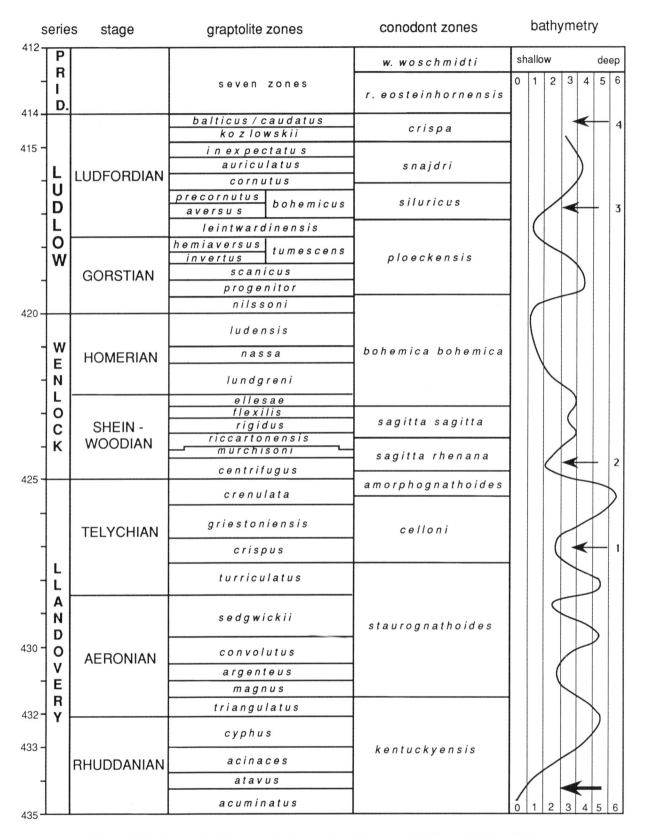

Figure 6. Modification of a Silurian sea-level curve from Johnson and McKerrow (1991), with lower heavy arrow indicating the Ordovician-Silurian low stand in sea-level correctly interpreted by Grabau, and the four smaller arrows pointing to separate eustatic regressions which Grabau considered coeval.

ing regional implications and gradually expanded it into an original theory on eustasy. He was the first geologist to use a method for decoding information on sea-level changes from the rock record and achieve something approaching a global data base with the potential to correlate events from one continent to another. Although he did not make a great fuss about it, he also was influenced by John Joly's concept of radioactive heat cycles as a plausible mechanism accounting for eustatic patterns in his stratigraphic data. Grabau certainly would have welcomed more recent concepts of mid-ocean ridges and changing rates of sea-floor spreading as a stimulus to eustasy (Hays and Pitman, 1973; and subsequent refinements). He also would have delighted in stronger evidence favoring the interconnectedness between his "Pulsation Theory" and notions of continental drift. Unlike de Maillet, Chambers, and many others before him, the most fascinating aspect of Grabau's contribution is that he did not set out to prove eustasy but arrived at that conclusion towards the end of an unusually broad and experienced career spanning three continents.

ACKNOWLEDGMENTS

I am grateful to Robert H. Dott, Jr., for urging me to participate in the symposium on "Eustasy—The Ups and Downs of a Major Concept" sponsored by the History of Geology Division at the 1990 annual meeting of the Geological Society of America in Dallas. This exercise has forced me to look back on my own undergraduate education and it is a pleasure to acknowledge the influence of William M. Furnish, who brought the spirit of A. W. Grabau and E. O. Ulrich alive in his stratigraphy classroom at the University of Iowa. I am very much indebted to the insights of Wang Yu, formerly Professor at the Nanjing Institute of Geology and Palaeontology and formerly one of Grabau's students in Beijing. Finally, it was at the University of Chicago that I first discovered and took an interest in Grabau's work on the Silurian of China. I am most grateful to Alfred M. Ziegler for encouraging me to get abroad in the Silurian world.

REFERENCES CITED

Berry, W.B.N., and Boucot, A. J., 1973, Glacio-eustatic control of Late Ordovician-Early Silurian platform sedimentation and faunal changes: Geological Society of America Bulletin, v. 84, p. 275–284.

Chambers, R., 1848, Ancient sea-margins, as memorials of changes in the relative level of sea and land: London, W. S. Orr & Co., 335 p.

Darwin, C., 1839, Observations on the parallel roads of Glen Roy, and of other parts of Lochaber in Scotland, with an attempt to prove that they are of marine origin: Philosophical Transactions Royal Society London, v. 129, p. 39–81.

Goldring, W., Gazin, C. L. and Woodring, W., eds., 1952, Distribution of evolutionary explosions in geologic time: Journal of Paleontology, v. 26, p. 297–394.

Grabau, A. W., 1900, Siluro-Devonic contact in Erie County, New York: Geological Society of America Bulletin, v. 11, p. 347–376.

—— , 1901, Guide to the geology and paleontology of Niagara Falls and vicinity: New York State Museum Bulletin, v. 45, p. 1–284.

—— , 1906, Types of sedimentary overlap: Geological Society of American Bulletin, v. 17, p. 567–636.

—— , 1912, Uber die einteilung des nordamerikanischen Silurs: International Geological Congress of Stockholm 1910, v. 11, session E, 979–995.

—— , 1913, Principles of stratigraphy: New York, A. G. Seiler and Co., 1185 p.

—— , 1922, Ordovician fossils from North China: Palaeontologica Sinica, Series B, v. 1, p. 2–127.

—— , 1925, Summary of the faunas from the Sintan Shale: Geological Society of China Bulletin, v. 4, p. 77–86.

—— , 1933, Palaeozoic formations in the light of the pulsation theory: Vol. 1, Taconian and Cambrian pulsation systems, first edition 1933, second edition 1936, 680 p.; Vol. 2, 1936, Cambrovician pulsation systems, Part I, 751 p.; Vol 3, 1936, Cambrovician pulsation systems, Part II, 850 p. (vols. 1 to 3, University of Peking Press); Vol. 4, 1938, Ordovician pulsation system, Part I, 941 p., Henri Vetch, Peking.

—— ,1936a, Revised classification of the Palaeozoic System in the light of the pulsation theory: Geological Society of China Bulletin, v. 15, p. 23–51.

—— , 1936b, Oscillation or pulsation: International Geological Congress, Report of the 16th session, United States of America 1933, v. 1, p. 539–553.

—— , 1936c, Classification of Paleozoics on pulsation theory: Pan-American Geologist, v. 66, p. 19–38.

—— , 1938, The significance of the interpulsation periods in Chinese stratigraphy: Geological Society of China Bulletin, v. 18, p. 115–120.

—— , 1940, The rhythm of the ages: Peking, Henri Vetch, 561 p.; 2nd printing in 1978 with an introduction by A. V. Carozzi: Huntington, New York, Krieger, 561 p.

Grabau, A. W., and Shimer, H. W., 1909–1910, North American Index Fossils: Cambridge, Massachusetts Institute of Technology Press, v. 1, 853 p.; v. 2, 727 p.

Hayes, J. D., and Pitman, W. C., III, 1973, Lithospheric plate motion, sea-level changes and climate and ecological consequences: Nature, v. 246, p. 18–22.

Heckel, P. H., 1986, Sea-level curve for Pennsylvanian eustatic marine transgressive-regressive depositional cycles along midcontinent outcrop belt, North America: Geology, v. 14, p. 330–334.

Henbest, L. G., 1952, Significance of evolutionary explosions for diastrophic division of earth history—Introduction to the symposium: Journal of Paleontology, v. 26, p. 299–318.

House, M. R., 1983, Devonian eustatic events: Ussher Society Proceedings, v. 5, p. 396–405.

Hsieh, C. Y., and Chao, Y. T., 1925, A study of the Silurian section at Lo Jo Ping, I Chang District, W. Hupeh: Geological Society of China Bulletin, v. 4, p. 39–44.

Jamieson, T. F., 1863, The 'parallel roads' of Glen Roy and their palce in the history of the Glacial period: Quarterly Journal Geological Society of London, v. 19, p. 235–259.

Johnson, J. G., Klapper, G., and Sandberg, C. A., 1985, Devonian eustatic fluctuations in Euramerica: Geological Society of America Bulletin, v. 96, p. 567–587.

Johnson, M. E., 1985, A. W. Grabau and the fruition of a new life in China: Journal of Geological Education, v. 33, p. 106–111.

Johnson, M. E., and McKerrow, W. S., 1991, Sea level and faunal changes during the latest Llandovery and earliest Ludlow (Silurian): Historical Biology, v. 5, p. 153–169.

Johnson, M. E., Kaljo, D., and Rong, J. Y., 1991, Silurian eustasy, *in* Bassett, M. G., Lane, P. D., and Edwards, D., eds., The Murchison Symposium: Proceedings of an International Conference on the Silurian System: Special Papers in Palaeontology, v. 44, p. 145–163.

Joly, J., 1924, Radioactivity and the surface history of the earth, Halley Lecture, May 28, 1924: Clarendon Press, Oxford, 40 p.

—— , 1930, The surface-history of the earth (second edition): Clarendon Press, Oxford, 211 p.

Kay, M., 1972, Grabau, Amadeus William: Dictonary of Scientific Biography, v. 5, p. 486–488.

Longwell, C. R., ed., 1949, Sedimentary facies in geologic history: Geological

Society of America Memoir 39, 171 p.

Maillet, B., de, 1748, Telliamed, ou entretiens d'un philosophe Indien avec un missionnaire Francios sur la diminution de la mer: Amsterdam, Chex L'honore & Fils, Libraires; English translation by A. V. Carozzi in 1968, University of Illinois Press, Urbana, 465 p.

Middleton, G. V., 1973, Johannes Walther's law of the correlation of facies: Geological Society of America Bulletin, v. 84, p. 979–988.

Ross, C. A. and Ross, J.R.P., 1988, Late paleozoic transgressive-regressive deposition, in, Wilgus, C. K., and others, eds., Sea-level changes: An integrated approach: Society of Economic Paleontologists and Mineralogists Special Publication 42, p. 227–247.

Shimer, H. W., 1947, Memorial to Amadeus William Grabau: Proceedings of the Geological Society of America Annual Report for 1946, p. 155–166.

Sun, Y. C., 1947, Professor Amadeus William Grabau, biographical note: Geological Society of China Bulletin, v. 27, p. 1–26.

Taylor, F. B., 1910, Bearing of the Tertiary mountain belt on the origin of the Earth's plan: Geological Society of America Bulletin, v. 21, p. 179–226.

Ulrich, E. O., 1911, Revision of the Paleozoic systems: Geological Society of American Bulletin, v. 22, p. 281–680.

Umbgrove, J.H.F., 1939, On rhythms in the history of the earth, v. 76, p. 116–129.

Vaslet, D., 1990, Upper Ordovician glacial deposits in Saudi Arabia: Episodes, v. 13, p. 147–161.

Walther, J., 1893–1894, Einleitung in die Geologie als historische Wissenschaft: Jena, Verlag von Gustav Fischer, 3 vols., 1055 p.

Wegener, A., 1924, The origin of continents and oceans: Methusen & Co., LTD., London, 212 p.

Zhang, D., and Faul, C., 1988, A history of geology and geological education in China (to 1949): Earth Sciences History, v. 7, p. 27–32.

MANUSCRIPT ACCEPTED BY THE SOCIETY JANUARY 14, 1992

Geological Society of America
Memoir 180
1992

Chapter 6

The cyclothemic concept in the Illinois Basin: A review

Ralph L. Langenheim, Jr.
Department of Geology and Museum of Natural History, University of Illinois, Urbana-Champaign, Urbana, Illinois 61801
W. John Nelson
Illinois State Geological Survey, 615 E. Peabody St., Champaign, Illinois 61820

ABSTRACT

Although earlier workers had noted Carboniferous sedimentary cycles in passing, the Illinois geologists J. A. Udden, J. Marvin Weller, and Harold Wanless in 1912 to 1932 were the first to explicitly describe and explain these cycles. They demonstrated that Pennsylvanian rocks of the North American craton are characterized by thin cyclically repeated sequences of both marine and nonmarine rock. To explain the phenomenon, Udden proposed periodic subsidence and basin-filling, Weller advocated diastrophic uplift and depression, and Wanless and Shepard advanced the notion of eustatic sea-level changes caused by waxing and waning of glaciers in Gondwanaland.

The cyclothemic concept in the Illinois Basin was established on outcrop data from the basin margins. The concept developed as abundant subsurface data from the deep basin became available. From the 1930s through the 1950s, cyclothems were widely mapped, and attempts were made to extend cyclothems into many other regions and facies.

Enthusiasm for cyclothems declined in the mid-1950s through the 1970s, as cyclothems were relegated to informal usage in stratigraphic codes, and viewed by some as purely local products of delta shifting. More recently, interest in cyclothems has revived. Their lateral continuity and contemporaneity with Gondwana glaciations now are widely, if not universally, accepted. After several decades of neglect, the idea of glacially driven eustasy has returned as a favored explanation for the cyclothemic phenomenon.

INTRODUCTION

The cyclothem concept is essentially an Illinois product, arising from the work of J. A. Udden in 1912 (Fig. 1A). The concept reached full flower during the 1930s with the work of J. Marvin Weller (Fig. 1B), Harold Wanless (Fig. 1C), and Francis Shepard (Fig. 1D). These scientists fully amplified the concept and enunciated two of the most important competing explanations of how cyclothems form: Weller's diastrophic (tectonic) model versus Wanless and Shepard's model of glacially induced eustasy. These models were based almost entirely on studies of Pennsylvanian rocks in the Illinois Basin. Wanless spent the rest of his life enlarging, testing, and seeking to explain the cyclothem model in the Illinois Basin and elsewhere. Although Weller continued to participate in discussions of cyclothemic theory, he soon shifted his emphasis in field and laboratory study

to other topics, especially after he left the Illinois State Geological Survey. Shepard left Illinois and Pennsylvanian studies entirely soon after his collaboration with Wanless.

Cyclothemic study may be divided into five phases: (1) 1912, initial recognition of cyclic repetition of beds in Pennsylvanian rocks; (2) 1925 to 1936, rapid growth of cyclothemic studies and theories; (3) 1937 to 1964, refinement of cyclic stratigraphy and establishment of the interregional contemporaneity of cyclothems; (4) 1964 to 1975, emphasis on paleoenvironmental interpretation of cyclothems; and (5) 1975 to present, renewed testing of theories of how cyclothems were formed.

At the time cyclothems were first recognized, only the most generalized environmental interpretation of cyclothemic members was possible, given existing knowledge of sedimentology and sedimentary petrology. Stratigraphy was largely restricted to de-

Langenheim, R. L., Jr., and Nelson, W. J., 1992, The cyclothemic concept in the Illinois Basin: A review, *in* Dott, R. H., Jr., ed., Eustasy: The Historical Ups and Downs of a Major Geological Concept: Boulder, Colorado, Geological Society of America Memoir 180.

Figure 1. Four individuals who played key roles in early development of the cyclothemic concept. A, Johan August Udden in the field in the Big Bend country of Texas. Heiman (1963) dates this picture as taken prior to 1911. She also reports that Udden began his Big Bend field work in 1903. Inasmuch as his Illinois and early Texas work overlapped in time, this picture probably gives a fair impression of Udden's appearance at the time of his Peoria Quadrangle work. Photograph courtesy of the Archive of the Big Bend Country, Sul Ross State University, Alpine, Texas. B, J. Marvin Weller, photographed in China circa 1937. Photograph courtesy of Harriet Weller. C, Harold R. Wanless at work on his paleoenvironmental maps, circa 1967. Photograph from University of Illinois Archives. D, Francis Shepard, photographed at a reunion held in his honor in 1980 at the Scripps Institution of Oceanography, LaJolla, California. Photo courtesy of Robert Dietz.

fining rock units for geologic mapping. Biostratigraphic studies of Pennsylvanian fusulinids were in their infancy; Pennsylvanian conodonts were essentially unknown. Subsurface geology was rudimentary, being based almost entirely on drillers' descriptions of well cuttings. Finally, the vast majority of geologists adhered firmly to T. C. Chamberlin's (1909, p. 693) dictum that, diastrophism "seems to be the ultimate basis of correlation." As cyclothemic studies proceeded from Udden's first efforts, the rise of petroleum geology and geophysics yielded massive quantities of new data and forced growth of new concepts on the origin and deposition of sedimentary rocks. Thus, growth of the cyclothemic theory and the work of our predecessors paralleled developments in geology as a whole and must be evaluated in light of the prevailing knowledge.

1912: RECOGNITION OF CYCLICITY

The first person to describe and interpret cyclicity in the Pennsylvanian rocks of Illinois was Johan August Udden (1912, Fig. 1A). Udden was interested in many facets of geology and held summer and ancillary appointments with many organizations. He began his career in 1881 to 1888 at Bethany Academy in Lindsborg, Kansas, where he probably saw rocks of the Kansas Pennsylvanian section. In addition to teaching at Augustana College from 1888 through 1911, he served as a special agent for the U.S. Geological Survey from 1908 through 1914. Udden was a special assistant at the Iowa Geological Survey from 1897 through 1903 and a geologist for the Illinois State Geological Survey from 1907 to 1911 (Baker, 1933; Heimann, 1963). He also served part-time with the Texas Bureau of Economic Geology from 1902 through 1911, and became a full-time employee of that institution in 1911. His work in west Texas led to, among other things, the discovery of oil in the Permian Basin (Baker, 1933). He was concerned with areal mapping and stratigraphic correlation, being an early exponent of subsurface stratigraphy. He mapped six quadrangles for the Iowa Survey prior to 1903, and prepared maps and reports for the U.S. Geological Survey on the Peoria (Udden, 1912), Belleville, and Breese Quadrangles (Udden and Shaw, 1915) in Illinois. Udden completed the field work in the Illinois quadrangles prior to his departure for Texas in 1912. The mapping involved detailed description of Pennsylvania coal-bearing rocks, and gave him a broad knowledge of Pennsylvanian rocks in the western part of the Illinois Basin.

Udden (1912) described and interpreted four cycles in the exposed Pennsylvanian rocks of the Peoria Quadrangle (Fig. 2). The sequence includes three coals: the Springfield (No. 5), Herrin (No. 6), and Danville (No. 7) of current terminology. The topmost cycle contains discontinuous thin coal beds presently referred to the Gimlet Coal. According to Udden (1912, p. 47), each cycle is composed of rocks representing "four successive stages, namely (1) accumulation of vegetation; (2) deposition of calcareous material; (3) sand importation; and (4) aggradation to sea level and soil making." He observed that coal thickness decreases upward in each successive cycle and that each coal is

succeeded by laminated carbonaceous shale or "bone coal," which he interpreted as resulting from marine water invading the coal swamp. The succeeding stage of marine sedimentation yielded differing thicknesses of limestone and fossiliferous shale. The calcareous beds in turn were succeeded by sandstone; which, according to Udden (1912), built up to sea level as sand filled the submerged area. Thereafter, shale and underclay (a claystone that underlies a coal seam and contains root casts) accumulated as a result of decay and weathering of the upper surface of the last sand deposit.

Udden (1912, p. 49) concluded "that the four cycles represent recurrent interruption of a progressive submergence." His explanation of the cycles, involving subsidence followed by sedimentary filling, reappears in later studies and remains acceptable. The 21 units comprising the four cycles were correlated by Udden throughout the Peoria 30-minute Quadrangle. In addition, the coal beds, as well as some other units, had been recognized by him and by others throughout much of western Illinois. Udden (1912, p. 50) stated, "Everything considered, the most remarkable feature bearing on the physical conditions prevailing at the time of deposition of the coal measures of this quadrangle is the horizontal extent and uniformity of thickness of each deposit."

1925 TO 1936: FLOWERING OF CYCLOTHEMS

Cyclothemic studies were not pursued seriously in the Illinois Basin after Udden's efforts in 1912 until those of Harold Wanless and J. Marvin Weller beginning in the mid-1920s. Wanless (Fig. 1C) received his undergraduate and graduate training at Princeton University. His doctoral dissertation concerned the White River Formation (Tertiary) of South Dakota, including its lateral and vertical facies changes, environments of deposition, source of sediments, and paleoecology. He joined the staff of the University of Illinois at Urbana-Champaign in 1923, and remained there for his entire professional career. Wanless steadily worked on problems of Pennsylvanian stratigraphy to the end of his life in 1970 (White, 1973).

J. Marvin Weller (Fig. 1B) was the son of Stuart Weller, an eminent paleontologist at the University of Chicago who worked extensively with the Illinois State Geological Survey and is noted particularly for his studies of Mississippian rocks and fossils. By ten years of age, the younger Weller accompanied his father in the field; and he was employed as a field assistant by the Illinois State Geological Survey at the age of 16. J. M. Weller received his undergraduate and graduate training at the University of Chicago. Upon completing his doctorate in 1925, he joined the staff of the Illinois State Geological Survey. He worked at the survey through 1945, when he succeeded his father as Professor of Invertebrate Paleontology at the University of Chicago, where he remained until his retirement in 1965 (Willman, 1978).

Both Wanless and Weller began their post-doctoral careers working on Pennsylvanian geology in the Illinois Basin. By 1925, Wanless was mapping the Alexis Quadrangle in western Illinois near Rock Island (Wanless, 1929), where he recognized five

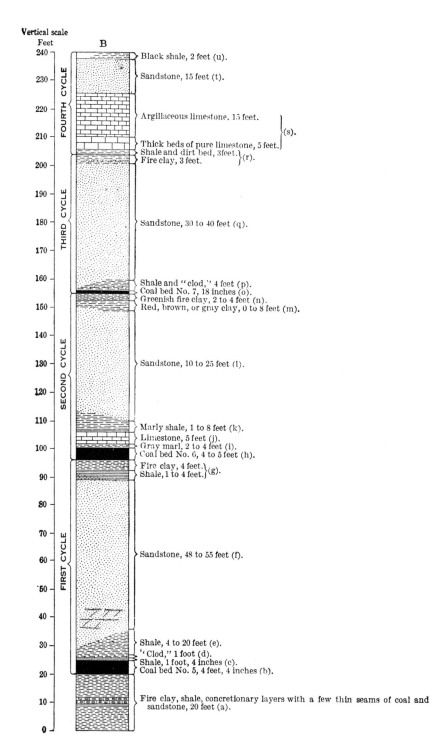

Figure 2. Udden's (1912) stratigraphic column of Pennsylvanian rocks exposed in the Peoria Quadrangle. The upper part of unit "r" is referred to as "vegetation represented by carbonaceous shale" by Udden (1912, p. 48).

cycles in the Pennsylvanian. In 1927 and 1928, he mapped in the Havana Quadrangle southwest of Peoria (Wanless, 1957a,b). In 1925, Wanless heard J. M. Weller speak on his discovery of an ascending succession of sandstone, underclay, coal, marine limestone and/or shale, and thick, unfossiliferous shale that characterized Pennsylvanian strata of Illinois. Wanless also heard Weller's description of the cycles that he had observed and the fossils that he had collected from Pennsylvanian rocks over much of Illinois. Wanless, in turn, revealed that he had observed similar cyclicity in his mapping (Wanless, personal communication to R. L. Langenheim, circa 1965). Wanless continued his mapping and Weller his regional collecting and, in the fall of 1927, they displayed their findings during a field trip from LaSalle to Peoria, Illinois, held by the Association of American State Geologists. Inspired by what they saw on this field trip, R. C. Moore of the Kansas Geological Survey and David Reger of the West Virginia Geological Survey immediately began searching for and finding cyclicity in Pennsylvanian rocks of their respective states. In 1928, Weller continued his stratigraphic and paleontologic studies in both Illinois and Indiana, while Wanless undertook detailed physical correlation between the Havana and Alexis Quadrangles. In this manner Wanless and Weller, early in their professional careers, hammered out their ideas about cyclothemic stratigraphy and its significance, informally comparing ideas and observations. Wanless concentrated on stratigraphic correlation and sedimentologic phenomena in western Illinois, while Weller mainly studied the faunal succession (Wanless, personal communication to R. L. Langenheim, circa 1965).

Weller (1930) published the first paper that was concerned with cyclical sedimentation in Illinois since Udden's (1912) report. Weller's paper was based on "detailed geologic investigations in western Illinois, which have been conducted during the last few years by various members of the State Geological Survey (Illinois), and reconnaissance studies in other areas" (Weller, 1930, p. 97).

Weller concluded that Pennsylvanian strata of Illinois and neighboring regions are cyclically repeated in a typical succession (Fig. 3A). The "typical cyclical formation" of Weller (1930) contained eight members: (1) shale (at the top), (2) marine limestone, (3) calcareous shale, (4) black fissile shale, (5) coal, (6) underclay, (7) sandy shale, and (8) sandstone, with an unconformity at the base. He further proposed that "each cyclical repetition of beds be considered a formation of the Pennsylvanian System" (Weller, 1930, p. 101), with the formations separated at the unconformity at the base of the sandstone. With this proposal, Weller rejected Udden's (1912) use of the base of the coal as the division point. After discussing the wide lateral extent of some cycles and their constituent members, Weller proposed that detailed correlations of Pennsylvanian strata between Missouri, Kansas, Illinois, and Ohio should be possible "through comparison of cyclical formations" (Weller, 1930, p. 110). Weller postulated that recurrent tectonic uplift and depression caused these sedimentary cycles. He envisioned a mechanism of repetitive uplift and downwarp in Appalachia that induced corresponding

smaller vertical movements in the cratonic interior. Regional differences in magnitude of uplift and downwarp produced regional facies changes within cycles. Weller suggested that the timing of uplifts in the Alleghenian and Ouachita-Marathon orogenic belts might have differed from one another. In consequence, according to Weller, cycles in the Eastern Interior might not correlate with cycles of the Western Interior. Finally, Weller tentatively suggested that the average Pennsylvanian cycle lasted approximately 400,000 years. He derived this figure by dividing the probable number of cyclothems in Illinois and Ohio (50) into Barrell's (1917) estimate of the length of the Pennsylvanian Period (20 m.y.).

The Wanless-Weller collaboration culminated in the 1930 symposium on the Pennsylvanian System held at the Illinois State Geological Survey. At this symposium Weller gave a paper "The Conception of Cyclical Sedimentation During the Pennsylvanian Period," and Wanless presented "Pennsylvanian Cycles in Western Illinois" (Weller, 1931; Wanless, 1931). Wanless by this time had identified 15 cycles (Fig. 4) in western Illinois, a substantial increase from Udden's four. Additional papers on Ohio (Stout, 1931), West Virginia (Reger, 1931), and Kansas (Moore, 1931) supported the cyclothem concept, but Ashley (1931) of Pennsylvania and Plummer (1931) of Texas were either lukewarm or opposed. In large part this reflected a generational, as well as a philosophical conflict, as other older men such as T. E. Savage also were critical (personal communication from Harold Wanless to R. L. Langenheim, Jr., circa 1965). Weller (1961, p. 32) wrote that, "The principal opponents were G. H. Ashley, T. E. Savage and David White" and commented that "These gentlemen appeared to rely mainly on their recollections and because they never noted cycles, they denied the existence of them." Cady (1934) "also was a more or less consistent critic" of the idea of Pennsylvanian cycles (Weller, 1961, p. 132). An unpublished

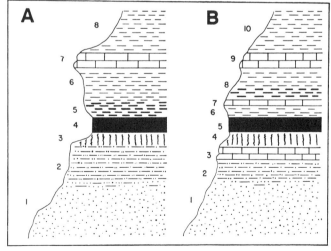

Figure 3. Pennsylvanian cyclothems of Illinois. A, As described by Weller (1930); B, As described by Willman and Payne (1942). Figure from Weller (1958, Fig. 1).

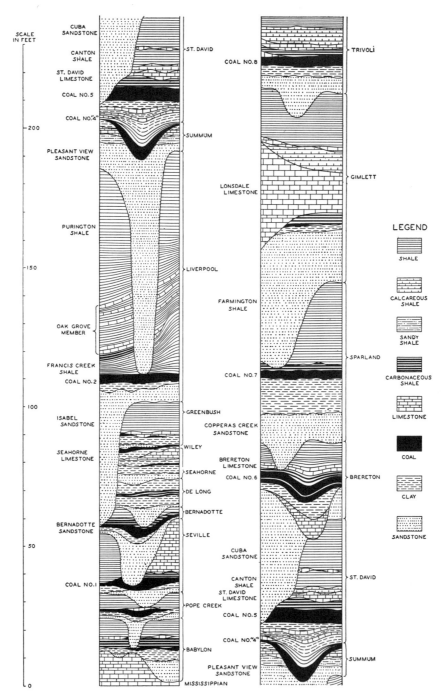

Figure 4. General section of proposed cyclical formations constituting the Pennsylvanian rocks of the western Illinois coal field (Wanless, 1931, Fig. 46).

manuscript in the files of the Illinois State Geological Survey outlines some of Cady's counterpoints, many of which remain pertinent. For example, he doubted the presence of a significant unconformity at the base of the sandstone in the cyclothem, an essential component in Weller's conception of the cycles. Nevertheless, Wanless and Weller demonstrated the cyclic nature of Pennsylvanian rocks throughout much of the eastern and central

United States. At this point, the concept of cyclicity was based almost entirely on study of exposed rocks, coal mines, and cores around the margins of the Illinois Basin. Geologically usable subsurface information would not be widely available until the late 1930s, with the advent of geophysical logging during the oil boom in deeper parts of the Illinois Basin.

The term "cyclothem" was introduced by J. M. Weller, in

Wanless and Weller (1932, p. 1003). The root is two Greek words: *cyclos,* or cycle, and *thema,* or deposit. Weller stated, "The word cyclothem is therefore proposed to designate a series of beds deposited during a single sedimentary cycle of the type that prevailed during the Pennsylvanian Period. A cyclothem ranks as a formation in the scale of stratigraphic nomenclature," replacing cyclical formation of previous usage. Cyclothems were accepted for many years as formal lithostratigraphic units, equivalent to formations, in the Pennsylvanian of Illinois.

Francis P. Shepard, a colleague of Harold Wanless at Illinois during the 1930s, was engaged in study of sea-level changes induced by Pleistocene glaciation. In 1935, Wanless and Francis Shepard (Fig. 1D) introduced a new explanation for upper Paleozoic cyclothems: eustatic rise and fall of ocean levels in response to the waxing and waning of Gondwanaland glaciation (Wanless and Shepard, 1935, 1936). These papers outlined the second major explanation of cyclicity in upper Paleozoic rocks. Wanless and Shepard wrote before any precise knowledge was available on the timing of Gondwana glaciation or of the number of glacial epochs that were involved. Their glacial-eustatic model was criticized by some, including Weller (1956, 1961), who pointed out that the number of proven glacial cycles did not match the number of observed cyclothems, and that the timing of glaciation was in doubt. In reponse to this criticism, Wanless mustered all available information on Gondwana glaciation, and visited Australia and South Africa to gather field evidence. Ultimately, he published an account of glaciation in the Southern Hemisphere, concluding that glaciation could have been responsible for cyclothems (Wanless and Cannon, 1966).

Intense interest in basinal versus marginal facies was beginning to develop in the mid-1930s, but most stratigraphers considered formations to be time-bounded and called on crustal movements to explain marine transgressions and regressions. The main challenge to these ideas awaited the explosion in the amount of data available for analysis and the rapid development of new concepts in stratigraphy yet to come.

1937 TO 1964: REFINEMENT OF CYCLOTHEMIC STRATIGRAPHY

Weller took a two-year leave in 1937 and 1938 to conduct a geological evaluation of petroleum and other minerals in northwestern and western China. Upon his return to the Illinois State Geological Survey, Weller shifted much of his attention to Mississippian and Devonian stratigraphy and the preparation of a state geological map. Although he continued to concern himself with cyclothems, he did little hands-on work with Pennsylvanian rocks after leaving the Illinois State Geological Survey in 1945. His major contributions consisted of philosophic and historical reviews of cyclothemic patterns and origins (Weller, 1956, 1964), stratigraphic reports involving description of additional cyclothems (Weller, 1940), correlation (Weller and others, 1942), and contributions to biostratigraphy (Dunbar and Henbest, 1942; Cooper, 1946). Wanless, on the other hand, actively continued to

seek more precise information on the sedimentology, stratigraphy, and biostratigraphy of Pennsylvanian rocks in the Illinois Basin and elsewhere, as applied to the cyclothemic concept. In this work Wanless collaborated with his graduate students at the University of Illinois and colleagues at the Illinois State Geological Survey and elsewhere.

Wanless and Weller were major contributors to the Pennsylvanian correlation chart published by the Pennsylvanian Subcommittee of the National Research Council's Committee on Stratigraphy (Moore and others, 1944). In addition to correlated columns from 58 localities in North America, the chart includes a stratigraphic cross section from West Virginia through Ohio, Illinois, and Kansas to Oklahoma (Fig. 5). Although cyclothems are not labeled on the chart, principal limestone units, coals, and major sandstone bodies are traced through their extent on the line of traverse. Because coals and limestones are among the most readily recognized and widespread members of cyclothems, their correlation is a de facto recognition of cyclothemic stratigraphy.

To test his hypothesis of glacial-eustatic control of cyclicity, Wanless (Wanless and Patterson, 1952) examined 70 Permo-Carboniferous sequences of shallow-marine carbonate rocks in west Texas, New Mexico, Colorado, Utah, Nevada, and California. Obviously, eustatic changes would affect all marine rocks, especially those deposited in shallow waters. Tectonism in the Appalachian and Ouachita orogens, in contrast, would have little or no influence in the far western United States. Wanless observed cyclicity in carbonate rocks of the far western United States, and suggested that such thick, continuously marine sequences might serve as a standard of correlation for cycles that occur in less complete sections. He followed up this work by sending several graduate students to examine selected western United States sections in detail, but apparently never attempted to correlate individual cycles from the west with those of the midwest.

Following establishment of the cyclothemic concept, geologists of the Illinois State Geological Survey and in the Department of Geology at the University of Illinois began describing Pennsylvanian sequences statewide in the framework of those concepts. Papers that describe and correlate cyclothems include Weller's (1940) work in southern Illinois; Dunbar and Henbest's (1942) monograph of the fusulinidae of the Illinois Basin; Weller's stratigraphic summary in Cooper's (1946) report on ostracodes; Wanless's (1957a) report on the geology of four quadrangles in western Illinois (work done prior to 1944); Willman and Payne's (1942) report on the Marseilles, Ottawa, and Streator Quadrangles; Simon's (1946) work in Bond County; and Ball's (1952) map and report on the Carlinville Quadrangle (field work done in 1929). By 1956 a total of 39 cyclothems in central and western Illinois and 38 cyclothems in southern Illinois had been described or proposed (Wanless, 1956; Siever, 1956). Furthermore, many of the Illinois cyclothems had been correlated with cycles in Missouri, Indiana, and Kentucky. These correlations were made primarily on the basis of outcrop study, although subsurface data (mainly from electric logs) were also used (Wan-

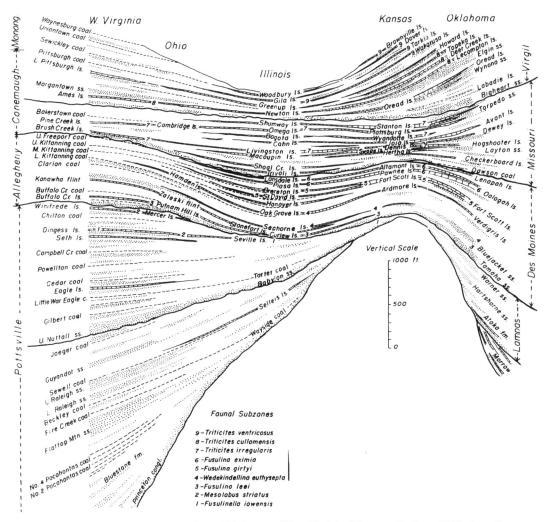

Figure 5. Stratigraphic cross section from Oklahoma to West Virginia (Moore and others, 1944, chart 6).

less, 1955). Cycles in the Virgilian Series (uppermost Pennsylvanian) in east-central Illinois, however, remained poorly known because of inadequate exposure and lack of subsurface data. Also, significant facies changes and lack of data prevented development of a standard classification between western and southern Illinois, even though many individual units were correctly correlated.

Wanless' (1957a, b) definitive work on the cyclothems of western Illinois, essentially the rocks in which Udden (1912) first recognized cyclicity, was published after a long delay. Wanless mapped the region in 1927 and 1928, prepared a comprehensive report in 1937 through 1944, and revised and modernized the manuscript in 1955 and 1956. The 1957 reports include geologic maps of four 15-minute quadrangles, 69 detailed measured sections, 10 well logs, and a comprehensive list of 525 taxa from 399 collections from 49 fossiliferous beds. One hundred and fifty-four individual rock units belonging to eighteen cyclothems are described in detail. This effort may be taken as *the* basic field report on the "type area" of the cyclothem concept.

Use of cyclothems as formations began with Wanless and Weller's (1932) correlations within the Carbondale and McLeansboro Groups in the Illinois Basin. Wanless (1939) extended the use of cyclothems with correlations from the Illinois Basin into the Appalachian Basin. Wanless (1956) and Siever (1956) later subdivided the Tradewater and Caseyville Groups of Illinois into cyclothems. In 1929 to 1930, Ball (1952) mapped cyclothems in the Carlinville Quadrangle, and Newton and Weller (1937) mapped them in six counties of southeastern Illinois. Wanless (1957a) mapped in western Illinois in 1937 and 1940 to 1944, and Willman and Payne (1942) mapped in northern Illinois. In addition, prior to 1937, Weller produced an unpublished map showing the subcrop belts of cyclothems in the southern two-thirds of Illinois at a scale of 1:500,000. This map was exhibited at the annual meeting of the Geological Society of America in 1988 and is presently in the map room of the Illinois State Geological Survey. The map appears to be an early stage of the compilation leading to the 1945 (Weller and others, 1945) edition of the state geological map. The 1945 map does not show cyclothems. It does, however, show the distribution of certain limestone beds in the Pennsylvanian.

Other significant contributions during this period were made by Paul E. Potter and David H. Swann of the Illinois State Geological Survey. In a series of papers, Potter and co-authors discussed provenance, transport, and deposition of Chesterian and Pennsylvanian sediments of the Illinois Basin (Potter and Siever, 1956; Potter and Glass, 1958; Potter and others, 1958; Potter, 1962, 1963). Meanwhile, Swann (1963, 1964) considered the same aspects of Chesterian rocks, which exhibit crude cyclicity of alternating siliciclastic and carbonate units. Both Potter and Swann envisioned southwesterly transport of clastic sediment to a broad shallow shelf. They proposed that strandline and deltaic dispersal centers shifted repeatedly, controlling sedimentation. Swann (1964) believed that variation in rainfall primarily controlled cyclicity, and that glacial-eustatic effects were secondary. He correlated Chesterian carbonate sedimentation with rainy periods, during which lush vegetation on land reduced the sediment yield. Clastic units were related to drier periods of increased runoff, erosion, and transport. Potter had relatively little to say regarding causes of cyclicity, although he wrote (1963, p. 86), "The widespread occurrence of cyclic deposition in late Paleozoic sediments in widely separated areas points to a world-wide control. Climatic controls seem plausible."

Beginning in 1947, the American Commission on Stratigraphic Nomenclature led a nationwide movement to standardize stratigraphic usage. Spurred by these developments, Willman and others (1958) formulated a new stratigraphic policy for the Illinois State Geological Survey. Cyclothems were removed from formal rock-stratigraphic classification and placed in a separate category relieved "from the restrictions imposed by the practical requirements of rock stratigraphic classification" (Willman and others, 1958, p. 11). Kosanke and others (1960) reclassified the Pennsylvanian rocks of Illinois, defining formations and groups on the basis of gross lithology and key beds. Each new formation contains several cyclothems, which are considered informal stratigraphic units. Kosanke and other's (1960) classification has persisted to the present day with little change. In the *Handbook of Illinois Stratigraphy,* cyclothems are retained as "much smaller units than formations . . . most useful in detailed differentiation and field mapping of the Pennsylvanian sediments," but "not entirely adequate for rock-stratigraphic classification" (Willman and others, 1975, p. 173). The current North American Stratigraphic Code (1983, Article 22j) likewise considers cyclothems as informal units. Cyclothems are set apart from formations, which, among other things, must be mappable "at the scale of geologic mapping practiced in the region when the formation is proposed" (Code, 1983, Article 25d).

Types of cyclothems

From the beginning it was recognized that cyclothems were, by no means, uniform. Although the eight units (Fig. 3A) originally described by Weller (1930) occurred in the same sequence in most cyclothems, some units might be absent and additional units might appear in individual cases. In addition, facies changes were apparent within the Illinois Basin and the changes were pronounced between the Illinois Basin and the Western Interior Basin. As a consequence, attempts were made to define an "ideal cyclothem" and to classify and define significant divergent types. Willman and Payne (1942, p. 87, Fig. 42) defined and illustrated an "ideally complete cyclothem" (Fig. 3B) for the Marseilles-Ottawa-Streator area, stating that, "this complete sequence rarely occurs." They also pointed out that, "with one exception the cyclothems in northern Illinois are universally present where they should be although they vary laterally in thickness and altitude" (Willman and Payne, 1942, p. 87). This idealized cyclothem of ten units has been reproduced in many Illinois State Geological Survey publications, including the *Handbook of Illinois Stratigraphy* (Willman and others, 1975).

J. M. Weller (1942) recognized four different types of cyclothem in the McLeansboro Group of Illinois. Type a cyclothems were characterized by prominent basal sandstones resting on a well-marked unconformity, generally were coal-bearing, and included a prominent black sheety shale overlain and underlain by marine limestone. Type b cyclothems were "very imperfect and were generally indicated only by a more or less persistent horizon of marine fossils" (Weller, 1942, p. 145). Type c cyclothems were well developed, had a well-developed basal sandstone, lack freshwater limestone, and coal seams were inconspicuous. Black sheety shale was not uniformly present, but the upper marine limestone was light-colored and thick. Type d cyclothems were thin and incomplete, lacked truly marine limestone, and were difficult to recognize because of their variability and lack of distinguishing characters" (Weller, 1942, p. 146).

Having defined four types of cyclothems, Weller (1942) went on to suggest that these types themselves recurred in order, comprising larger "groups" of cyclothems. Weller designated six such "groups" of cyclothems in Illinois. Three of the "groups" were complete, containing cyclothems of types a, b, c, and d in ascending order. Two other "groups" were incomplete, lacking one of the four types. The sixth and uppermost "group" contained only the basal type a cyclothem, younger cyclothems having been eroded.

Weller (1958) revised his 1942 classification, designating cyclothem type a as the Macoupin type, type c as the LaSalle type, and type d as the Bogota type (Fig. 6). Type b cyclothems apparently no longer were recognized. Weller now adopted the term "Illinois megacyclothem" for his "groups" of cyclothems, and he correlated Illinois megacyclothems with the Kansas megacyclothems of Moore (1936, 1949).

The Kansas megacyclothems of Moore each ideally contained five limestone-shale couplets (Fig. 6). Moore believed that each couplet recorded a rise and fall of sea level and was, therefore, a cyclothem. Four megacyclothems, each containing five cyclothems, were defined in the Shawnee Group of Kansas (Moore, 1936, 1949). Weller (1958, 1961) pointed out the many differences between the Kansas and Illinois megacyclothems, but

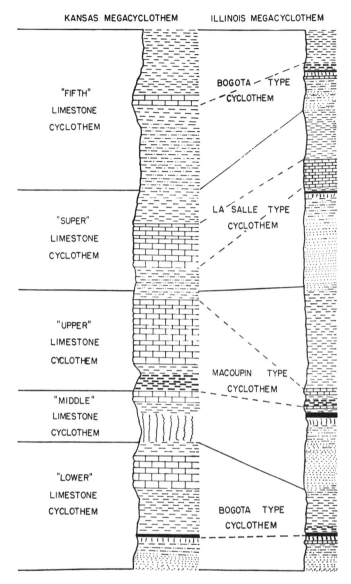

KANSAS MEGACYCLOTHEM   ILLINOIS MEGACYCLOTHEM

Figure 6. Weller's correlation of Illinois and Kansas megacyclothems (Weller, 1958, Fig. 3).

ascribed them to facies changes, stating, "The Kansas megacyclothem and the Illinois cycle of cyclothems appear to be coordinate and fundamentally similar. Each consists of three or more differently constituted simple cyclothems that are repeated in regular order. It seems logical and proper, therefore, to term the large Illinois cycle a megacyclothem also" (Weller, 1961, p. 151–152). Wanless (1964, p. 605), however, disagreed with this interpretation, stating, "It is proposed that the megacyclothem of the northern Midcontinent is the equivalent of the cyclothem of the Illinois basin formed in regions nearer sources of marine transgression and farther from frequent sources of clastic sediment."

Heckel (1980, 1984) and Heckel and others (1980) analyzed Moore's megacyclothems, applying concepts of detailed carbonate petrology and faunal analysis unavailable to Moore.

The new analysis demonstrated that sea level rose rapidly to maximum depth during deposition of the black fissile shale, then fell slowly during deposition of the "upper" limestone, "super" limestone, and "fifth" limestone (cited as rare and fortuitous). On this basis, Heckel agreed with Wanless (1964), likening the Kansas megacyclothem to the Illinois State Geological Survey "Ideal Cyclothem" as well as to the "LaSalle" cyclothem and all of the other Illinois types (Fig. 7). Heckel and others (1980) showed that "types" of cyclothems may have merely local, rather than regional significance. For example, the lower, transgressive limestone (below the black shale) is lenticular at the type locality of the Fithian cyclothem near Danville, Illinois. Within an exposure 30 m (100 ft) long, the Fithian cyclothem changes from a "Kansas-type (Macoupin) cyclothem" to an "Illinois-type (LaSalle) cyclothem" as the limestone pinches out.

1964 TO 1975: REGIONAL STRATIGRAPHIC ANALYSIS AND PALEOENVIRONMENTAL STUDY

The studies discussed previously established a reasonably reliable succession of cyclothems within all but the uppermost Pennsylvanian of the Illinois Basin and adjacent regions. During the 1950s, attention began to focus on paleogeographic and paleoenvironmental studies. Starting in 1937 electric logs became available in the Illinois Basin and by 1960, Wanless had a collection of more than 18,000 electric logs (Wanless, 1962). Using this newly available subsurface data in conjunction with all of the accumulated outcrop data, Wanless prepared his first paleogeologic, isopachous, and structural maps of the Eastern Interior Basin (Wanless, 1955, 1962). In these early works, he described regional differences in cyclothems, and defined a series of different types of cyclothems within the Illinois Basin and in adjacent basins. Cyclothems closer to the Appalachians generally contain little or no marine limestone and fossiliferous shale, in contrast to those of Kansas and Nebraska, which are composed almost entirely of marine shale and limestone (Wanless, 1947; Weller, 1956).

Murray (1953) proposed that early Allegheny coal beds in western Indiana were deposited during both the transgressive and regressive phases of an individual marine invasion. Thus the "transgressive" coal rested on nonmarine rocks and was succeeded by marine rocks, whereas the "regressive" coal rested on marine rocks and was overlain by non-marine strata. This suggestion was followed by a more elaborate theoretical paper (Wheeler and Murray, 1957) which argued that each cyclothem recorded not one, but two transgressive-regressive cycles (Fig. 8). Their model was based on Simpson's (1940) hypothesis of long-term fluctuations in solar radiation. According to Simpson, each solar cycle would produce two glacial and two interglacial events, and corresponding eustatic effects. Applying their model to the "typical Illinois cyclothem," Wheeler and Murray (1957) envisioned the following sequence of events: (1) base level strongly down, producing an unconformity; (2) base level moderately up, lower non-marine clastic portion of cyclothem deposited; (3) base

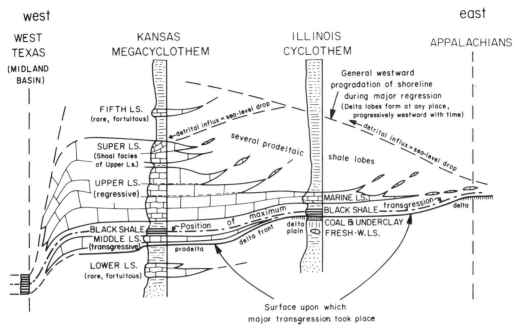

Figure 7. Inferred facies changes as a Kansas cyclothem (megacyclothem of Moore, 1936) grades eastward into an Illinois "typical" cyclothem—in this case the LaSalle Type of Weller (1961) (Heckel, 1977, Fig. 4).

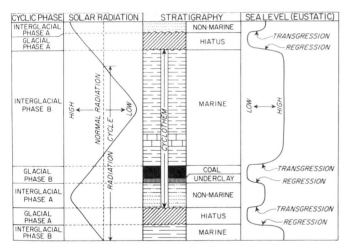

Figure 8. Inferred relationship between an ideal Illinois cyclothem (Macoupin Type of Weller, 1961) and Simpson's theoretical solar radiation curve (Wheeler and Murray, 1957, Fig. 3).

cies, and paleoenvironmental maps for individual units of cyclothems throughout the Illinois Basin, as well as in Missouri, Iowa, eastern Kansas, and northeastern Oklahoma. These maps ultimately incorporated data from theses by about 20 graduate students. A first report on the Summum, St. David, and Brereton cyclothems and their equivalents (Wanless and others, 1963) included a cross section of interpreted environments from northeastern Oklahoma to western Kentucky, looping across northern Missouri and the Illinois Basin. Wanless's maps showed superposed deltas and coal basins, limits of black shale deposition and of marine limestone beds, thicknesses of the three cyclothems, lithofacies of the Brereton Cyclothem, and 31 paleoenvironmental maps (Wanless and others, 1963) of individual cyclothemic units. An example of one of Wanless and others' (1963) maps is illustrated here (Fig. 9). Data for the maps consisted of surface sections, driller's logs, coal-test cores and shafts, and geophysical logs. Records were sought from each township in the area, a ideal generally achieved in the Illinois Basin, except in a belt from 32 to 64 km (20 to 40 mi) wide along the northern and northeastern margin of the basin. Later studies cover younger strata: the Liverpool through Millersville cyclothems (Carbondale, Modesto, and Bond Formations) and their equivalents, and rocks from the Plattsburg Limestone of the Lansing Group through the Severy Shale of the Wabaunsee Group of Kansas. The average number of datum points per map increased to nearly 2,500 (Wanless and Wright, 1978). A total of 154 paleoenvironmental maps ultimately appeared in the final, posthumous work of Wanless (Wanless and Wright, 1978). In the early maps, coal beds were

level moderately down, underclay and peat (coal) developed; and finally (4) base level strongly up, upper marine shales and limestones deposited. Wheeler and Murray's hypothesis is carefully argued, but it lacks parsimony. Perhaps for this reason, it has gained few supporters.

Continuing the line of study begun in his 1955 and 1962 regional syntheses, Wanless began compiling isopachous, lithofa-

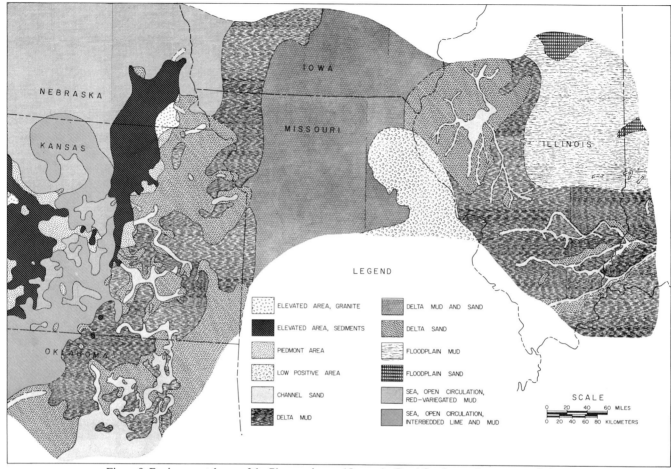

Figure 9. Environmental map of the Pleasantview and Lagonda (Prue) Sandstone, Summum cyclothem (Wanless and Wright, 1978, Fig. 24).

the key units in correlation. Later maps were keyed upon the black fissile shales, which Wanless (Wanless to R. L. Langenheim, personal communication, circa 1965) asserted could be traced much farther west than the coals, ultimately pinching out at the eastern limit of arkosic arenite derived from the ancestral Rockies. Wanless also determined that individual marine limestone beds persisted regionally and were readily traceable in geophysical logs. Remaining units of the idealized cyclothem were found to be discontinuous and to undergo abrupt facies changes. Wanless also defined numerous clastic wedges, related to deltaic incursions, interrupting the succession of cyclothemic units.

Another significant effort from this period was Zangerl and Richardson's (1963) monographic study of two black shales, the Mecca Quarry and Logan Quarry Shales, in west-central Indiana. This study featured lamina by lamina disassembly of large volumes of shale that had been painstakingly reassembled in the Field Museum of Chicago after being brought in from the field. Thus Zangerl and Richardson recorded the character and distribution of organic remains, chiefly fossil fish, and noted successional differences in lithology. Drawing analogies to swamp and

bayou sediments in Louisiana, Zangerl and Richardson concluded that these black shales were deposited in very shallow water and under a semipermanent floating mat of vegetation. Periodic, perhaps seasonal, fluctuation in water level was invoked to explain lamination and successional changes in shale character, as well as periodic trapping of large numbers of fish in shallow stagnant pools (Zangerl and Richardson, 1963). All of this was ascribed to incursion of marine waters into the coal swamp, reaching a depth of not more than 1 m for the black layers, and 3 to 5 m for the gray layers (Zangerl, 1980).

A new model of cyclothemic origins, popularly called delta-switching, arose to challenge the diastrophic and glacial-eustatic models in the late 1960s. Based on sedimentologic studies of Recent deltas, the new model sought to explain cyclicity as the product of recurrent progradation, abandonment and submergence of delta lobes. The concept of delta-switching apparently originated with British geologists. D. Moore (1959) used this mechanism to explain cyclothems in the Lower Carboniferous Yoredale Series of northern England and Scotland. In his abstract, Moore proclaimed "The mechanism of cyclic advance of the delta is sufficient to account for all of the observed features of the Yoredale Series cyclothems without recourse to more fanciful ideas." In another British paper, Duff and others (1967, p. 243) stated, "the system is largely self-regulating and incorporates an in-built feed-back mechanism." However, on a more cautious note they also wrote, "In summary, a theory of cyclothem development which includes only delta-switching as a mechanism we conclude is inadequate" (Duff and others, 1967, p. 156). Others, however, embraced delta-switching as the primary control of cyclicity. Notable among these were John Ferm and associates, who worked in the Appalachian area, Fort Worth Basin, and elsewhere from the 1960s onward. In two representative papers, Ferm (1970, 1975) concluded that cyclicity of Pennsylvanian strata was better explained by episodic progradation and decay of deltas rather than by tectonic or eustatic effects. Such a model implies that cyclothems and their constituent units are relatively local features that cannot be correlated among different basins of deposition. The provocative ideas of Ferm have been hotly contested, but because the debate is centered mainly outside of the Illinois Basin, it will not be recapitulated here.

Interestingly enough, Ferm came to Illinois in 1949 to 1950 to work with Wanless after completing a Master's degree with P. D. Krynine at Pennsylvania State University and a year of studying sedimentology and paleobotany at Michigan. He left in July 1950 to accept a Shell Fellowship at the Pennsylvania State University after a full year as a research assistant with Wanless. Although Ferm never published research on the Illinois Basin, his views on the generation of cyclothems through deltaic shift were strongly supported by many, including Glen Merrill, one of his students. Merrill spent a short time teaching at Monmouth College, during which time he investigated conodont biostratigraphy and paleoecology in western Illinois. Merrill (1975) viewed various members of cyclothems as having formed concurrently in different parts of a delta complex. Specifically rejecting tectonic and eustatic models of cyclicity, he wrote (Merrill, 1975, p. 5), "Granted an ongoing, but gentle, subsidence of the basin, the normal processes of deltaic progradation, avulsion, compaction and repeated progradation would suffice to produce the preserved sedimentary record." In Merrill's model all cyclothemic members are laterally discontinuous and in facies relationship with one another. This model directly opposes Wanless's interbasinal correlation of dozens of cyclothemic members in vertical succession.

Charles Shabica also applied delta-switching models to Illinois cyclothems. He is best known for his studies of depositional environments and paleoecology of the Francis Creek Shale (Desmoinesian) of northern Illinois. Shabica (1979) postulated that the Francis Creek and associated strata were deposited by deltas of low gradient under generally static sea-level conditions.

The role of deltas was acknowledged by Wanless (1967) and Wanless and Wright (1978). Among the conclusions of Wanless and Wright are:

1. Cyclothems comprise a few thin, widespread units—underclay, coal, black shale, and limestone—preceded and succeeded by more variable clay and sand.

2. The areal distribution of any widespread units reflects patterns of sediment distribution in preceding units.

3. The many widespread units traceable throughout the Illinois Basin and northern Midcontinent indicate free connection between the areas and suggest that the whole central United States was remarkably flat. A sea-level change of a few tens of meters might shift the strandline by hundreds of kilometers. Sharp contacts between many widespread units suggest rapid changes in the position of the seas.

4. Clastic wedges may interrupt the succession of widespread units. Some wedges are composed of the uppermost shale of a lower cyclothem and the basal sandstone of the next, originating at a time of regression. Others may develop at almost any point within a cycle. All resulted from differential uplifts in highlands surrounding the depositional basin, indicating local tectonism.

5. The basal sandstone of the cyclothem, originally interpreted as a subaerial channel deposit on the surface of unconformity at the base of the cyclothem (Weller, 1930), now was seen as a product of deltaic maturation. Shale was initially deposited offshore in the prodelta, and overlain by distributary-channel and sheet sands, which formed on top of the prograding delta.

6. Underclays were seen as forming on deltaic platforms in the late stages of delta growth.

7. Extensive coal beds formed only on suitable platforms, generally those constructed by one or more deltas. Less extensive coal beds formed in estuaries, coastal lagoons, oxbow lakes, and in unfilled channels.

8. Wedges of gray shale overlying several coals are deltaic in origin and formed in response to local or nearby tectonic events.

9. Black shale beds overlying coal beds record initial marine invasion of the coal swamp.

10. Marine limestone beds are thickest and most prominent in the Kansas-Nebraska region; some have Illinois Basin counterparts and some are represented by thin argillaceous limestone units.

11. The upper gray shale of a cyclothem may be marine at the base, but the upper portion is generally deltaic in origin (see No. 5).

12. Transgressions and regressions responsible for the cyclothems seem to result from eustatic rise and fall of sea level in response to glacial growth and wasting in Gondwanaland. Local irregularity in subsidence and sediment supply, however, determine the amount and type of sediment deposited in each cycle.

1975 TO PRESENT: RECENT DEVELOPMENTS

Heckel's (1977) hypothesis for a relatively deep-water (up to 200 m) origin for phosphatic, black fissile shales in Pennsylvanian cyclothems, although developed in the northern Midcontinent, profoundly affected workers in the Illinois Basin. Heckel challenged the conclusions of both Wanless and Wright (1978) and Zangerl and Richardson (1963). This conflict was highlighted at the 10th Annual Field Conference of the Great Lakes Section, Society of Economic Paleontologists and Mineralogists (Langenheim and Mann, 1980). During this meeting, Zangerl and Heckel visited Zangerl's localities at Barren Creek, near Mecca Quarry in Parke County, Indiana (Zangerl, 1980), and the black shale outcrop at the Fithian site in Vermilion County, Illinois (Heckel and others, 1980), in company with a large field trip group. The shallow-water versus deep-water models for black shales were vigorously debated on the field trip. Some participants concluded that both shallow-water and deep-water black shales might exist. Recent support for that idea was given by Coveney and others (1991), who documented strikingly different trace-element occurrences between basin-margin and more seaward black shales.

The continuity of black shales from the Illinois Basin to the Western Interior Basin is sufficiently well established that in two cases (Anna and Excello Shales) the same names are used in both basins. The same shale might have been deposited in significantly deeper water in Kansas than in Indiana. The essential factor for black shale is not water depth per se, but oxygen deficiency.

The only remaining substantial gap in knowledge of cyclothemic succession in the Illinois Basin, Virgilian rocks at the top of the sequence, was recently filled by the work of Weibel (1986, 1988, 1991; Weibel and others, 1989). These rocks are poorly exposed and generally are not logged by petroleum drillers. They had not been studied intensively since Newton and Weller (1937) first defined cyclothems in the area. Even the basic succession of units was not established. At least 13 different stratigraphic columns were published for these rocks between 1937 and 1986 (Weibel, 1986). Weibel used recently available gamma-ray logs, which unequivocally highlight the black fissile shale beds in the cyclothems. Also, he used a series of coal and oil exploration logs, unavailable to earlier workers, and applied new stratigraphic and sedimentologic concepts to these data (Weibel, 1986, 1988; Weibel and others, 1989). Weibel redescribed and reinterpreted the individual cyclothems, arranging them in a well-documented stratigraphic order for the first time. Also he argued for returning cyclothemic boundaries to the "top of the coal or the base of the marine portion" (Weibel and others, 1989, p. 143). When defined in this fashion cyclothemic boundaries become more readily recognizable at the surface and in most geophysical logs. They also relate to a readily detectable geologic event: initiation of marine deposition. Weibel (1991) further proposed use of his "modified cyclothems" as basinwide lithostratigraphic units in an application of sequence stratigraphy. Finally, Virgilian cyclothems of Illinois have now been more securely correlated with those of Kansas and Texas, using newly refined conodont biostratigraphy (Heckel and others, 1991; Weibel and others, 1989).

Eustasy as a cause for cyclothemic deposition was recently related to possible "forcing" by Milankovitch cycles by Heckel (1986) and others. This concept was based on work outside of the Illinois Basin. Klein and Willard (1989) took exception to the notion of eustasy as the only cause of cyclicity in Pennsylvanian rocks. Although they attributed Kansas cyclothems to eustatic

changes of a "periodicity comparable to Milankovitch orbital parameters" (Klein and Willard, 1989, p. 152), they also asserted that foreland flexing was responsible for Appalachian cyclothems and that Illinois cyclothems are "intermediate between the two end member processes." They concluded (p. 152) that "the Pennsylvanian coal-bearing cyclothems of North America owe their origin to the remarkable coincidence of supercontinent development, concomitant glaciation and eustatic sea-level change, and associated episodic thrust loading and foreland basin subsidence of small magnitude on progressively more rigid crust."

Klein and Willard's model encompasses both a tectonic process reminiscent of Weller's (1930) idea of diastrophic control of cyclicity and Wanless and Shepard's (1936) concept of glacial-eustatic control. The implied temporal correlation between glacial-eustatic and thrust-loading events seems quite remarkable.

Klein (1990) cast doubt on correlations between Milankovitch orbital cycles and the time elapsed during deposition of Kansas cyclothems as postulated by Heckel (1986). Klein pointed out the potential for error in calculating Milankovitch cycle periods that have lengths of thousands of years, by using radiometric dates that have error margins of millions of years. In addition, he (Klein, 1990, p. 456) called attention to Lippolt and others (1984) and Hess and Lippolt (1986), who showed that the Pennsylvanian may, in fact, have lasted for only 19 m.y. rather than the 30 to 40 m.y. proposed by other authors. Klein (1990, p. 456) stated the opinion that "their time scale appears to be constrained far better" than other current time scales, reducing the length of the Pennsylvanian by 45% and that this "poses serious consequences for (Heckel's) calculations of Pennsylvanian cycle periodicities." Also, the applicability of Holocene orbital parameters to the Carboniferous was challenged by Klein.

Each of Klein's arguments has been challenged. Langenheim (1991), Heckel (1991), and deBoer (1991) questioned many aspects of the time scales favored by Klein and maintained that, even granting Klein's assumptions, cycle lengths still fall within the range of Milankovitch parameters. Klein (1991) responded to all three critics, and the issue remains in controversy.

The cyclothemic concept has experienced many ups and downs in its history. The fact that it still evokes controversy after nearly 80 years proves the subject to be lively and durable. The debate of tectonics versus eustasy remains as vigorous today as when introduced in the 1930s. New contenders including climate and delta-switching have joined the fray. Whatever course the debate may take in the future, much of it will be set in the birthplace of the cyclothem, the Illinois Basin.

ACKNOWLEDGMENTS

We thank R. H. Dott, Jr., Philip H. Heckel, and Daniel F. Merriam, who reviewed this manuscript and offered many helpful suggestions. Also, we thank Heinz Damberger and Pius Weibel for reading an earlier version of the manuscript. Harriet Weller, Augustana College, the University of Illinois Archives, the Illinois State Geological Survey Library, Robert Dietz of

Arizona State University, Gerry Kuhn of the University of California at San Diego, and the Sul Ross State University Archives helped us obtain portraits of the "old timers." Elwood Atherton, William Newton, Heinz Damberger, and Pius Weibel also gave freely of their memories and/or ideas.

Pam Cookus was most helpful in preparing the manuscript from rough copy on short notice.

REFERENCES CITED

Ashley, G. H., 1931, Pennsylvanian cycles in Pennsylvania: Illinois Geological Survey Bulletin 60, p. 241–245.

Baker, C. L., 1933, Memorial of Johan August Udden: Geological Society of America Bulletin, v. 44, p. 402–413, pl. 13.

Ball, J. R., 1952, Geology and mineral resources of the Carlinville Quadrangle, Illinois: Illinois State Geological Survey Bulletin 77, 110 p., 4 pls.

Barrell, J., 1917, Rhythms and estimates of geologic time: Geological Society of America Bulletin, v. 28, p. 795–905.

Cady, G. H., 1934, Alternative interpretation of the subdivision of the Pennsylvanian series in the Eastern Interior Province [abs.]: Geological Society of America Proceedings for 1973, p. 71.

Chamberlin, T. C., 1909, Diastrophism as the ultimate basis of correlation: Journal of Geology, v. 17, p. 685–693.

Cooper, C. L., 1946, Pennsylvanian ostracodes of Illinois: Illinois State Geological Survey Bulletin 70, 177 p.

Coveney, R. M., Jr., Watney, W. L., and Maples, C. G., 1991, Contrasting depositional models for Pennsylvanian black shale discerned from molybdenum abundances: Geology, v. 19, p. 147–150.

deBoer, P. L., 1991, Comment *on* 'Pennsylvanian time scales and cycle periods': Geology, v. 19, no. 4, p. 408–409.

Duff, P.McL.D., Hallam, A., and Walton, E. K., 1967, Cyclic sedimentation: Elsevier Publishing Company, Developments in Sedimentology 10, 280 p.

Dunbar, C. O., and Henbest, L. G., 1942, Pennsylvanian fusulinidae of Illinois: Illinois State Geological Survey Bulletin 67, 218 p.

Ferm, J. C., 1970, Allegheny deltaic deposits, *in* Morgan, J. P., ed., Deltaic sedimentation, modern and ancient: Society of Economic Paleontologists and Mineralogists Special Publication 15, p. 246–255.

—— , 1975, Pennsylvanian cyclothems of the Appalachian Plateau, a retrospective view: U.S. Geological Survey Professional Paper 853, p. 57–64.

Heckel, P. H., 1977, Origin of black shale facies in Pennsylvanian cyclothems of Mid-Continent North America: American Association of Petroleum Geologists Bulletin, v. 61, p. 1045–1068.

—— , 1980, Paleogeography of eustatic model for deposition of midcontinent Upper Pennsylvanian cyclothems, *in* Fouch, F. D., and Magathan, M. R., eds., Paleozoic paleogeography of west-central United States: Society of Economic Paleontologists and Mineralogists, Rocky Mountain Section Symposium 1, p. 197–215.

—— , 1984, Changing concepts of Midcontinent Pennsylvanian cyclothems, North America: Neuvieme Congres International de Stratigraphie et de Geologie du Carbonifere, Compte Rendu, v. 3, p. 535–553.

—— , 1986, Sea-level curve for Pennsylvanian eustatic marine transgressive-regressive depositional cycles along Midcontinent outcrop belt, North America: Geology, v. 14, p. 330–334.

—— , 1991, Comment *on* 'Pennsylvanian time scales and cycle periods': Geology, v. 19, no. 4, p. 406–407.

Heckel, P. H., Price, R. C., and Schutter, S. R., 1980, Glacial eustatic models for black-shale-bearing Pennsylvanian cyclothems of Midcontinent and Illinois, *in* Langenheim, R. L., Jr., and Mann, C. J., eds., Middle and Late Pennsylvanian strata on margin of Illinois Basin: Society of Economic Paleontologists and Mineralogists, Tenth Annual Field Conference, Great Lakes Section, p. 139–157.

Heckel, P. H., Barrick, J. E., Boardman, D. R., Lambert, L. L., Watney, W. L.,

and Weibel, C. P., 1991, Biostratigraphic correlation of eustatic cyclothems (basic Pennsylvanian sequence units) from Midcontinent to Texas and Illinois [abs.]: American Association of Petroleum Geologists Bulletin, v. 75, p. 592.

Heimann, M., 1963, A pioneer geologist: Biography of Johan August Udden: Kerrville, Texas, Sam M. Udden, 215 p.

Hess, J. E., and Lippolt, J. J., 1986, $^{40}Ar/^{39}Ar$ ages of tonstein and tuff sanidines: New calibration points for the improvement of the upper Carboniferous time scale: Isotope Geoscience, v. 59, p. 143–154.

Klein, G. deV., 1990, Pennsylvanian time scales and cycle periods: Geology, v. 18, no. 5, p. 455–457.

—— , 1991, Reply *to* Comments *on* 'Pennsylvanian time scales and cycle periods': Geology, v. 19, no. 4, p. 405–410.

Klein, G. deV., and Willard, D. A., 1989, Origin of the Pennsylvanian coal-bearing cyclothems of North America: Geology, v. 17, no. 2, p. 152–155.

Kosanke, R. J., Simon, J. A., Wanless, H. R., and Willman, H. B., 1960, Classification of the Pennsylvanian strata of Illinois: Illinois State Geological Survey Report of Investigations 214, 84 p., 1 pl.

Langenheim, R. L., Jr., 1991, Comment *on* 'Pennsylvanian time scales and cycle periods': Geology, v. 19, no. 4, p. 405.

Langenheim, R. L., Jr., and Mann, C. J., eds., 1980, Middle and Late Pennsylvanian strata on margin of Illinois Basin: Society of Economic Paleontologists and Mineralogists, Tenth Annual Field Conference, Great Lakes Section, 238 p.

Lippolt, H. J., Hess, J. C., and Burger, K., 1984, Isotopische alter von pyroklastischen sanidinen aus kaolin-Kohlentonstein als korrelationsmarken fur das mittelueroaische Oberkarbon: Rheinland und Westfalen Forschfirst Geologisches, v. 32, p. 119–150.

Merrill, G. K., 1975, Pennsylvanian conodont biostratigraphy and paleoecology of northwestern Illinois: Geological Society of American Microform Publication 3, 128 p.

Moore, D., 1959, Role of deltas in the formation of some British Lower Carboniferous cyclothems: Journal of Geology, v. 67, no. 5, p. 522–539.

Moore, R. C., 1931, Pennsylvanian cycles in the northern Mid-Continent Region: Illinois Geological Survey Bulletin 60, p. 247–257.

—— , 1936, Stratigraphic classification of the Pennsylvanian rocks of Kansas: State Geological Survey of Kansas Bulletin 22, 256 p.

—— , 1949, Divisions of the Pennsylvanian System in Kansas: State Geological Survey of Kansas Bulletin 83, 203 p.

Moore, R. C., and 27 others, 1944, Correlation of Pennsylvanian formations of North America: Geological Society of America Bulletin, v. 55, p. 657–706.

Murray, H. H., 1953, Transgressions and regressions of the early Allegheny (Pennsylvanian) seas in Indiana [abs]: Geological Society of America Bulletin, v. 64, p. 1456.

Newton, W. A., and Weller, J. M., 1937, Stratigraphic studies of Pennsylvanian outcrops in part of southeastern Illinois: Illinois State Geological Survey Report of Investigations 45, 31 p.

North American Stratigraphic Code, 1983, The North American Commission on Stratigraphic Nomenclature: American Association of Petroleum Geologists Bulletin, v. 67, no. 5, p. 841–875.

Plummer, F. B., 1931, Pennsylvanian sedimentation in Texas: Illinois Geological Survey Bulletin 60, p. 259–269.

Potter, P. E., 1962, Late Mississippian sandstones in Illinois: Illinois State Geological Survey Circular 340, 36 p.

—— , 1963, Late Paleozoic sandstones of the Illinois Basin: Illinois State Geological Survey Report of Investigations 217, 92 p.

Potter, P. E., and Glass, H. D., 1958, Petrology and sedimentation of the Pennsylvanian sediments in southern Illinois: A vertical profile: Illinois State Geological Survey Report of Investigations 204, 60 p.

Potter, P. E., and Siever, R., 1956, Sources of basal Pennsylvanian sediment in the Eastern Interior Basin: Journal of Geology, Part I, Cross-bedding, v. 64, no. 3, p. 225–244; Part II, Sedimentary petrology, v. 64, no. 4, p. 317–335; Part III, Some methodological considerations, v. 64, no. 5, p. 447–455.

Potter, P. E., Nosow, E., Smith, N. M., Swann, D. H., and Walker, F. H., 1958,

Chester cross-bedding and sandstone trends in Illinois Basin: American Association of Petroleum Geologists Bulletin, v. 42, no. 5, p. 1013–1046.

Reger, D. B., 1931, Pennsylvanian cycles in West Virginia: Illinois Geological Survey Bulletin 60, p. 217–239.

Shabica, C. W., 1979, Pennsylvanian sedimentation in northern Illinois: Examination of delta models, *in* Nitecki, M. H., ed., Mazon Creek fossils: New York, Academic Press, p. 13–40.

Siever, R., 1956, Correlation chart, *in* Wanless, H. R., ed., Classification of the Pennsylvanian rocks of Illinois as of 1956: Illinois State Geological Survey Circular 217, 14 p.

Simon, J. A., 1946, Correlation studies of Upper Pennsylvanian rocks in southwest-central Illinois [M.S. thesis]: Urbana, University of Illinois, 56 p.

Simpson, G. C., 1940, Possible causes of change in climate and their limitations: Proceedings, Linnaean Society London, v. 152, p. 190–219.

Stout, W. E., 1931, Pennsylvanian cycles in Ohio: Illinois Geological Survey Bulletin 60, p. 195–216.

Swann, D. H., 1963, Classification of Genevievian and Chesterian Late Mississippian rocks of Illinois: Illinois State Geological Survey Report of Investigations 216, 91 p.

—— , 1964, Late Mississippian rhythmic sediments of Mississippi Valley: American Association of Petroleum Geologists Bulletin, v. 48, no. 5, p. 637–658.

Udden, J. A., 1912, Geology and mineral resources of the Peoria Quadrangle: U.S. Geological Survey Bulletin 506, 103 p., with geological and economic geology maps.

Udden, J. A., and Shaw, E. W., 1915, Description of the Belleville and Breese Quadrangles, Illinois: U.S. Geological Survey Atlas Belleville-Breese Folio, no. 195, 13 p., maps.

Wanless, H. R., 1929, Geology and mineral resources of the Alexis Quadrangle: Illinois State Geological Survey Bulletin 57, 230 p., 6 pls.

—— , 1931, Pennsylvanian cycles in western Illinois: Illinois Geological Survey Bulletin 60, p. 179–193.

—— , 1939, Pennsylvanian correlations in the Eastern Interior and Appalachian coal fields: Geological Society of America Special Paper 17, 130 p., 9 pls.

—— , 1947, Regional variations in Pennsylvanian lithology: Journal of Geology, v. 55, p. 237–253.

—— , 1955, Pennsylvanian rocks of Eastern Interior Basin: American Association of Petroleum Geologists Bulletin, v. 39, p. 1753–1820.

—— , 1956, Classification of the Pennsylvanian rocks of Illinois as of 1956: Illinois State Geological Survey Circular 217, 14 p., correlation chart.

—— , 1957a, Geology and mineral resources of the Beardstown, Glasford, Havana and Vermont Quadrangles: Illinois State Geological Survey Bulletin 82, 233 p., 7 pls.

—— , 1957b, Pennsylvanian faunas of the Beardtown, Glasford, Havana and Vermont Quadrangles: Illinois State Geological Survey Report of Investigations 205, 59 p.

—— , 1962, Pennsylvanian rocks of Eastern Interior Basin, *in* Branson, C. C., ed., Pennsylvanian System in the United States: American Association of Petroleum Geologists, p. 4–59.

—— , 1964, Local and regional factors in Pennsylvanian cyclic sedimentation, *in* Merriam, D. F., ed., Symposium on cyclic sedimentation: Kansas Geological Survey Bulletin 169, v. II, p. 593–606.

—— , 1967, Eustatic shifts in sea level during the deposition of late Paleozoic sediments in the central United States *in* Elam, J. G., and Chuber, S., 1967: Cyclic sedimentation in the Permian Basin: Midland, Texas, West Texas Geological Society, p. 41–54.

Wanless, H. R., and Cannon, J. R., 1966, Late Paleozoic glaciation: Earth Science Review, v. 1, p. 247–286.

Wanless, H. R., and Patterson, J., 1952, Cyclic sedimentation in the marine Pennsylvanian of the southwestern United States, *in* Troisieme Congres pour l'advancement des Etudes de Stratigraphie et de Geologie du Carbonifere: Herleen, Netherlands, Compte Rendu, v. 2, p. 653–664.

Wanless, H. R., and Shepard, F. P., 1935, Permo-Carboniferous coal series related to Southern Hemisphere glaciation: Science, v. 81, p. 521–522.

—— , 1936, Sea level and climatic changes related to late Paleozoic cycles: Geological Society of America Bulletin, v. 47, p. 1177–1206.

Wanless, H. R., and Weller, J. M., 1932, Correlation and extent of Pennsylvanian cyclothems: Geological Society of America Bulletin, v. 43, no. 4, p. 1003–1016.

Wanless, H. R., and Wright, C. R., 1978, Paleoenvironmental maps of Pennsylvanian rocks: Illinois Basin and northern Midcontinent region: Geological Society of America MC-23, 32 p., 165 figs.

Wanless, H. R., Tubb, J. B., Jr., Gednetz, D. E., and Weiner, J. L., 1963, Mapping sedimentary environments of Pennsylvanian cycles: Geological Society of America Bulletin, v. 74, p. 437–486.

Weibel, C. P., 1986, Resolution of stratigraphic disarray, Virgilian of Illinois Basin: Geological Society of America Abstracts with Programs, v. 18, no. 4, p. 330.

—— , 1988, Stratigraphy, depositional history, and brachiopod paleontology of Virgilian strata of east-central Illinois [Ph.D. thesis]: Urbana, University of Illinois, Department of Geology, 228 p.

—— , 1991, Cyclothem revival! (Sequence stratigraphy of Upper Pennsylvanian strata, east-central Illinois): Geological Society of America Abstracts with Programs, v. 23, no. 3, p. 65.

Weibel, C. P., Langenheim, R. L., and Willard, D. A., 1989, Cyclic strata of the Late Pennsylvanian outlier, east-central Illinois, *in* Vineyard, J. D., and Wedge, W. K., eds., Geological Society of America 1989 Field Trip Guidebook: Missouri Department of Natural Resources Division of Geology and Land Survey Special Publication 5, p. 141–169.

Weller, J. M., 1930, Cyclical sedimentation of the Pennsylvanian Period and its significance: Journal of Geology, v. 38, p. 97–135.

—— , 1931, The conception of cyclical sedimentation during the Pennsylvanian Period: Illinois Geological Survey Bulletin 60, p. 163–177.

—— , 1940, Geology and oil possibilities of extreme southern Illinois: Illinois State Geological Survey Report of Investigations no. 71, 71 p.

—— , 1942, Rhythms in Upper Pennsylvanian cyclothems: Transactions Illinois State Academy of Science, v. 75, no. 2, p. 145–146.

—— , 1956, Argument for diastrophic control of late Paleozoic cyclothems: American Association of Petroleum Geologists Bulletin, v. 40, no. 1, p. 17–50.

—— , 1958, Cyclothems and larger sedimentary cycles of the Pennsylvanian: Journal of Geology, v. 66, no. 2, p. 195–207.

—— , 1961, Patterns in Pennsylvanian cyclothems: Nova Scotia Department of Mines and Research Foundation, 3rd Conference on the Origin and Constitution of Coal, Crystal Cliffs, Nova Scotia (1956), p. 129–171.

—— , 1964, Development of the concept and interpretation of cyclic sedimentation, *in* Merriam, D. F., ed., Symposium on Cyclic Sedimentation: Kansas Geological Survey Bulletin 169, v. 2, p. 607–621.

Weller, J. M., Wanless, H. R., Cline, L. M., and Stookey, D. G., 1942, Interbasin Pennsylvanian correlations, Illinois and Iowa: American Association of Petroleum Geologists Bulletin, v. 26, p. 1585–1593.

Weller, J. M., Workman, L. E., Cady, G. H., Bell, A. H., Lamar, J. E., and Ekblaw, G. E., 1945, Geologic map of Illinois: Illinois State Geological Survey, scale 1:500,000.

Wheeler, H. E., and Murray, H. H., 1957, Base-level control patterns in cyclohemic sedimentation: American Association of Petroleum Geologists Bulletin, v. 41, p. 1985–2011.

White, G. W., 1973, Memorial to Harold Rollin Wanless 1898–1970: Geological Society of America Memorials, v. 2, p. 116–128.

Willman, H. B., 1978, Memorial to James Marvin Weller, 1899–1976: Geological Society of America Memorials, v. 8, 12 p.

Willman, H. B., and Payne, J. N., 1942, Geology and mineral resources of the Marseilles, Ottawa and Streator Quadrangles: Illinois State Geological Survey Bulletin 66, 388 p.

Willman, H. B., Swann, D. H., and Frye, J. C., 1958, Stratigraphic policy of the Illinois State Geological Survey: Illinois State Geological Survey Circular 249, 14 p.

Willman, H. B., and 8 others, 1975, Handbook of Illinois stratigraphy: Illinois State Geological Survey Bulletin 95, 261 p.

Zangerl, R., 1980, The Pennsylvanian black, carbonaceous, sheety shales of the Illinois and Forest City Basins, *in* Langenheim, R. L., Jr., and Mann, C. J., eds., Middle and Late Pennsylvanian strata on margin of Illinois Basin: Society of Economic Paleontologists and Mineralogists, Tenth Annual Field Conference, Great Lakes Section p. 225–238.

Zangerl, R., and Richardson, E. S., Jr., 1963, The paleoecological history of two Pennsylvanian black shales: Fieldiana, Geology Memoir 4, 152 p.

MANUSCRIPT ACCEPTED BY THE SOCIETY JANUARY 14, 1992

Geological Society of America
Memoir 180
1992

Chapter 7

R. C. Moore and concepts of sea-level change in the midcontinent

Rex C. Buchanan and Christopher G. Maples
Kansas Geological Survey, 1930 Constant Avenue, Lawrence, Kansas 66047

ABSTRACT

Raymond C. Moore was among the most important stratigraphers and paleontologists of the twentieth century. Yet, he was among the last of his contemporaries (1892 to 1974) to accept the importance of glacial eustasy for sea-level changes during the late Paleozoic. Moore staunchly defended the concept that sea-level changes and resultant lithologic changes were caused primarily by orogenic and diastrophic processes, noting that orogeny in one part of the world could affect sea level globally. Our impression is that Moore was loath to change his mind once he had reached a decision and was a commanding force who could not be ignored easily. Moore was among the many geologists who operated under an epistomological paradigm of their time—if a single action could explain all results, they refused to complicate the issue by invoking multiple causes. Moore's principal concerns were not the causes of sea-level change, but the effects, especially the great lateral persistence of thin stratigraphic units throughout the midcontinent.

INTRODUCTION

In September, 1958, Raymond C. Moore delivered the presidential address to the annual meeting of the Geological Society of America. The address dealt with the "Stability of the Earth's Crust." Although a popular account holds that an earthquake shook the room during the address, in reality the earthquake was small and occurred within a few hours after the talk. Twelve years later, that address was printed in the *Bulletin of the Geological Society of America* (Moore, 1970). Its subject seems a little afield for Moore, well known for work in paleontology and stratigraphy, but not particularly noted as a structural geologist. Yet the address took on a topic, the source of cyclic deposits, that was central to much of Moore's thought and to much of midcontinent geology. The address was another salvo in a debate that was actually carried on in much greater detail in the 1930s (a period that one geologist of the time remembers as days of "miracles and wonder"), but lingered for several decades thereafter.

Moore studied Pennsylvanian and Permian cyclic deposits, which are the most striking examples of cyclic sedimentation preserved in the rock record. One can hardly live in the midcontinent without being awed by the repetitive nature and the lateral persistence of very thin beds. Why and how did these beds form—these questions have been almost inescapable for geologists in the midcontinent for nearly a century. Our paper traces the debate about the mechanism for cyclic deposits in the midcontinent, focusing particularly on the role of sea-level change. Although we touch on most of the major players in this discussion, we pay particular attention to the contribution of R. C. Moore. Moore was perhaps less interested in the mechanism behind sea-level change than some of the other people involved, but he was nonetheless instrumental in the development of theories concerning cycles of deposition, and thus a crucial player.

RECOGNITION OF CYCLICITY:
THE DEBATE RISES

Previous papers (particularly Heckel, 1984) have developed the history of observations of geologic cyclicity in the midcontinent. Workers in Kansas implied a sense of cyclic deposition in the Upper Pennsylvanian of Kansas in the late 1800s (West, 1990), but explicit recognition of the cyclicity of interbedded limestones and shales is generally credited to Johann Udden, who, in a U.S. Geological Survey *Bulletin* on the Peoria Quadrangle in Illinois, reported on the cyclicity of Pennsylvanian deposits and even postulated a eustatic mechanism. "The cycles

Buchanan, R. C., and Maples, C. G., 1992, R. C. Moore and concepts of sea-level change in the midcontinent, *in* Dott, R. H., Jr., ed., Eustasy: The Historical Ups and Downs of a Major Geological Concept: Boulder, Colorado, Geological Society of America Memoir 180.

represent recurrent submergences, alternating with periods during which the sunken areas were filled to the level of the surface of the sea . . ." wrote Udden. The changes in deposition, he went on, "represent recurrent interruptions in a progressive submergence" (Udden, 1912, p. 49). Udden not only established the earliest concrete recognition of the cyclic patterns of deposition, he formulated a theory for the mechanism behind those cycles—a theory in which the land subsided and was inundated—that was developed later in far more detail. Coincidentally, Udden had a Kansas connection. Born in Sweden in 1859, Udden emigrated to the United States at the age of two. He graduated from Augustana College, Rock Island, Illinois, in 1881 and spent the next nine years teaching at Bethany College in Lindsborg on the eastern edge of the Cretaceous in central Kansas (Hansen, 1985). Although Udden did field work in Kansas and later published the results, his Kansas work concentrated on recent geology and the time in Kansas apparently had little influence on his later work in Illinois.

After Udden's observations, relatively little was published on cycles in the midcontinent until the late 1920s, when several authors began to discuss the issue. Among them was Raymond C. Moore, who was, at the time, the director of the Kansas Geological Survey. Moore was born in Washington State, earned an undergraduate degree in classics from Denison University, and, in 1916, received a Ph.D. (in geology) from the University of Chicago. Moore was undoubtedly influenced by faculty members such as T. C. Chamberlin and R. D. Salisbury, and his mentor, Stuart Weller, who probably affected his later notions about sea-level change. Moore went directly from Chicago to the Kansas Geological Survey as director and state geologist. He also served three terms as chairman of the University of Kansas geology department. Even though he retired as director of the survey in 1954, Moore continued to be active at the survey and in professional earth-science societies. In a previous paper (Maples and Buchanan, 1989), we divided Moore's accomplishments into four broad categories: administration of the Kansas Survey and the University of Kansas geology department; work in invertebrate paleontology, including the founding of the *Treatise on Invertebrate Paleontology*; professional presence in scientific societies; and contributions to ideas concerning stratigraphic classification and cyclic sedimentation in the midcontinent.

The first inkling of Moore's work on cycles came in a 1929 paper in the *Bulletin of the American Association of Petroleum Geologists* (Moore, 1929) on the environment of Pennsylvanian life in North America. With Moore's location in eastern Kansas, where the Pennsylvanian is the outcropping rock, the subject was a natural. Also, because Pennsylvanian and Permian rocks were petroleum-producing units in much of eastern and central Kansas at the time, and because the state geologist of Kansas had to have more than a tacit interest in oil, the Pennsylvanian was a perfect target. In the article, Moore discussed the interbedded continental and marine deposits in the midcontinent, and said that it was necessary to assume "innumerable up-and-down movements of the relative sea level, and each of these must have amounted to

hundreds or even thousands of feet. . . .There must have been very strongly differential upward and downward movements of the borders of the basin" (Moore, 1929, p. 485–486). In this long article about the Pennsylvanian, one that recognizes the constancy of sea-level change, this is all that Moore said about the mechanism. In some respects, that set the tone for Moore's later pronouncements on cyclic deposits. Although he occasionally commented on other proposed mechanisms for the sea-level change that led to cyclic deposits, and in some instances reacted at length to other authors, detailed theorizing about a mechanism was never a priority for Moore. Rather, Moore's goal was lithostratigraphic correlation; the mechanism that resulted in an ability to correlate rock units being entirely serendipitous, if not superfluous.

THE INTRODUCTION OF DIASTROPHISM

J. Marvin Weller (Stuart Weller's son) made the first detailed, systematic attempt at an explanation of midcontinent cyclicity in a 1930 paper in the *Journal of Geology,* a paper that set the stage for much of his thinking for the next two decades (Weller, 1930). Weller, who also had a Ph.D. from the University of Chicago, joined the Illinois Geological Survey in 1925. His 1930 paper began by establishing the connection between widely separated formations. "If the hypothesis of regional cycles be established, it will be possible to set up, in various widely separated Pennsylvanian areas, general geologic sections each of which is subdivided into a succession of comparable formations, and with the aid of paleontology these should be subject to precise correlation. Thus it should be possible to make definite, detailed correlations between the Pennsylvanian strata in Missouri-Kansas, Illinois, and Ohio, an accomplishment which has been heretofore impossible" (Weller, 1930, p. 110). Weller then examined the existing alternative explanations for the mechanism behind the cycles and found a single explanation. "Although climatic change may have been an important factor, evidence of its influence has not been recognized and therefore it may be ignored at this time, as diastrophism alone is capable of providing an adequate explanation for the cycle" (Weller, 1930, p. 131). Weller demonstrated an interesting and influential line of reasoning here. If an explanation could account for results of cyclic sedimentation, then it stood alone as an adequate explanation, even though other forces might admittedly be at work. For the remainder of this debate, the players were consistently devoted to a zealous application of Ockham's razor.

In 1931, the Illinois Geological Survey held a conference on the subject of Pennsylvanian cycles and published the papers, one of which was Moore's. This time he was far more explicit about both the cycles of deposition in the Pennsylvanian and their cause, commenting on the "regular alternation of shale and limestone beds and in the regular and peculiar sequence of certain types of limestone and shale in parts of this alternating series" (Moore, 1931, p. 251). Then he postulated a reason: "The alternation of marine and nonmarine units implies an oscillation or rhythmic advance and retreat of the sea. Such oscillation may have been caused by periodic subsidence accompanied by intervening outbuilding of the land until the shallow sea was displaced, or it may mean actual alternating positive and negative movements of the sea bottom with the sum total strongly negative, for it is clear that there was a gradual subsidence in the area of Pennsylvanian sedimentation as time elapsed" (Moore, 1931, p. 256). He wrote latter that he first recognized cyclicity in rocks of the Shawnee Group, formations in the Upper Pennsylvanian that crop out in eastern Kansas (Moore, 1936a, p. 26).

There are two simple and obvious end-member explanations for apparent sea-level change. One is that the seas are going up and down, while the land remains still. The other is that the land is going up and down, while relative sea level adjusts concomitantly. Moore chose the latter, with an emphasis on subsidence, until late in his career. Continents in the Pennsylvanian subsided, they were inundated with sea water, sediment was deposited in shallow, near-shore areas, which eventually resulted in a progradation of the land seaward (Fig. 1).

Moore and Weller were hardly the only people thinking about the question, however. Other notables were H. R. Wanless and F. P. Shepard of the University of Illinois. Wanless, who had published an article on Pennsylvanian cycles in that same bulletin of the Illinois Geological Survey in 1931, earned a Ph.D. from Princeton and came to the University of Illinois in 1925 (see White, 1971). Wanless and Weller in an article in 1932 discussed the similarity of Pennsylvanian deposits both east and west of the Mississippi River. Their theory was that "the cyclical repetition of strata in the different basins was controlled by the same series of diastrophic movements which must have affected the entire eastern half of North America" (Wanless and Weller, 1932, p. 1016). This notion of sea-level change as a result of continental uplift and subsidence—sea-level change as a result of

diastrophism—became associated with Weller in particular, in part because Wanless spent more time considering nondiastrophic mechanisms.

Another figure in the formulation of ideas about cyclic deposition was Maxim K. Elias (Fig. 2), who worked at the Kansas Geological Survey. Elias, an emigrant from Russia, speculated briefly on the source of cyclicity in the midcontinent in 1934. Describing Permian units in Kansas, he wrote that ". . . it seems quite obvious that periodic change of sea-level was the main controlling factor that produced the observed cyclic repetition of stratigraphic units. The gradual rise and fall of sea level due to major changes in the ocean bottoms or to epeirogenic (sic) movements of the continents are quite sufficient to produce the faunal and lithologic changes which are observed in the cycles" (Elias, 1934, p. 29–30). Elias and Moore collaborated for three years on midcontinent stratigraphy and occasionally speculated on mechanisms for cyclicity. However, a personal falling out between the two that began in 1936 ended their scientific cooperation (see correspondence from Elias to University of Kansas Chancellor Ernest H. Lindley, and from Moore to Lindley, Lindley Collection, Lindley Correspondence 1936/37, Box 2/9/5, 3, University of Kansas Archives, Spencer Research Library, Law-

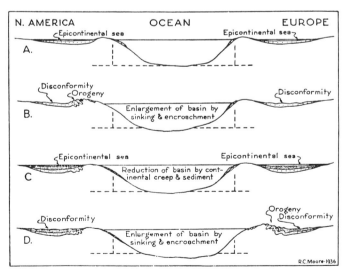

Figure 1. Diagrammatic depiction used by Moore (1936b, p. 1806) to explain the intercontinental correlability of stratigraphic breaks using diastrophism.

Figure 2. Maxim K. Elias, an early progenitor of ideas about cyclic deposition in Kansas, in a 1933 photograph. Elias eventually left the Kansas Geological Survey after a particularly bitter dispute with Moore. Courtesy of the University of Kansas Archives, Spencer Research Library, University of Kansas.

rence, Kansas). Elias did little further work on cyclic deposition or the mechanisms behind it (see Elias, 1937).

Moore, on the other hand, embraced, but did not really develop, a mechanism that was only slightly different from that of Weller (probably because they had such similar graduate backgrounds, but this is only speculation). He discussed it simply and at length in his 1933 book, *Historical Geology.*

Because of the repeated alternation of sea and land conditions that is evidenced in so much of the Pennsylvanian deposits, it is especially desirable to ask (1) whether the depth of the Pennsylvanian seas, on the average, was of the order of 500 or 600 feet and, accordingly, whether there were repeated up and down movements of the earth's crust of approximately this amount, or, on the other hand, (2) whether the depth of the seas was very small and the amount of crustal movements correspondingly slight. In the latter but not the former case, it is possible that movement of the crust may have been almost wholly downward, change from sea to land being effected by sedimentation. The assumption that large parts of the continental areas were many times evenly raised and lowered several hundreds of feet is much less reasonable than that the vertical movements of the crust were small and perhaps mainly movement of sinking only. (Moore, 1933, p. 285–286)

Diastrophism continued to be Moore's mechanism for sea-level change. Moore initially believed that cyclic deposits resulted from sea-level change based on slight subsidence of the continents, followed by sedimentation in shallow, near-shore areas that prograded land seaward (Moore, 1935b). He revised this idea in 1935 in another paper in the *Bulletin of the American Association of Petroleum Geologists.* The article was titled "Late Paleozoic Crustal Movements of Europe and North America," a topic not too far afield from his 1970 Geological Society of America address.

It appears possible—indeed, it is very probable—that the widespread withdrawal of epicontinental seas and the interruption of sedimentation that is indicated by disconformities within the stable platform areas of the continents, do not signify upward movement of these parts of the crust. Subequal elevation of enormous crustal segments is much more difficult to conceive of as an actual epirogenic movement than as a result of depression of mean sea-level. If uplift of mountains in some geosynclinal belt is accompanied by crustal changes that for a time somewhat increase the capacity of oceanic basins, it is easy to understand that lowered sea-level should result in simultaneous withdrawal of shallow seas from different continental platforms. (Moore, 1935b, p. 1256)

In other words, mountain building in some places results in sea-level changes in other, tectonically stable areas. This was Moore's answer to evidence of seemingly synchronous cyclicity on different continents and to lack of evidence for tectonic activity in continental interiors where cyclothems are preserved. Bear in mind that this was 30 years before plate tectonics began to influence geologic thought.

GLACIERS

Perhaps the best job of developing a sea-level change mechanism in the 1930s in the midcontinent came from Wanless and Shepard in 1936. They methodically examined the possible explanations for cyclic deposition, and came to the conclusion that "Earth movements appear to be inadequate to explain the peculiar sedimentary cycles under consideration" (Wanless and Shepard, 1936, p. 1189–1190). They agreed with Moore that subsidence was a possible mechanism, but they said it was only part of the story and they added a twist. "The authors favor the interpretation of a more or less continuous subsidence of the sedimentation basin, resulting, at least in part, from the weight of the accumulating sediment" (Wanless and Shepard, 1936, p. 1189). In other words, Wanless and Shepard postulated the notion of sediment loading as a factor in continuing the subsidence and thus the deposition. Basins subside and are inundated, sedimentation begins, causing the seas to become shallow, then the weight of the sediment causes the subsidence to continue.

But perhaps more importantly, Wanless and Shepard went beyond that to look for an additional mechanism that could account for the sedimentation that "earth movements" could not. They found it in glaciers, citing relatively recent work on Quaternary marine terraces and estimates of modern sea-level changes should ice caps melt: "The formation of continental glaciers appears to be an adequate cause of the lowering of sea level to the amounts required" (Wanless and Shepard, 1936, p. 1191). In the end, they settled on an explanation that required a mix of earth movement and glacial flux: "The hypothesis of glacially-controlled sea level oscillations appears more satisfactory as an explanation of the cycles than previously developed diastrophic hypotheses, (1) because of widespread cyclic sedimentation in late Paleozoic rocks, (2) because of the great extent of individual strata, and (3) because of the complicated diastrophic hypothesis which would be required to explain these successions. On the other hand local diastrophism was no doubt important and the depositional basins are thought to have subsided slowly as sediment accumulated, the cyclic fluctuation being due to the rise and fall of sea level during this setting" (Wanless and Shepard, 1936, p. 1205–1206). In doing this, Wanless and Shepard avoided resorting to a single process—crossing an epistomological barrier by invoking multiple causal mechanisms.

Moore, not surprisingly, continued to dance with the girl he brung. In a 1936 *Kansas Geological Survey Bulletin* (Moore, 1936a), in a 1936 guidebook to a field trip of the Kansas Geological Society (Moore and others, 1936), and at the Second International Carboniferous Congress in 1937 (Moore, 1937a), Moore continued to defend diastrophism. And in a *Geological Society of America Bulletin* in late 1936, he took on Wanless and Shepard directly. "One may immediately rule out the first suggestion, that there was no subsidence of the floor of the basins and that rise of sea level kept approximate pace with the increasing thickness of sediments, because the actual thickness of equivalent sediments in different basins and in different parts of the same basin varies considerably" (Moore, 1936b, p. 1792). Moore's reasoning was that if all the seas were connected to the ocean, a change in sea level would be worldwide, and the result should be uniform deposition. He noted their proposal of "oscillatory changes of sea level in Late Paleozoic time, due to waxing and waning of continental glaciers," but insisted again that "differential subsidence in the basins cannot be ignored. As differential subsidence is clearly indicated, it is reasonable to conclude that subsidence alone is adequate to account for return of the sea to a basin after it has been expelled by previous infilling" (Moore, 1936b, p. 1793). He did not respond directly to Wanless and Shepard's suggestion of "local diastrophism" that might account for variety in deposition, or that two factors—diastrophism and glacial flux—might be at work. This combination, climatically influenced sea-level fluctuation and episodic tectonism, remains a relatively popular explanation today (e.g., Klein and Willard, 1989).

However, in the 1936 *Kansas Geological Society Guidebook,* Moore (in collaboration with M. K. Elias, F. C. Greene, and N. D. Newell) observed that "The Pennsylvanian and Lower 'Permian' rocks of the northern Mid-Continent area are now divided into successive series on the basis of obscure but widely persistent and stratigraphically important disconformities. . . . Some of these breaks in the Kansas-Missouri region appear, when traced southward into the southern Oklahoma region, to be represented by larger breaks associated with folding. They (the breaks) thus define epochs of orogenic disturbance in the geosynclinal area" (Moore and others, 1936, p. 7). Cratonic subsidence alone was adequate for marine transgression of epiric seas; sediment filling and ocean basin adjustments were adequate for marine regression. Any degree of intercontinental sea level synchroneity was dismissed with statements such as "a lowering of sea level that is associated with or due to an orogenic movement in an American geosyncline should be expected to affect the position of strand lines on continents in other parts of the globe" (Moore, 1937a, p. 673).

This argument was more than academic to Moore. It had a direct bearing on the definition of formations, and the resulting stratigraphic nomenclature that was being established in Kansas at the time. In 1935 Moore published the first reasonably complete and detailed stratigraphic column of Kansas (Moore, 1935a), based on work done by the survey, and in 1937 he was co-author of the first large-format, full-color geologic map of Kansas ever published (Moore and Landes, 1937). In making decisions related to stratigraphic nomenclature, Moore was driven by his view that the cycles were pervasive and geographically widespread. He wanted to use the breaks in deposition created by changes in sea level to define major stratigraphic units, a concept that is one of the basic building-blocks of the "new" genetic/sequence stratigraphy (e.g., see papers in Schlee, 1984; and Franseen and others, 1991). These decisions were often hotly debated on field trips (Figs. 3 to 5), and in the 1937 *Kansas Geological Society Guidebook,* Moore wrote, "Disconformities that are evident in some places, obscure in others, divide these units. It seems clear that they have essential characters of series, and if, as I have indicated in published papers, they are genetically related to crustal movements in different continents, certainly they cannot be considered as merely local stratigraphic divisions" (Moore, 1937b, p. 11).

Moore's personality undoubtedly had a bearing on his ob-

Figure 3. R. C. Moore, pick and pipe in hand, in an undated photo probably taken in the mid-1930s. Photo courtesy of the University of Kansas Archives, Spencer Research Library, University of Kansas.

servations of cyclicity and eustasy. Moore seems to have been obsessed with leaving a legacy, and one way to do that was to erect a stratigraphic classificatory scheme that others had to use. There is, for example, the persisting story that Moore named the Aarde Shale Member in Kansas for exposures (poor that they were) on the Aarde Farm, solely because he desired to have the first name in the *U.S.G.S. Lexicon of Stratigraphic Nomenclature* (Wilmarth, 1938). It still is first, by the way (M. E. Mac Lachlan, personal communication, 1990). For Wanless and Shepard (1936) to imply that diastrophic controls were merely local in extent was a blow to Moore, who either was determined to be famous himself, or was determined to make the University of Kansas famous—thus, lines had been drawn in the sand. Moore later admitted that, indeed, some stratigraphic units in Kansas had only regional or local extent, but this, he explained, was the result

Figure 4. Moore at a stop on the 1932 field conference of the Kansas Geological Society. Trips such as this one, which included stops in Kansas, Nebraska, and Missouri, were instrumental in debating evidence related to midcontinent cyclicity. Photo courtesy of the University of Kansas Archives, Spencer Research Library, University of Kansas.

of sea-level transgression from the west and earlier deposition of units in Kansas as opposed to Illinois.

THE DEBATE SUBSIDES

Those positions—Weller and Moore on the side of subsidence and global diastrophic effects and Wanless and Shepard in favor of glacial change and local diastrophism—were formulated in the 1930s. Perhaps because of World War II and more pressing and practical matters, the debate itself subsided during the 1940s. But it blossomed again briefly in the 1950s. In 1945, Weller moved to the University of Chicago, and in 1956, he published a careful, methodical review of the theories of sea-level change. Weller began with an almost mournful appraisal of the impossibility of determining absolutely, once and for all, the

mechanism behind sea-level change. "If a simple and adequate mechanism that would produce the postulated oscillations of Pennsylvanian time could be offered, this explanation might win more general acceptance. Unfortunately, however, the framing of any hypothesis to account for such oscillations is an expedition into almost pure speculation" (Weller, 1956, p. 45). He proceeded to examine the speculation, and came down on the side of diastrophism. Then he began to look for the mechanism behind the mechanism, the reason for diastrophism. "These oscillations probably were produced by vertically acting forces. Present knowledge of the geophysics and geochemistry of the earth's crust is inadequate to explain the operation of such a mechanism but the idea comes to mind at once that it might be related to thermal contraction and expansion" (Weller, 1956, p. 47).

Moore, as if to prove that his mind remained unchanged in 20 years, briefly discussed cyclic sedimentation in the second edition of his book *Introduction to Historical Geology,* published in 1958. ". . . sea level throughout the world may be affected by crustal deformation on any continent, and, if this is so, geologic effects may be recorded by simultaneous sea-and-land changes throughout the world" (Moore, 1958, p. 242). Weller (1960) agreed in his big book, *Stratigraphic Principles and Practice,* published two years later. He admitted that "The origin of megacyclothems and hypercyclothems is not understood." However, "The occurrence of larger cyclic sequences in basins adjacent to the stable Ozark region probably indicates that the larger sequences were related to a longer period of rhythmicity in the subsidence of the basins" (Weller, 1960, p. 379).

In 1964, the debate over cyclic deposition, and the reason for it, reached its third decade. To commemorate the 100th anniversary of the first geological survey of Kansas, the Kansas Geological Survey invited the heavyweights to spar once more, this time with a series of contributed papers on the subject. But by now the major entrants seem to have softened their hard lines somewhat, admitting that no single theory seemed likely to explain it all. They seem almost to have adopted Weller's melancholy realization that consensus was not only elusive, but probably not possible (Fig. 6). Weller himself reviewed the different competing theories, and then summed it up. "Almost every conceivable factor that might have influenced the development of late Paleozoic sedimentary cycles has been incorporated ingeniously into one theory or another. Many of the views expressed are irreconcilable, and it is obvious that no agreement is presently in prospect" (Weller, 1964, p. 618).

Moore was finally willing to admit that sea level changed because of glacial flux, and seemed willing to incorporate it into an overall theory, but wasn't willing to abandon subsidence altogether. He wrote, "Eustatic fluctuations of sea level correlated with recurrent glaciation must be admitted, but for reasons given by Weller, not to mention other objections, Pennsylvanian and Permian cyclothems and water depths of their marine phases from place to place almost certainly do not reflect such fluctuations alone. To a large extent, the hypothesis of diastrophic control of cyclothems advocated by Weller is plausible but I can find

Figure 5. Some of the principals in the debate over cyclicity on a field trip, probably in the 1920s, probably in the Appalachians. Photo courtesy of University of Kansas Archives, Spencer Research Library, University of Kansas.

Figure 6. Figure from Moore's 1964 paper on Pennsylvanian and Permian cyclothems, Kansas. Moore drew the figure and noted in the caption that it depicts a view "looking west from site of Douglas County courthouse in Lawrence, Kansas." While not exactly a melancholy view, it does poke fun at the efforts of the stratigraphic gladiators to that point.

no good reasons for postulated upward movements of the crust in such areas as the Illinois Basin and Kansas platform alternating with current subsidences" (Moore, 1964, p. 368–369). In other words, by 1964, Moore had decided to give glaciers partial credit for sea-level change, and took issue with some of Weller's notions of diastrophism. By now Moore was 72 years old. His major achievements were behind him, and more and more his publications were dominated by work in the *Treatise on Invertebrate Paleontology,* although he managed to publish 120 more articles after 1964. Among those publications was the 1970 appearance of the Geological Society of America address that he gave in 1958. The fact that he published that speech 12 years after its delivery shows that Moore's thinking had not changed drastically. "Taking account of the geographic spread of these conditions in North America and occurrence of like cyclic sedimentation contemporaneously on other continents, one cannot escape the conclusion that small eustatic fluctuations of sea level primarily controlled the nature of sedimentation," Moore wrote. "It follows that during millions of years continental segments of the crust maintained almost incredible stability while large areas alternately were slightly submerged by marine waters and then uncovered, all the while with accompanying very gradual subsidence of regionally differing amounts that severally matched rates of sedimentary accumulation" (Moore, 1970, p. 1311). Moore still did not know what to do about glaciers.

CONCLUSIONS

The major entrants in this debate are gone now, but the competing theories of cyclic deposition, and its causes, are still around, although the concept of global importance of diastrophically induced sea-level control did suffer severely. The discussions in the midcontinent continue today, with the introduction of ideas about punctuated aggradational cycles, genetic stratigraphy, and climate change. However, many of the paradigms for today's discussions were established 50 years earlier by such notables as Raymond C. Moore. Indeed, debate over causes of sea-level changes continues to wax and wane much like the seas themselves. Some would contend that geologists today are simply "reinventing the wheel" when it comes to theories about cyclic sedimentation. We prefer to think that Udden, Wanless, Weller, Moore, Chamberlin, and others were all partially correct and the addition of new data has refined and sharpened ideas of thoughtful and influential geologists who established the paradigm of stratigraphic thought in the midcontinent.

ACKNOWLEDGMENTS

We appreciate the comments of D. F. Merriam, G. deV. Klein, and R. R. West on early versions of this paper. Thanks go to R. H. Dott, Jr., for organizing the GSA symposium at the 1990 annual meeting in Dallas, Texas, of which this paper was a part, and for his perceptive and helpful comments on this paper. We also thank Barry Bunch, Ed Kehde, and John Nugent of the University of Kansas Archives, Spencer Research Library, for their assistance and tolerance.

REFERENCES CITED

Elias, M. K., 1934, Stratigraphy of the Big Blue Series in north-central Kansas: Kansas Geological Survey Open-file Report 34–1, 168 p.
—— , 1937, Depth of deposition of the Big Blue (late Paleozoic) sediments in Kansas: Geological Society of America Bulletin, v. 48, p. 403–432.
Franseen, E. K., Watney, W. L., Kendall, C. G. St. C., and Ross, W. C., eds., 1991, Sedimentary modeling: Computer simulation and methods for improved parameter definition: Kansas Geological Survey Bulletin 233, 524 p.
Hansen, W. B., 1985, Dust in the wind: J. A. Udden's turn-of-the century research at Augustana, *in* Drake, E. T., and Jordan, W. M., eds., Geologists and ideas: A history of North American geology: Geological Society of America, Centennial Special Volume 1, p. 203–214.
Heckel, P. H., 1984, Changing concepts of Midcontinent Pennsylvanian cyclothems, North America, *in* Neuvième Congres International de Stratigraphie et de Geologie du Carbonifère: Southern Illinois University Press, v. 3, p. 535–553.
Klein, G. deV., and Willard, D. A., 1989, Origin of the Pennsylvanian coal-bearing cyclothems of North America: Geology, v. 17, p. 152–155.
Lindley Collection: Lawrence, Kansas, University of Kansas Archives, Spencer Research Library.
Maples, C. G., and Buchanan, R., 1989, Raymond C. Moore (1892–1974): Memorial and bibliography (in celebration of the 100th anniversary of the Kansas Geological Survey): Paleontological Society Memoir 25, 29 p.
Moore, R. C., 1929, Environment of Pennsylvanian life in North America: American Association of Petroleum Geologists Bulletin, v. 13, p. 459–487.
—— , 1931, Pennsylvanian cycles in the northern Mid-continent region: Illinois Geological Survey Bulletin 60, p. 247–257.
—— , 1933, Historical geology (first edition): McGraw-Hill Book Company, Inc., 673 p.
—— , 1935a, Rock formations of Kansas: Kansas Geological Survey, Open-file Report 35–1, 1 pl.
—— , 1935b, Late Paleozoic crustal movements of Europe and North America: American Association of Petroleum Geologists Bulletin, v. 19, p. 1253–1307.
—— , 1936a, Stratigraphic classification of the Pennsylvanian rocks of Kansas: Kansas Geological Survey Bulletin 22, 256 p.
—— , 1936b, Stratigraphic evidence bearing on problems of continental tectonics: Geological Society of America Bulletin, v. 47, p. 1785–1808.
—— , 1937a, Comparison of the Carboniferous and Early Permian rocks of North America and Europe, *in* Congres pour l'Advancement des Etudes de Stratigraphie Carbonifère, Deuxieme: Heerlen, Comptes Rendues, v. 2, p. 641–676.
—— , 1937b, Upper Carboniferous rocks of southeastern Kansas and northeastern Oklahoma, *in* Kansas Geological Society, Eleventh Annual Field Conference: Kansas Geological Society, p. 9–16.
—— , 1958, Introduction to historical geology (second edition): McGraw-Hill Book Company, Inc., 656 p.
—— , 1964, Paleoecological aspects of Kansas Pennsylvanian and Permian cyclothems, *in* Merriam, D. F., ed., Symposium on cyclic sedimentation: Kansas Geological Survey Bulletin 169, p. 287–380.
—— , 1970, Stability of the Earth's crust: Geological Society of America Bulletin, v. 81, p. 1285–1324.
Moore, R. C., and Landes, K. K., 1937, Geologic map of Kansas: Kansas Geological Survey, 1 sheet, scale 1:500,000.
Moore, R. C., with collaboration of Elias, M. K., Greene, F. C., and Newell, N. D., 1936, Pennsylvanian and Lower 'Permian' rocks of the Kansas-Missouri region, *in* Kansas Geological Society, Tenth Annual Field Conference: Kansas Geological Society, 73 p.
Schlee, J. S., ed., 1984, Interregional unconformities and hydrocarbon accumulation: American Association of Petroleum Geologists Memoir 36, 184 p.
Udden, J. A., 1912, Geology and mineral resources of the Peoria Quadrangle, Illinois: U.S. Geological Survey Bulletin 506, 103 p.
Wanless, H. R., and Shepard, F. P., 1936, Sea level and climatic changes related

to late Paleozoic cycles: Geological Society of America Bulletin, v. 47, p. 1177–1206.

Wanless, H. R., and Weller, J. M., 1932, Correlation and extent of Pennsylvanian cyclothems: Geological Society of America Bulletin, v. 43, p. 1003–1016.

Weller, J. M., 1930, Cyclical sedimentation of the Pennsylvanian Period and its significance: Journal of Geology, v. 38, p. 97–135.

—— , 1956, Argument for diastrophic control of late Paleozoic cyclothems: American Association of Petroleum Geologists Bulletin, v. 40, p. 17–50.

—— , 1960, Stratigraphic principles and practice: Harper and Row, 725 p.

—— , 1964, Development of the concept and interpretation of cyclic sedimentation, *in* Merriam, D. F., ed., Symposium on cyclic sedimentation: Kansas Geological Survey Bulletin 169, p. 607–622.

West, R. R., 1990, Thoughts on the upper Palaeozoic history of Kansas, *in* Cunningham, C. R., and Maples, C. G., eds., 1990, Society of Vertebrate Paleontology upper Paleozoic of eastern Kansas excursion guidebook: Kansas Geological Survey Open-file Report 90–24, p. 5–15.

White, G. R., 1971, Memorial to Harold Rollin Wanless, 1898–1970: Geological Society of America Memorial Series, 13 p.

Wilmarth, M. G., 1938, Lexicon of geologic names of the United States (including Alaska): U.S. Geological Survey Bulletin 896, 2 vols.

MANUSCRIPT ACCEPTED BY THE SOCIETY JANUARY 14, 1992

Geological Society of America
Memoir 180
1992

Chapter 8

The evolution of seismic stratigraphy and the global sea-level curve

Peter R. Vail
Department of Geology and Geophysics, Rice University, Houston, Texas 77251

ABSTRACT

Truly new research ideas are generally unpopular when first proposed; therefore, many of our best ideas have had long incubation periods. The environment conducive to new ideas and to their acceptance must integrate creativity with a well-defined research program. Generally this is optimized in small, highly motivated working groups of mutually supportive people with varied experiences and skills. Such was the group at Exxon in which we developed our concepts of sequence seismic stratigraphy during the 1960s and 1970s. These concepts evolved from L. L. Sloss' ideas of stratigraphic sequences first espoused in 1949; they integrated seismic stratigraphy, well logs, and biostratigraphy. Mathematical modeling in the later 1970s then allowed us to relate sea level, subsidence, and sediment supply to produce the curves on our global cycle chart, which implies a major role for eustasy throughout Phanerozoic time. The sequence approach has the potential to provide a unifying concept for stratigraphy and basin evolution similar to what plate tectonics has already accomplished for structural geology.

INTRODUCTION: OPTIMIZING RESEARCH CREATIVITY

The business of research is new ideas. Few things, however, are more unpopular with researchers than truly new ideas. As a result, some of our best ideas have exceedingly long incubation periods before they are accepted by researchers and put into operational practice, or, worse yet, they are not developed until competitors are way ahead. How can this problem of recognizing and developing worthwhile, truly new ideas be solved? I believe to solve this problem, it is necessary to establish an environment that will stimulate new ideas and encourage their acceptance. The integration of creativity with a well-defined research program is fundamental to this environment.

In my experience, creativity is sparked by relatively small working groups made up of 5 to 30 people with the necessary experience and skills to attack a problem that they can mutually define. Creativity flourishes when the individuals within a gorup are highly motivated by having the responsibility for reaching their own goals. It is also my experience that the work of such creative groups may not always be in the best interest of their

employer. They may be outward-looking and overly competitive or become inward-looking and overly protective. This degenerative outcome can be avoided, I believe, by fostering a working environment wherein the problems are accurately defined and interrelated so that relatively small creative groups can flourish in a mutually supportive manner. To do this, it is important to establish what we define as a thematic research program. Such a program is established by first defining clear-cut goals for the overall research, and then planning the projects that are needed to reach the goals. The thematic research program outlines the major project areas and how they interrelate; the projects form the basic or organizational structure for the small creative groups. Within this structure, individual researchers can fit both their goals and group goals to the objectives of the research themes. This will achieve the necessary integration of the creative groups within the overall research program.

This framework of small creative groups working on mutually defined project goals is, I believe, ideally suited for efficiently developing the latest technology that should keep an organization abreast of the competition. Although this form of organization is desirable, in my experience it will not put any group ahead of the

Vail, P. R., 1992, The evolution of seismic stratigraphy and the global sea-level curve, *in* Dott, R. H., Jr., ed., Eustasy: The Historical Ups and Downs of a Major Geological Concept: Boulder, Colorado, Geological Society of America Memoir 180.

competition unless we go one step further and define the concepts that drive the thematic research. It is important to recognize these underlying concepts, henceforth called driving concepts, because it is then possible to acknowledge and nurture ideas that challenge, and may prove superior to the existing driving concepts. These new ideas must be allowed to challenge the already accepted concepts that drive the established thematic research program. Otherwise, the thematic organizational structure could deteriorate into an idea-stifling, management-by-objective bureaucracy.

In general, new ideas based on accepted driving concepts can be developed and applied fairly rapidly within the framework of thematic research. However, truly new, worthwhile ideas based on competing driving concepts may not be accepted within the framework of thematic research. These competing driving concepts are commonly ignored or put aside because of the priority of other work. What is needed is a means to identify worthwhile competing driving concepts and develop those independently from the directed thematic research. When proven, these new ideas may lead to breakthrough research, which could significantly change the way we operate. These conclusions suggest that projects should be planned with a thorough understanding of the driving concepts that underlie the research. Moreover, the organizational structure should embody enough flexibility to allow individuals to pursue innovative approaches that lie outside established driving concepts. In this way, we can efficiently develop our thematic or applied research, yet still create the climate for rapidly testing and developing new concepts that may significantly change the way we do our research.

If we can create such a working environment, an organization will then be provided with its needed technology in a timely manner, as well as have the ability to originate and quickly recognize, develop, and apply new ideas based on both accepted and competing driving concepts. Let me further explain my understanding of a driving concept by giving an example. When I went to college, the underlying driving concept to explain tectonics and structure was vertical tectonics. We learned about eugeosynclines, miogeosynclines, taphrogeosynclines, and the like. Then, in the early 1960s, Vine and Matthews (1963) documented symmetrical magnetic stripes in the center of the Atlantic, proving a competing driving concept, sea-floor spreading, that had been around a long time under the name "Continental Drift." The acceptance of this competing driving concept, now elaborated into "Plate Tectonics," revolutionized the way we think about tectonics and structure.

A principal application of the plate-tectonic concept to research is the concept of structural styles, an area of investigation now in a fairly mature stage of development. Driving concepts that are built on the accepted concepts, such as the ideas of ramp tectonics to better understand and interpret thrust faults, are developed and applied rapidly. Driving concepts that use structural styles as a basis, but require an expanded understanding of stratigraphy, such as the concept of subsidence cycles developed from geohistory analysis, which help explain the timing of the structur-

al styles, tend to be applied more slowly. Driving concepts, such as the expanding earth theory, which compete directly with the plate-tectonic concepts, are not believed to be worthwhile, and are hardly worked on at all. As the above discussion illustrates, driving concepts are hierarchical. There generally is an overall concept that breaks down into subsidiary concepts, which deal with smaller and smaller parts of the overall problem.

SELF EXAMINATION OF A RESEARCH PHILOSOPHY

I have asked myself three questions: What makes a researcher, how does one relate to other people, and what is one's research philosophy? The first question can be put another way, namely what are the inherited traits that make a researcher? I conclude that in my own case there is nothing very obvious, and I believe that this is often the case for successful researchers. As my close colleagues will testify, I am not a great whiz in the three Rs: reading, writing, and arithmetic. In fact, when I was working on a report long ago with Dutchman Jan Hardenbol, he told me that the European educational system would have weeded me out years ago. My most serious problem was my inability to write a readable report. My first report, written on stratigraphic mapping techniques, sat on the corner of my supervisor's desk for months, finally was moved to a corner behind his desk, and eventually disappeared. At first, I blamed him for not handling the report, but it finally dawned on me it was not his fault, but mine. A supervisor should not be burdened with a poorly written report. To solve that problem, I talked with a company editor and technical writer, Jerry Murrey. For some reason, she thought I was worth saving, and literally spent days teaching me to write a creditable report. I consider what I learned about report writing and organization in general from her to be one of my most important career experiences.

Obviously, I had trouble with my three Rs, but other than that, do I have a special inherited ability to do research? If I do, it is my ability to visualize and to think in four dimensions. It is especially important for geologists to visualize the earth in three dimensions, as well as to understand how it changes through time. This ability is also useful when visualizing the parts of a whole and understanding how these may develop through time.

The second question, "How do I relate to other people?," is a tough one; obviously a great variety of different types of people do good research. However, I do believe my most important trait in my relations with other researchers is my ability to listen to what they are saying and still be able to communicate with them, even if we have major disagreements.

As for the third question, "What is my research philosophy?," I can be more specific. I believe it is very important for a geologist to have a research philosophy that balances observation with developing and testing a working hypothesis to explain those observations. It is of critical importance to observe and then understand the working hypothesis, or we could say the driving concept, upon which your observations are based. If there is one thing I have learned from seismic data, it is that we tend to see only what we understand or think we understand. A geophysicist trained in the seismic process will see, besides the major reflections, multiples, diffractions, and coherent and incoherent noise patterns. A geologist trained in structural geology will see block edges, growth faults, and upthrusts. A geologist trained in depositional processes will see prograding shelf edges and submarine fans. I believe that the same principle applies also to well-log stratigraphy and to outcrops. A geologist observing outcrops based on an episodic depositional concept will see turbidites, point bars, tidal deposits, and shoreface sands. A geologist observing outcrops on the basis of a eustatic cycle concept will see sequences, downward shifts of coastal onlap, lowstand deposits, and highstand deposits. We see what we are trained to see. It is necessary, therefore, when making observations, to understand the driving concept that underlies your observations, critically test it, present it to others, and listen to what they say. You must try to understand their problems with your concept, and evolve or change the concept as you acquire more feedback and observations. Do not be afraid to reassess any driving concept and start over again if the observations do not fit. If your observations do fit your driving concepts, you must believe in yourself and trust your observations. This is true even if the observations run against popular lore. With our good communication today, it is easy for any group of experts to build up a common lore that the group accepts as fact. The group will then vigorously defend it against all competing ideas on the basis of group lore rather than observed fact.

In conclusion, I have found the most productive research philosophy is first to observe and then to apply and test existing concepts carefully. If they work, fine. If not, do not be afraid to modify them or develop new ones. Next, listen patiently to what others say or write in order to find problems with your own concepts. If you do have problems, modify or change your driving concepts as necessary to explain your observations. Then, observe again in light of this new or modified concept. You will now see more. The whole procedure snowballs, especially when your driving concept becomes known to other groups. It will be tested by others, and problems and solutions will begin to flow to you. You then become more and more knowledgeable, and as a result you learn more in less and less time. The trick is not to fall too deeply in love with your concepts. Be constantly ready to adapt and improve, or drop them altogether.

THE DEVELOPMENT OF SEISMIC STRATIGRAPHY

Now I will use my research career as an example to illustrate the importance of knowing the problems you're trying to solve and developing the driving concepts to solve them. To do this, I have divided my career into six overlapping phases. The first phase I call "Learning the Driving Concepts Behind Exploration Activities." As the title implies, I had the opportunity early in my career to learn what driving concepts lay behind the geologists' and geophysicists' exploration efforts. The second phase I call

"Discovering and Developing New Driving Concepts as an Individual Researcher." It was during this phase of my career that I first learned how difficult it was to get new driving concepts accepted by fellow researchers. The third phase I call "Discovering and Developing Driving Concepts as a Supervisor." It was during this phase that I learned the importance of group definition of goals and group planning to meet those goals, as well as the importance of motivating people by giving each individual the maximum amount of responsibility possible. The fourth phase I refer to as "Learning the Hard Way about the Importance of Working Effectively with Other Research Groups." During this phase, I learned that highly productive groups may not be in the best interest of a company if they are overly competitive or overly protective. In my fifth phase, which I call "Readapting to Individual Research," I learned how rewarding a technical career in corporate research can be. Finally, in my sixth and current phase, I am struggling with the question, "How can I best contribute as a senior researcher in an academic setting?"

With this background, let us now look at P. R. Vail's career and see what we can learn from it about driving concepts and research effectiveness. Learning the driving concepts behind existing exploration efforts was my first career phase. I was fortunate when in 1956 I first joined the Carter Oil Company research division (a predecessor of Exxon Production Research Company) because I was hired to do a specific research project for which the objective was to evaluate, develop, and apply new mapping techniques to exploration problems. My first assignment was working with Bob Mitchum on mapping Pennsylvanian strata of the Paradox Basin. Bob and I had previously spent two years as officemates at Northwestern University, and have worked together as close friends ever since.

Early stratigraphic mapping

One of my professors at Northwestern University was Professor W. C. Krumbein, who was also a consultant for Carter Oil Company. The first two summers I was with Carter, I traveled with Krumbein and visited all of the many regional Carter offices in the United States from Mattoon to Durango, plus Imperial Oil Company in Calgary. I visited all of these offices at least once over the course of two summers. First Krumbein lectured on mapping techniques and I showed a series of maps made from Mitchum's Paradox Basin data illustrating and contrasting all different types of mapping techniques. Then the explorationists reviewed their work, mostly regional seismic sections, well-log cross sections and maps that they used to locate their prospects.

Following this work with Carter and Imperial, Cecil Rix and I did two large research application projects for Creole in Venezuela applying the techniques we had used for Carter. As a result of these early experiences, I received an excellent early indoctrination in how three companies explored for hydrocarbons. This early understanding of existing exploration techniques was critical to my later career. I knew the projects that I subsequently worked on were important because I understood how they could improve exploration efforts, whether other people thought so or not. I learned the importance of understanding the accepted driving concepts that direct the stratigraphically oriented exploration operations.

While still working on mapping projects with Carter, Imperial, and Creole, I began the second phase of my research career as an individual researcher working with a number of different groups and people. In this phase, beginning about 1958, I built my research on existing driving concepts. However, those concepts did not always lead to accurate facies maps. I then looked for new ways to define the mapping unit. There is a common thread through this early stage of my research career. I worked on stratigraphically oriented projects and then tried to quantify them with some computer technique. I attribute this directly to my graduate school education. I did my thesis on a regional stratigraphic mapping project under Professor Dapples, and became very interested in stratigraphy through this work. Professor Krumbein, at Northwestern, was the leader in the quantification of geology, and he had drummed into my head the importance of the computer in geologic work. As I said earlier, my first research project was with Robert Mitchum working on stratigraphic mapping techniques, which resulted in a research report specific to the Paradox Basin. Additionally, a more general use of stratigraphic mapping techniques was later published in another coauthored report. That first research report I wrote on Stratigraphic Mapping Techniques and presented to my supervisor never did reappear.

In the course of my mapping work, I teamed with a reservoir computer programmer, Tom Needham, and he wrote a program in stratigraphic mapping techniques for me that would calculate the values needed for plotting and contouring stratigraphic maps. The computer was an IBM 650, one that brings back fond memories. After this, when I visited various exploration offices, I would show the output of this program and demonstrate how it would calculate the mapping values they needed. This was before the days of plotters, but we could list them in order for manual plotting. The explorationists were very interested in this program, and we built at Carter Research a brisk business of calculating map values from data forms sent in by the explorationists. We key punched the data forms, processed them through the computer, and sent the explorationists printouts listing their mapping values. However, we only charged for computer processing time, which was, of course, only a fraction of the true cost. As our business grew and became more time-consuming, management decided that we should charge overhead. That ended our mapping-values calculation business, but not without leading to two larger projects—one for the Illinois Basin and another for Venezuela.

As I worked on the mapping techniques project, I soon realized that the problem wasn't in developing new mapping techniques. The real problem was mapping the right unit, and I became obsessed with the problem (and still am). In dealing with stratigraphy or facies, one needs geologic time-rock correlations, and then must select the proper mapping interval. At this point, I

realized that the existing driving concepts for well-log correlations were inadequate, so I concentrated my efforts on correlation techniques. In this work, I got to know Charles V. Campbell, who taught me one of the most important things in my career— how to determine geologic time from physical stratigraphy. When I tell others of the importance of this discovery, most think that I am crazy. Anybody knows that the rocks above are younger than the ones below, and what's so neat about that? As I thought about it, however, I realized that Chuck had taught me a new driving concept.

When I went to college, what we did was to examine the rocks by measuring sections. We first identified the rock type, textures, and structures. Then, from these observations, we interpreted how the rocks were deposited—by storms, floods, or tides—and finally we determined the depositional environments and named the facies. Not until then did we draw our time lines using biostratigraphy. The biostratigraphic time lines were ephemeral horizons that supposedly were different from the rock surfaces. What Chuck taught me was that one could determine time lines from the physical stratigraphy. Then one interprets facies within the time-stratigraphic framework determined earlier from bedding-surface correlations, whether working with outcrops or well logs. One uses biostratigraphy to determine ages and make sure that correlations are in the correct intervals, but then time-stratigraphy is established by the physical stratal patterns of the rocks. This has been a major driving concept of mine and still is. Based on this concept, Campbell, John Sangree, and I worked up a technique for correlating well-log marker horizons that we called "pattern correlation of well logs." I then worked diligently to try to expedite this correlation with a computer well log correlation program. Computer correlation of well logs has always been a pet project of mine, at which I utterly failed.

Birth of seismic stratigraphy

An associate, Paul Tucker, encouraged me to look at seismic reflections as an additional aid to correlating well logs. This eventually led me into the seismic area, and in 1960 I came to Humble's Houston Research Center and attended a school on seismic interpretation. In 1961, I transferred from the geological division to the geophysical division to pursue the correlation of well logs with seismic data. One of the first things I did in geophysics was to study a seismic section from what was then Portuguese Guinea (now Guinea Bissau). Three wells had been drilled. The most landward well had hit the top of a major Cretaceous reservoir sand, overlying an unconformity with Paleozoic rocks below. When a second well was drilled downdip, it was predicted that this sand would be high in the well, but it was actually encountered much lower. As a result, it was a dry hole. A similar experience occurred in the third well. Then we looked at the seismic section, and saw that the reflection from the top of the sand in the first well was two reflections above the reflection of the top of the sand in the second well and even higher in the third well. There was no miscorrelation of the seismic data with the well-logs, so I consulted the paleontologist, Lou Stover, who was studying microfossils from the wells. We confirmed that the seismic reflections were following the time lines based on his paleontology rather than the top of the sandstone reservoir objective. Our work on the pattern correlation of well-log marker horizons showed that the real physical surfaces cross the facies of time-transgressive rock units, suggesting that the seismic reflections do not follow massive time transgressive formational boundaries where strong impedances occur, but instead they follow the detailed bedding patterns or the real physical surfaces in the rocks. Thus, they cross time-transgressive facies and rock-formation boundaries, which are not continuous physical surfaces.

At the time, this was a revolutionary basic driving concept. It provided a new driving concept for interpreting seismic data. Before, such data had been considered a low-resolution tool for mapping major rock units because seismic reflections were thought to follow the major impedance contrasts. Our research showed, however, that this was not true. No matter what the resolution, seismic-reflection continuity was not an accurate method for mapping facies and rock type because reflections cross time-transgressive facies and formation boundaries at any resolution. What this new driving concept showed was that *seismic sections are a high-resolution tool for determining chronostratigraphy—the time lines in rocks*. This was a "Eureka" at that time. We had found the tool and developed the methodology to make regional chronostratigraphic correlations and to put stratigraphy into a geologic time framework for mapping and the understanding of paleogeography. In addition, this concept explained seismic data's usefulness in structural mapping: the reflections follow the horizons that were deposited at the same time, no matter what the lithology. The fact that seismic reflections follow time lines is the second basic driving concept for interpreting stratigraphy to develop from this well-correlation research.

The development of a third driving concept in seismic stratigraphy involved the total interpretation of a seismic section. What we found was that, besides correlating the major reflectors, you could correlate all the reflectors, and thus build up a very detailed chronostratigraphic pattern. We interpreted all the reflection patterns that we could not demonstrate to be some kind of coherent noise. From this detailed interpretation of the seismic reflections, we later developed the seismic sequence and seismic facies interpretation techniques based on the reflection patterns of onlap, downlap, and all the other patterns that we have come to recognize as old friends.

In our seismic interpretation research, I worked closely with F. Branisa and R. Zimmermayer on the stratigraphic interpretation of amplitude, frequency, and continuity of seismic records. During this time, Frank Branisa took me under his wing and taught me geophysics using a graphical, nonmathematical approach, which was very effective for me. His patience and diligence in teaching provided me with the basic understanding of geophysics that was critical for my interpretation research. As we developed the seismic stratigraphic interpretation techniques based on the total interpretation of seismic lines in a number of

different basins around the world, we began to recognize prominent discontinuities that appeared over and over again at approximately the same age. This triggered my memories of working on my Ph.D. dissertation with another of my Northwestern professors, Lawrence L. Sloss, who, of all my professors, had the greatest impact on my career. He not only provided me with the basic stratigraphic insights—especially the introduction to sequence stratigraphy—upon which I have built my scientific career, but he inspired me to attack any problem, no matter how difficult, and diligently work it out.

One of my scholastic victories was to convince Sloss that the unconformity he had called a sequence boundary at the base of the Mississippian Chesterian Series should be near the top. This experience, plus my training by Sloss and my work on well-log correlation, taught me to think in terms of interregional unconformities or sequence boundaries. I discovered in the early sixties that seismic data was the best means to identify and map them. I noticed, as I worked with data from around the United States, Venezuela, Sumatra and northwest Africa, that we could always recognize unconformities, or what we have come to call seismic sequence boundaries, on any grid of reasonable quality seismic data. As we tied these boundaries into wells, we began to study the geologic age at the time the unconformities became conformable. There were formidable age-dating problems in those days. For example, what was called Oligocene in most of the world was lower Miocene in the Gulf Coast. Nonetheless, there was a basic recognizable pattern or stratigraphic signature that we could chart. In 1959, I drew my first Phanerozoic global cycle chart based on well log studies. In 1963, I gave my first talk on the cycle chart at a company forum, which was based on seismic as well as well-log data. At that time I called the chart an onlap chart and interpreted the sawtooth cycles as caused by eustatic changes of sea level. In 1966, I delivered a talk coauthored with Robert Wilbur to the AAPG annual convention in St. Louis on this subject.

The second phase of my career culminated in 1964 with a large research applications project involving the Tertiary of the North Sea. The Geneva Agreement had been signed, so Exxon could now explore the North Sea. There was a widely spread exploration grid of seismic data over the central and southern North Sea. The main exploration interest in the North Sea was the Permian Rotliegende sands, but there was also an interest in the Tertiary. However, there were no "through-going" reflections in the Tertiary. Our operations people said "Why don't we let this guy, Vail, have a try. He says you shouldn't make regional correlations by following reflections, you should correlate the discontinuities, and there sure are a lot of discontinuities." So I got the chance to take a crack at the Tertiary of the North Sea. I worked a whole year on that project. It was the first major application of seismic stratigraphy and it contributed to a number of blocks being leased by Shell/Esso in the central North Sea.

So much for my second research career phase. In hindsight, it is not too bad a list of accomplishments for a junior researcher. But how were these accomplishments received? I'll give three examples that I believe illustrate their acceptance. First, my job rating, as reflected in my promotion record, provides some measure. I was hired as a Research Geologist in 1956, and six years later I was still a Research Geologist. Also, near the end of this second career phase, I had a performance appraisal, and my supervisor told me that I probably would never make it in research because I did not have the necessary skills. Obviously, my accomplishments were not very well accepted. I have a strong belief in the fairness of our merit system, and I don't believe that it was to blame for the problem. The problem was caused more by the difficulty we have in recognizing the importance of new driving concepts, especially those of our fellow researchers. The third example illustrates this point. In the early 1960s, I presented a talk on the relation of seismic reflections to geologic time to a major company research review. Talks were given in a large auditorium with several hundred people in attendance. After my talk, one of the senior people stood up and proceeded to ridicule me and my research. This included goading the audience into howling laughter by suggesting that the reflections must bounce off the backs of fossils. I tell this story to make the point that it is often very difficult to get a new research idea accepted.

Evidently I was not ranked high in the company ratings. What I discovered, however, was that it is not always bad being low in the merit rankings. If one can get along with less money and less prestige, you can accomplish a lot more research, and can build much stronger peer relationships. My father used to tell me that during lulls in your career, work hard and prepare for the busy times ahead. I believe this is good advice.

DEVELOPING DRIVING CONCEPTS AS A SUPERVISOR

What did I learn about driving concepts in my second career phase? I learned the importance of believing in your own research even if it challenges existing lore. I also learned that it is critical to listen to others for valuable insight about the validity of your ideas. Near the end of my second career phase, a major reorganization of company research occurred, and a small section was created in the geology division to investigate and develop what is now called seismic stratigraphy. Geophysicist Dan Skelton, the instigator of this arrangement, knew that the driving concepts that we were developing for seismic stratigraphy would never have a chance in the geophysics division as it existed at that time. Within a year I became supervisor of the new section.

My appointment as supervisor started my third career phase, which I call "Developing Driving Concepts as a Supervisor." We had a busy few years, and had a number of accomplishments, mainly in the areas of seismic stratigraphy and computer applications to geology. One of our early successes guided by Howard Yorston had great potential value. It was the ability to predict gas occurrence directly from seismic data using our models of impedance variation with depth for gas-filled reservoirs.

The major accomplishment of our group, however, was the development of seismic sequence and seismic facies interpretation

procedures and the application of the global or eustatic cycle chart to exploration. It was a group accomplishment. Howard Yorston and I started the group with R. M. Touring as supervisor. We were joined over the next couple of years by geologists Mike Widmier, John Sangree, Bob Mitchum, John Bubb, Sam Thompson and Carlton Johnson, by geophysicist Frank Branisa, and by programmers M. B. Ward, Janet Teagarden-Wilbur, and Russell Herron. In addition, we always had one or more affiliate interpreters working with us on temporary assignments. Our first studies were in the Fairview area in east Texas, where we worked with previously acquired seismic data, and in the San Juan Basin, New Mexico, where we shot our own seismic lines. These studies provided the initial data base upon which we developed the seismic sequence and seismic facies interpretation procedures, together with the application of the global cycle chart to exploration. The name *seismic sequences* was derived from L. L. Sloss's original work on unconformity-bounded sequences (Sloss and others, 1949; Sloss, 1963), and the name *seismic facies* was coined by John Sangree. Typically, each affiliate interpreter, while he or she was with us, worked on a seismic stratigraphic problem provided by an affiliate company. An ever-increasing data base led us to upgrade our procedures continually and to develop and document the global cycle chart. Near the end of this period, we were involved in two large projects. One headed by Sangree (offshore Louisiana and Texas) and Mitchum (offshore Florida) was a high resolution seismic and core study of the Gulf of Mexico slope from Northern Florida to the Rio Grande. The second, by Mitchum, was a post mortem of northwest Africa. These two studies systematized our seismic stratigraphy and eventually led to a series of company research reports, which evolved into a company redbook series on seismic stratigraphy.

We also worked very hard to improve the seismic data and the ties to well logs so we could better apply our techniques. Mike Widmier developed a well-log synthetics program that reproduces the individual reflection wavelets. Frank Branisa developed a well-log filtering program so we could filter logs to the resolution of the seismic data in order to tie the individual reflection wavelets accurately to stratigraphy. He also developed an inverse seismic modeling program, which produced synthetic logs from seismic data. This work was years ahead of its time and suffered from seismic data quality problems; the procedure was evidently independently duplicated years later by another company. We also worked hard to get high resolution for better stratigraphic definition. As a result, Branisa developed a frequency domain inverse filtering program and a phase coherence method for picking the upper limits of the coherent signal in order to obtain a broad band signal. Mike Widmier developed a velocity program with potential for stratigraphic interpretation. We also developed an amplitude enhancement program, a depth section program, and a datum section program.

As a result of applying computer programs with our seismic interpretation procedures to new data, we began to develop a number of new geologic concepts. The principal ones related to global sea level changes, submarine fans, and lowstand deltas.

One interesting example is the recognition of submarine fans in the North Sea. In a 1965 company report, I was able to identify a number of lower Tertiary submarine fan prospects (that we came to call "crabs") in the central North Sea, and this work was updated and extended to the Viking Graben by Carl Swanson, an Esso interpreter, as new seismic data became available. Our submarine fan interpretation was accepted by Esso until the first well was drilled on the Grandad or Balder prospect. The geologists insisted that the thick sands interbedded with dark shales containing an arenaceous Foraminifera fauna must be shallow-water deltas. We made numerous studies to try to solve this problem in the late sixties and early seventies. Eventually, our paleontologist pointed out that arenaceous faunas occur in both shallow and deep water, and one can be told from the other by the diversity of species. The Balder arenaceous species were not diverse, and therefore were deep water. This discovery was the turning point for the debate in Esso, but it was not until the mid- or late seventies, after we began teaching our seismic stratigraphy schools in Norway, that other companies revised their interpretations from deltaic to deep-sea fans (e.g., Heritier and others, 1979).

Our group saw the importance of computer applications to geology for seismic interpretation work, so we started a major effort in computer mapping under the guidance of Mark MacElroy and Carlton Johnson. This evolved rapidly, especially in applications to reservoir mapping and surface mine mapping. We also moved from two-dimensional to three-dimensional programs, and thence to interactive workstations for prospect identification under the guidance of Carlton Johnson.

I believe that our seismic stratigraphy research group was one of the most creative research sections that I have ever known. Many of the ideas developed there are still in the mainline of research today, and are techniques widely used by operations. What made it work? We had a multidisciplinary group, which had most of the skills necessary to solve the problems we were working on. We regularly had group planning sessions, which assumed we had all the time and money needed to do the research projects suggested. We met in the evenings as well as during the day. As a group, we developed an overall plan. We would then try to identify the person who was most interested and knowledgeable for each task, and then endeavor to give each person a maximum amount of responsibility for his or her project area. What worked best was an overlapping concept of management. We tried to develop a situation wherein each researcher had a clear-cut area of responsibility, but we made sure it overlapped with as many other areas as possible. This insured good communication, because each person was vitally interested in what the others were doing. Some researchers were able to assume a lot more responsibility than others. Even when the section had over 30 people, I had no group leaders. Certain people, such as John Sangree, became natural leaders and were sought out by the group. The seismic people got along very well, but the computer people did not get along at all. Both groups, however, were very motivated, and the interpersonal relationships did not make a lot of difference. I believed at that time that my role as supervi-

sor was primarily to create opportunity for the researchers and to keep them informed of how they and their work were being received by the company. My guidelines were for each researcher to keep me informed of everything I should know. I did not want to be surprised, and I wanted to take advantage of new opportunities as they developed. What did I learn about driving concepts in my third career phase? I learned the importance of creating an environment where both teamwork and individual responsibility prevailed.

INTERACTING WITH OTHER RESEARCH GROUPS

What happened to the accomplishments of our section? My fourth research career phase represents what happened. I've called this phase "Learning the Hard Way about the Importance of Working Effectively with Other Research Groups." What we did not do was to work effectively with other research groups. We got into everybody's hair. We got involved in a very destructive competition between different groups; most of what we developed went into a dormant period and was not effectively used. "Bright spots," seismic stratigraphy, and many of the computer programs were not applied until much later.

In March of 1971, we were broken up and most of us transferred to various groups in geophysics. In hindsight, this was probably the best thing that could have happened, although at the time it was a tremendous disappointment. I thought that we had figured out how to do high-volume, high-quality creative research. This may have been true, but we were not doing effective research. The only answer was that we had to disperse. It was difficult for me to readapt to individual research. I ended up with two offices, one in the geology end of the building and the other in geophysics, and I did a number of different things. I helped start a major project on lowstand deltas and submarine fans, and, for a 2-year period, I was supervisor of the structural geology section, which was a tremendous learning experience.

READAPTING TO INDIVIDUAL RESEARCH

I call my fifth career phase "Readapting to Individual Research," which has been the most rewarding to me personally. I was able to get control of my life and contribute both technically and organizationally, and to build a technical reputation in the public domain. My involvement in outside professional activities started with a performance appraisal, which suggested that I needed to develop an outside reputation if I was to progress. With an established professional reputation recognized both in and outside the company, I was no longer dependent on the company for my livelihood. Retirement no longer seemed like the end of my career, but the beginning of an exciting second career.

My fifth career phase involved two main themes: outside professional activity (e.g., Vail and Sangree, 1971) and the relearning of exploration problems through research applications projects and on-site teaching. Up to them, I had done very little public speaking or publishing. One of my first talks, coauthored by Don Seely and George Walton, was at a Penrose Conference in the early 1970s on our Trench Slope project. I have given many talks since then, but none have had such a dramatic effect on the audience. At that time, there was a minority group of earthquake specialists who believed that the Benioff Zone must be caused by underthrusting. The majority of scientists who were studying seismic refraction data, bathymetry, and cores, believed that the inner slopes of trenches were made up of down-dropped tensional fault blocks. I showed a seismic section that crossed the mid-America trench on the Pacific side of Guatemala. It showed reflections from the oceanic crust bending down under the shelf edge and trending right into the Benioff earthquake zone. This new evidence completely turned the group around. It was a very dramatic experience, and it inspired me to continue publishing and giving talks.

Following the Penrose experience, our group presented talks to the Geological Society of America meeting in Miami in 1974 on our seismic stratigraphy work (Mitchum and others, 1974; Vail and others, 1974). The public response to these presentations was very disappointing. Most of the audience was comprised of ex-Exxon employees wondering what was being released. Following that, Mike Widmier joined us, and the three of us gave talks at the American Association of Petroleum Geologists meeting. Here the response was overwhelming. Everybody, it seemed, wanted to know more about seismic stratigraphy. This favorable response led EPR's Howard Gould, who headed the AAPG's Education Committee, to ask us to present an AAPG Seismic Stratigraphy School, which we did. Our lecture notes eventually resulted in AAPG Memoir 26 on seismic stratigraphy (Payton, 1977). I was also invited to be an AAPG Distinguished Lecturer (Vail, 1975), which provided the opportunity to tour widely and speak to both industrial and academic groups. The public recognition associated with these talks and publications led to invitations to join a number of professional committees. To me the rewarding thing about getting outside recognition was becoming acquainted with many leading scientists, who worked in the areas of interest to me. There was a lot of outside interest in our work, so we received a tremendous amount of valuable feedback about problems, documentation, and applications of our concepts. My concurrent involvement with research application projects and on-site training schools also gave public exposure to our ideas, which also revealed problems associated with the driving concepts being developed by us.

It was during this phase, which I call readapting to individual research, that I worked closely with the biostratigraphers, especially Jan Hardenbol. Our key objective was to date the conformities associated with the sequence boundaries and condensed sections. In the sixties and seventies, all the age dates were derived from well data. In the early eighties, we started outcrop studies, in addition to the subsurface studies, to better define the age and facies relationships of the sequences. Our first outcrop studies took place in the Permian of the Guadalupe Mountains (Sarg, 1986, 1991). We selected the Guadalupe Mountains because the outcrops were the scale of seismic sec-

tions. Later we studied outcrops in Alabama (Baum and Vail, 1989) and Europe. These outcrops tended to be more the scale of well logs. We combined this work on biostratigraphic age dating with model studies to help understand the processes that created the rock patterns we observed. These model studies were started by M. T. Jervey in the seventies and continued in the eighties by Henry Posamentier and others (1989). Jan Hardenbol and I also developed an approach for separating the tectonic effects from the eustatic effects by using tectonic subsidence curves (Hardenbol and others, 1981). From these various studies, we learned how to apply the concept of shelf accommodation to recognize sequences and systems tracts. From this knowledge, we learned to recognize sequence and systems tracts not only on seismic data, but also on outcrops and well logs. This expanded application of concepts learned from seismic data to outcrop and well log studies we now call sequence stratigraphy.

CONTRIBUTING AS A SENIOR ACADEMIC RESEARCHER

My fifth career phase gradually came to a close as I steadily gained more confidence in myself as a researcher and scientist. What did I learn from this fifth career phase? I learned the importance of developing one's own sense of worth through technical competence. I refer to my sixth and present career phase as "Contributing as a Senior Researcher and Teacher." During this phase, I have endeavored to work in two areas. One is to contribute technically in sequence stratigraphy and the other is to become a competent teacher where learning is both creative and exciting.

STATUS OF SEQUENCE STRATIGRAPHY AND EUSTASY

Sequence stratigraphy has evolved from the early concepts of Sloss, Krumbein, and Dapples (1949) and Sloss (1963) through the addition in the 1960s of seismic and well-log data (Payton, 1977) to conventional outcrop and biostratigraphic data (Posamentier and others, 1989). Today, sequence stratigraphy implies also the mathematical modeling of subsidence and sediment supply to produce the curves of the global cycle chart (e.g., Haq and others, 1987). In its modern form, sequence stratigraphy has the potential for providing a unifying concept for stratigraphy and basin evolution similar to what plate tectonics has done for most of geology. My own technical thrust has been to work toward the achievement of this goal and its application to hydrocarbon exploration.

Early in our work at Exxon, we were struck by the similarities of certain age periods that produce similar stratigraphic patterns or signatures and by the apparent synchrony of seismic discontinuities on widely separated continental margins. As noted above, even when I drew my first onlap chart in the early sixties, I tentatively interpreted the sawtooth cycles as eustatic in origin (Vail and Wilbur, 1966). As our studies of seismic stratigraphy matured, we became increasingly convinced that eustasy was the principal cause of the onlap cycles (e.g., Vail, 1975; Mitchum and others, 1976; Payton, 1977; Haq and others, 1987). In spite of challenges to this position, we continued to feel that the eustatic hypothesis is a valuable guide for research and deserves our advocacy.

ACKNOWLEDGMENTS

This paper was adapted from a talk given in 1983 to a seminar in Exxon Production Research Corporation on "Ideas and Innovations." I appreciate the opportunity provided by the Eustasy Symposium to share it with a wider audience. The manuscript has profited from critical reviews by R. H. Dott, Jr., and William M. Jordan.

REFERENCES CITED

Baum, G. R., and Vail, P. R., 1989, Sequence stratigraphy concepts applied to Paleogene outcrops, Gulf and Atlantic basins, *in* Wilgus, C. K., ed., Sea-level changes and stratigraphy: Society of Economic Paleontologists and Mineralogists Memoir 42, p. 309–327.

Haq, B. U., Hardenbol, J., and Vail, P. R., 1987, Chronology of fluctuating sea levels since the Triassic: Science, v. 235, p. 1156–1167.

Hardenbol, J., Vail, P. R., and Ferrer, J., 1981, Interpreting paleoenvironments, subsidence history and sea-level changes of passive margins from seismic and biostratigraphy, *in* Proceedings, International Geologic Congress Meeting: Paris, 1980, Oceanologica Acta, p. 33–44.

Heritier, F. E., Lossel, P., and Wathne, E., 1979, Frigg Field—Large submarine-fan trap in lower Eocene rocks of North Sea Viking graben: American Association of Petroleum Geologists Bulletin, v. 63, p. 1999–2020.

Mitchum, R. M., Jr., Vail, P. R., and Sangree, J. B., 1974, Regional stratigraphic framework from seismic sequences [abs.]: Geological Society of America Program for Annual Meetings, p. 873.

Mitchum, R. M., Jr., Vail, P. R., Todd, R. G., and Sangree, J. B., 1976, Regional seismic interpretation using sequences and eustatic cycles [abs.]: American Association of Petroleum Geologists Bulletin, v. 60, p. 699.

Payton, C. P., ed., 1977, Seismic stratigraphy—Applications to hydrocarbon exploration: American Association of Petroleum Geologists Memoir 26, 516 p.

Posamentier, H. W., Jervey, M. T., and Vail, P. R., 1989, Eustatic Controls on clastic deposition; I, Conceptual framework, *in* Wilgus, C. K., ed., Sea-level changes and stratigraphy: Society of Economic Paleontologists and Mineralogists Memoir 42, p. 109–124.

Sarg, J. F., 1986, San Andreas/Grayburg Formations, Guadalupe Mountains, New Mexico and Texas, *in* Symposium and Guidebook: Permian Basin Section, Society of Economic Paleontologists and Mineralogists, no. 86-25, p. 83–93.

Sarg, J. F., 1991, Sequence stratigraphy, facies, and reservoir geometries of the San Andreas, Grayburg, and Queen Formations, Guadalupe Mountains, New Mexico and Texas, *in* Permian Basin Section, Society of Economic Paleontologists and Mineralogists Annual Field Conference Guide, Publication no. 91-32, 141 p.

Sloss, L. L., 1963, Sequences in the cratonic interior of North America: Geological Society of America Bulletin, v. 74, p. 93–114.

Sloss, L. L., Krumbein, W. C., and Dapples, E. C., 1949, Integrated facies analysis, *in* Geological Society of America Memoir 39, p. 91–124.

Vail, P. R., 1975, Eustatic cycles from seismic data for global stratigraphic analysis [abs. for an AAPG Distinguished Lecture]: American Association of Petroleum Geologists Bulletin, v. 59, p. 2198–2199.

Vail, P. R., and Sangree, J. B., 1971, Time stratigraphy from seismic data [abs.]: American Association of Petroleum Geologists Bulletin, v. 55, p. 367–368.

Vail, P. R., and Wilbur, P. O., 1966, Onlap, key to worldwide unconformities and depositional cycles [abs.]: American Association of Petroleum Geologists Bulletin, v. 50, p. 638.

Vail, P. R., Mitchum, R. M., Jr., and Thompson, S., III, 1974, Eustatic cycles based on sequences with coastal onlap [abs.]: Geological Society of America Program for Annual Meetings, p. 993.

Vine, F. J., and Mathews, D. H., 1963, Magnetic anomalies over ocean ridges: Nature, v. 199, p. 947.

MANUSCRIPT ACCEPTED BY THE SOCIETY JANUARY 14, 1992

Geological Society of America
Memoir 180
1992

Chapter 9

A challenge: Is it possible to determine eustasy and does it matter?

Christopher G. St. C. Kendall, Philip Moore, and Gregory Whittle
Geological Sciences, University of South Carolina, Columbia, South Carolina 29208
Robert Cannon
Computer Science, University of South Carolina, Columbia, South Carolina 29208

ABSTRACT

An interest in eustasy, after a long dormancy, has been revived by the development of seismic stratigraphy. Eustatic events signal their occurrence through the synchronous creation or loss of worldwide accommodation of the space available for sediment fill. Such events can only be recognized if this signal is large enough, and of worldwide extent. The signal is dependent on reliable stratigraphic markers spaced sufficiently closely in time to resolve the sea-level events. The amplitude cannot be determined. Evidence for eustatic events are widely separated synchronous sedimentary sequences and the unconformities which bound these features.

To unequivocally interpret the stratigraphic record, one must be able to disentangle the effects of changing tectonics, eustasy, and sediment supply. In practice it is impossible to accomplish a complete calibration of seismic sequences, therefore it will always be a matter of interpretation. However, a wide range of geological characteristics place limits on tectonism and eustasy. This allows the application of a family of reasonable tectonic and eustatic models to explain basin history. In most instances, models within the family are similar enough to reproduce the stratigraphic record at the level of resolution produced by seismic sections. In many cases this is due to the fact that tectonics, eustasy, and sediment supply are linked, rather than being independent of each other. Hence, although absolute values of bathymetry and tectonics may never be determined with precision, models can generate complex basinal sequences with high fidelity using plausible inputs. Thus assumptions heaped on assumptions work.

Examples used to demonstrate the above paradigm are from the Mesozoic and Tertiary of the Bahamas, the Gulf Coast of the United States, and the South Carolina Coast; and the Permian of the Midland basin of Texas.

INTRODUCTION

In this volume, most of the chapters provide a historical perspective to current studies on eustasy, and it is our contention that eustasy has played an important role in punctuating the character of the sedimentary section throughout the Earth's history. Geologists have long recognized that it is difficult, if not impossible, to prove a truly eustatic change of sea level from ancient strata because the magnitudes of the simultaneous influences of tectonics, sediment supply, and sea-level change could not be determined with certainty. What we have long known is that only evidence of a *relative change* of sea level is recorded in the rocks. Until the advent in the petroleum industry of high-resolution seismic cross sections in the 1960s, there has been a dormant period of at least three decades with regard to the study of eustasy. However, the rapid proliferation during the late sixties and seventies of seismic data from several continental margins has seen a mushrooming of interest in, and claims for, detailed documentation of ancient eustatic changes. These studies are so common that many believe we are in the midst of a revolution in geology similar to and as important as that which produced with the advent of plate tectonics. But is such a bold claim justified? In the present chapter, we look to the future and the use of graphical simulations to unravel the sedimentary section. We use

Kendall, C. G. St. C., Moore, P., Whittle, G., and Cannon, R., 1992, A challenge: Is it possible to determine eustasy and does it matter?, *in* Dott, R. H., Jr., ed., Eustasy: The Historical Ups and Downs of a Major Geological Concept: Boulder, Colorado, Geological Society of America Memoir 180.

the fact that sediment accommodation is the product of eustasy and tectonics, so that if one assumes the sea-level behavior, then the residual is tectonic behavior. This assumption of sea-level behavior has far-reaching implications in that it explains why one can use graphical simulations to predict facies and their geometry with great accuracy away from points with good geologic control. This assumption also explains why different sea-level curves and tectonic models can be equally successful in predicting geometries and facies.

This chapter is divided into three parts. We begin by showing that the size of the eustatic excursions cannot be measured. We then demonstrate that geometric simulations can be made that accurately predict the geometry and facies found within the geological record. These simulations use prescribed sea-level curves and prescribed tectonic behavior for the region being simulated. We conclude by demonstrating that prescribed tectonic behavior alone can be used to simulate geometries in the geologic record.

RECOGNITION OF EUSTATIC SIGNALS

Eustatic events signal their occurrence through the synchronous creation or loss of worldwide accommodation, that is, the space available for sediment fill (Jervey, 1988; Posamentier and others, 1988). The evidence for eustatic events consists of synchronous sedimentary sequences and the unconformities that bound them (Vail, 1988). An eustatic signal is recognized only if it is large enough and is of worldwide extent. The correlation of the signal to the stratigraphic record is dependent on reliable time markers spaced sufficiently close in time to resolve the sea-level events. Clearly, eustatic events do occur because we do see evidence of the synchronous creation of worldwide accommodation filled by sediment (Haq and others, 1987). Not all accommodation filled by sediment is synchronously created by eustasy but the Haq and others (1987) curve suggests that many of these sediment packages are synchronous (Figs. 1 and 2).

The problem with eustasy is that, though sea-level events can be recognized, the amplitude of their excursion cannot be determined. Thus, though there are several ways to measure sea level indirectly, there is no way to directly measure the magnitude of the change. This is so because the datum available from which we measure the sea-level variation varies itself. Relative sea level can be measured, but is dependent on the movement of the Earth's crust and eustatic position. Neither of these can be measured with respect to the other without assuming a model of the latter's behavior (Burton and others, 1987). There is simply no place to stand to make the measurement.

There are a number of methods, however, that purport to measure sea-level position indirectly (Vella, 1961; Burton and others, 1987). There is the use of tide gauges (Gutenburg, 1941), but these assume a tectonic behavior to determine the eustasy. For instance, if we compare the tidal gauges of Norway to those of the Bahamas, it is very clear that something is happening differently in either environment. We assume a tectonic behavior to explain the uplift of Norway with respect to a rather stable crustal behavior in the Bahamas. It should be realized, however, that these tectonic models are assumptions, reasonable as they might be (Burton and others, 1987).

We can use strandline position (Cogley, 1981; Harrison and others, 1981; Burton and others, 1987), but in order to use this to measure eustatic movement through geological time, we have to assume either continental relief as a function of time or tectonic behavior for the area, or both (Burton and others, 1987).

We also can use paleobathymetry to measure eustatic sea level (Barrell, 1917; Wanless and Shepherd, 1936; Wells, 1960; Harris and others, 1984); in this particular case we have to assume a tectonic behavior before we can actually extract the residual sea level (Burton and others, 1987).

The same criticism can be applied to the use of seismic sequence onlap. In this case, we assume we can see the relative position of individual sedimentary bodies or seismic sequences as they onlap continental masses to determine eustatic behavior (Vail and others, 1977, 1984; Hardenbol and others, 1981; Vail, 1988). To determine the size of these excursions, however, we have to assume a tectonic model (Hardenbol and others, 1981). The Haq and others (1987) curves require that one assumes a thermotectonic subsidence on extensional margins, and then extract sea level as the residual. However, as we show (Guidish and others, 1984) when we stack a series of crustal subsidence curves, these curves not only contain low-frequency signal but they also have a high-frequency signal. These curves bear little resemblance to the signals of the Vail and others (1977) and Haq and others (1987) curves, so they tend to be conveniently ignored. While a general low-order background thermal subsidence is demonstrably reasonable (Watts and Steckler, 1979), the cause of the erratic high-frequency signal is probably because the Earth's crust is brittle and thus has a jerky high-frequency response to the low-order effects of thermal subsidence. Cloetingh and others (1989) explain how the sea-level events of Vail and others (1977) and Haq and others (1987) may be a response to intermittent phases of accumulated tensional stresses "associated with rift episodes and subsequent rapid relaxation of these stresses." As we see it, these superimposed high-frequency variations in crustal behavior bear little relationship to the weight of the sea water on the crust

Figure 1. The Haq and others (1987) eustatic curves and their relationship to the stratigraphic column of the United Arab Emirates. For these correlations of sea level to basin stratigraphy it was assumed by Kendall and others (1991) that most of the Haq and others (1987) excursions took place at the times they specify. Where Kendall and others (1991) had access to paleontological age data they have based their correlations on these but where age data are absent, they have extrapolated between events of known ages using the philosophy of Van Hinte (1976a, b). The dashed horizontal lines are intended to coincide with rapid sea level rises, and the gray fill the general occurrence of onlapping seismic facies.

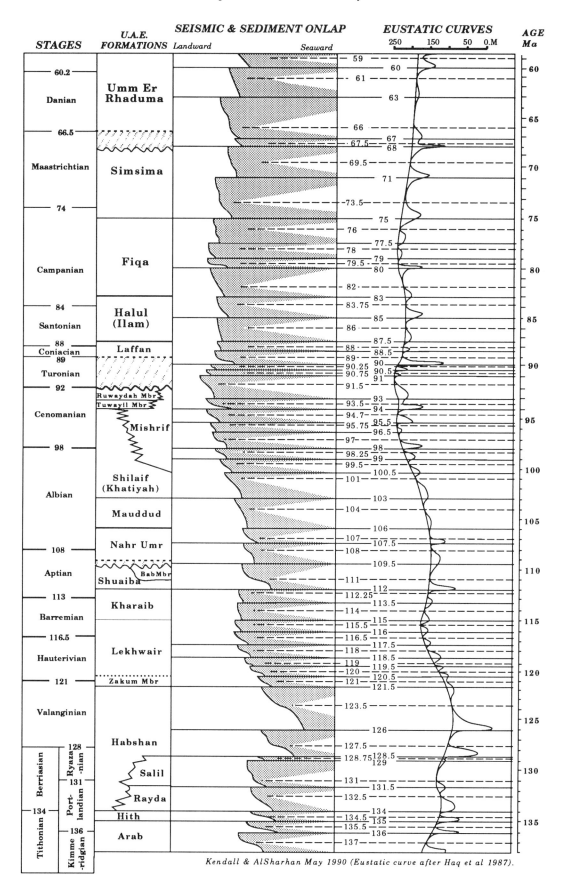

STAGES	U.A.E. FORMATIONS	SEISMIC & SEDIMENT ONLAP	EUSTATIC CURVES	AGE Ma

Kendall & AlSharhan May 1990 (Eustatic curve after Haq et al 1987).

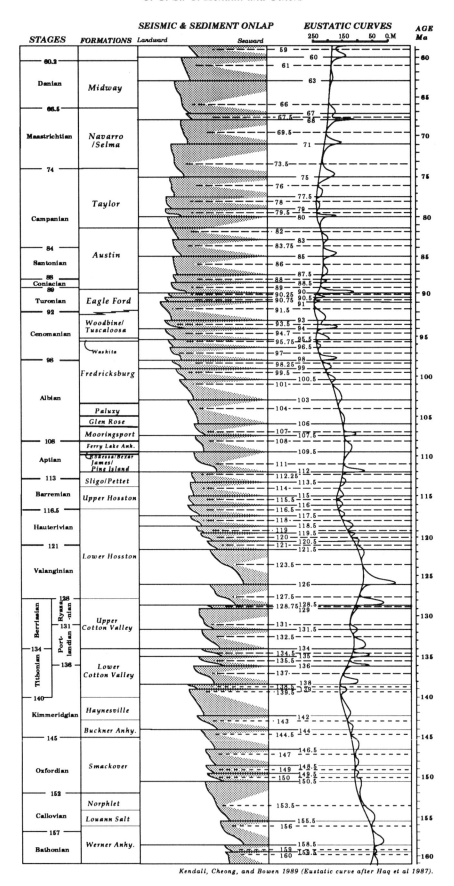

Kendall, Cheong, and Bowen 1989 (Eustatic curve after Haq et al 1987).

(Guidish and others, 1984), but may indeed be related to rapid crust and plate movement (Fig. 3).

Finally, we can use sedimentary simulations to match sea level and sequence geometry, but again, though we can do this with remarkable accuracy, we have to assume a sea-level curve to derive tectonic behavior or vice versa (Burton and others, 1987). The simulations derived from these assumptions are accurate and verifiable away from the areas of interest and measurement. The reason we can do this is that the geometry of the sediment is dependent on the rate of sedimentation and the sum of tectonic movement and sea-level position, in other words, the accommodation. Furthermore, if a tectonic model is assumed, then a sea-level model automatically is determined, or vice versa.

One can use an assumed sea-level curve to create accurate graphical simulations of the sedimentary fill of basins. The technology of graphical simulations is becoming more widely accepted and used within the geological community, particularly within university geological departments and oil companies. In the simulation we have designed (SEDPAK), we can track the evolving sedimentary geometry of carbonates and clastics as they fill a basin (Strobel and others, 1989; and Kendall and others, 1990 describe much of what follows; the readers are referred to these papers for more details). To do this, we assume an initial basin geometry, prescribe a sea-level curve, and plot tectonic behavior as a function of time and position. Then for clastic deposition, we determine the volume of clastic sediment as an area of sediment that enters the basin as a function of time, and the distance that it penetrates the basin as a function of time. This sediment deposition obeys simple laws, including the precept that clastic sediment may not be deposited if the sediment depositional surface is above a certain angle, or having been deposited, if compaction and tectonics now cause the sediment to rest at too high an angle, then the sediment is eroded and deposited downslope. The clastic sediments are deposited as either sand or shale (or both), within the marine setting, or upslope as alluvial sediments. The marine setting includes a coastal-plain shelf or the sediment may penetrate the basin below wave base as turbidites or collect as some form of pelagic deposits. Secondary variables handled within the simulation include regional subsidence, hinged subsidence, the isostatic response to sediment loading, the compaction of sediment, the subaerial and submarine erosion, submarine slumping, faulting, and two-sided fill of the basin.

For carbonate accumulation, we assume that its rate is dependent upon water depth, and so rates of accumulation are faster in shallow water and become slower in deeper water. The user must prescribe the rates of accumulation at certain depth positions, and the program interpolates these rates between the user-defined rates. Within the carbonate algorithm, we assume that the

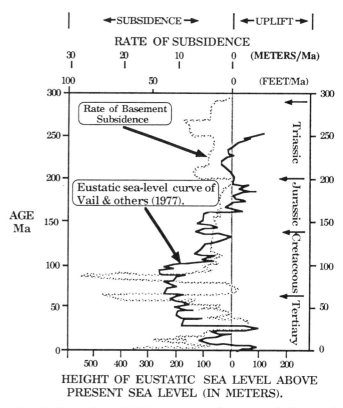

Figure 3. Comparison of global average rate of basement subsidence and eustatic curve of Vail and others (1977); after Guidish and others (1984).

rate of carbonate accumulation for a particular run is constant, while we vary the rate of pelagic carbonate input as a function of time. We also can prescribe the amount of sediment that forms on the shelf margin and may be distributed downslope as an apron or as a turbidite or may actually be carried from the break-in slope back onto the shelf to infill the lagoon. We assume that carbonate production for the slope is largely coming from the basin margin, and using this assumption, we have been very successful with our simulations. Not only do we accumulate carbonates, but we can damp their accumulation in response to the input of clastics or as a function of location. In other words, we can have faster or slower rates of accumulation in lagoons, and we can damp them as a function of wave energy. In the latter case, we can prescribe a fall in the rate of accumulation as a function of depth when waves start touching the sea floor. This wave-damping function is subtracted directly from the depth-dependent rate of accumulation.

SIMULATION RESULTS

Bahama Banks

Having described the simulation, we will now show how graphical simulations that assume a specific sea-level behavior can be used to model either carbonate geometries or clastics, or

Figure 2. The Haq and others (1987) eustatic curves and their relationship to the stratigraphic column of the northern Gulf of Mexico. (See also discussion and symbol definitions on Figure 1 caption.)

mixes of both with incredible accuracy. The first model is for the Bahamas. Here, Western Geophysical acquired a series of seismic lines on the northwestern side of the Great Bahama Banks. These were interpreted by Eberli and Ginsburg (1989), who demonstrated that, from the Late Cretaceous on, a series of carbonate platforms grew upward toward sea level (Fig. 4). Their rates of accumulation were faster over these banks, but the areas between banks accumulated carbonates rapidly enough to fill them to sea level. Here the carbonates aggraded and then prograded as the areas between the banks filled. Eberli and Ginsburg (1989, Fig. 11), recognizing the existence of unconformities, mapped a series of seismic sequences, which they lettered A to Q, and were able to correlate from the western margin of the Bahamas to a region they called the Straits of Andros, in the center of the Bahama Bank. They then related these sequences to the Haq and others

(1987) curve, using a well at Great Isaac to determine the position of two major breaks in the sedimentary section. One such unconformity was in the mid-Miocene, another at the Oligocene-Miocene boundary; the rest of the compilation was assumed to be directly correlatable to the events seen in the Haq and others (1987) curve.

Using the Haq and others' (1987) curves then as input to our simulation, varying tectonic subsidence across the section and assuming a particular rate of carbonate accumulation as a function of water depth, and varying pelagic accumulation as a function of time, we were able to match the geometries of the western Bahamas with some accuracy (Figs. 4 and 5; Eberli and others, 1990). Of particular significance was the fact that we were able to cause this sequence to aggrade and not to prograde during the major sea-level fall of the upper Oligocene, by making the fault

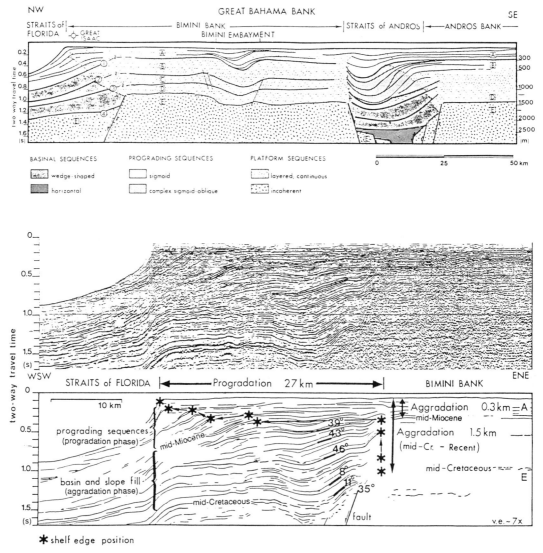

Figure 4. Schematic cross section of the northwest Great Bahama Bank after Eberli and Ginsburg (1987), and an interpreted seismic section of the western edge to the Great Bahama Bank after Eberli and Ginsburg (1987).

against the early western Bahama margin active during deposition as probably initiated by the collision of Cuba with the Bahamas. This prevented the rapid progradation of the sequence during the Oligocene sea-level low; however, during the mid-Miocene sea-level low, rapid progradation was initiated. The match between the seismic section and the simulation is remarkable. Individual unconformities can be matched, as can the timing of events. Low-stand onlapping and the high-stand progradation events are clear. Both the simulation and the seismic sections match beautifully. The interesting thing is that to acquire this match in geometries between the simulation and the actual seismic data, we varied only subsidence behavior and tried different accumulation curves. Eventually we were able to obtain a match between the seismic simulation of the western Bahamas (Fig. 5) and the seismic simulation of the Straits of Andros (Fig. 6) by using the same sea-level curve, similar carbonate accumulations, and tectonic models. Thus we were able to predict the geometries that

we see in the Straits of Andros using data from the western margin. In this test of the input parameters, we made very little variation in the sediment accumulation rates, but did change subsidence rates to be different from those we used for the western side of the Bahamas.

In conclusion, by using the Haq and others' (1987) sea-level curve, we are able to recreate the regional stratigraphic geometries from very simple assumptions that we have programmed in our simulation and get remarkable matches in the geometries from the seismic data. This has far-reaching implications with respect to the development of predictive production and exploration models for petroleum.

Gulf of Mexico

We can demonstrate a similar match that can be achieved when the clastic algorithm is used. Here, we used a seismic line from the Gulf of Mexico, provided by the TGS company (Fig. 7;

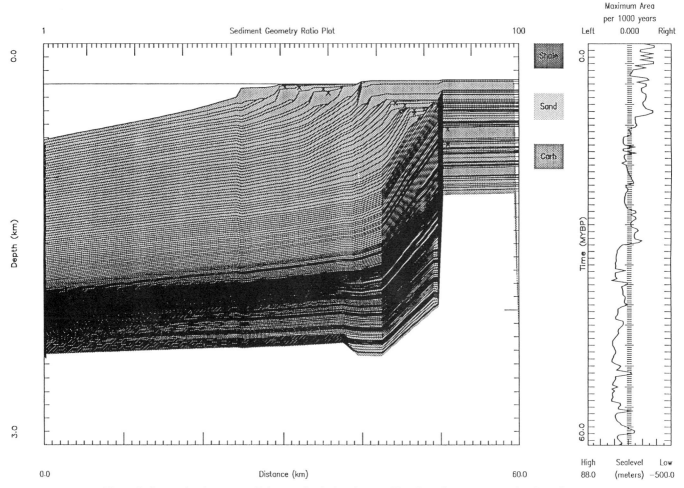

Figure 5. Output for the western Bahamas simulation data set. Note how the system aggrades through the lower Tertiary to the mid-Miocene and then progrades. At the same time, pelagic deposition rates varied. The subdivisions on the upper horizontal axis of the left diagram indicate the columns on which sediment deposition was simulated. The lower horizontal axis shows distances across cross section. The vertical axis is depth in meters. The xs mark the intersection of the coastal plain and sea level (the most seaward edge of the coast). The diagram to the right shows the sea-level curve.

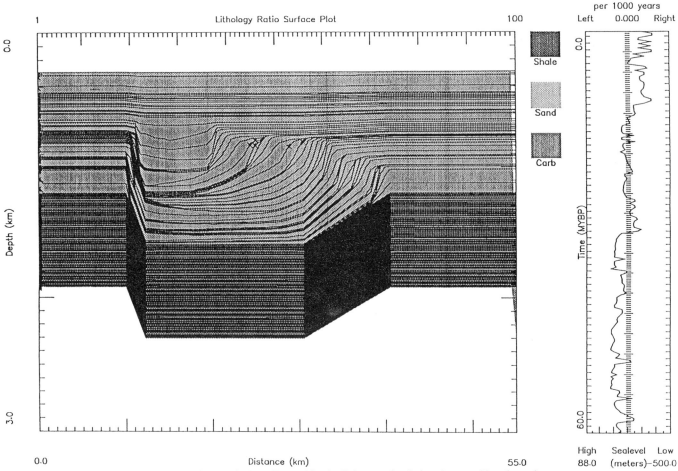

Figure 6. Output for the Andros Channel in the Bahamas simulation data set. Note how the system progrades through the lower Tertiary into the Miocene and then aggrades. At the same time, pelagic deposition rates varied. See Figure 5 caption for explanation.

Kendall and Lowrie, 1990). This line shows a series of small salt domes, which were active during the deposition of deltaic sequences in the late Pleistocene and early Holocene. By varying the amount of clastic input as a function of time expressed as shales and sands, we were able to recreate the general geometries that occur in this area using a sea level that we derived from the seismic line. The match between the seismic data and the clastic fill was not perfect, but suggested that this simulation, which was tied to the seismic section (Figs. 7 and 8), can be used to highgrade the sedimentary potential of the area.

Using the simulation, we should be able to model below the resolution of the seismic data in both the Bahamas and the Gulf of Mexico and produce stratigraphic models, which match with some accuracy.

TECTONICS AS THE SOLE CAUSE OF ACCOMMODATION

Despite the fact that we can reproduce a stratigraphic section through simulation, we are still faced with the problem of

separating fact from fantasy. Which sea-level curve do we use, or do we even need to use a sea-level curve? Below, we demonstrate how one can reproduce the geometries of stratigraphic sections, using either a sea-level curve tied to a tectonic signal, or reproduce the geometries using tectonics alone, and ignore the sea-level curve.

Permian Clear Fork Formation

In this particular case, we used seismic data and well logs in an interpretation put together by Sarg (1988) and others from Exxon, and modeled the Permian Clear Fork Formation at the margin of the Midland Basin. Here, a series of prograding clinoform carbonate bodies interfinger down-dip with clastic wedges (Fig. 9). We interpret this sequence to be a product of variations in sea level, and we derive our own sea-level curve for the region using the Ross and Ross (1988) sea-level curve and our own interpretations. We can show that initially there was a prograding, high-stand carbonate body filling the basin, but as sea

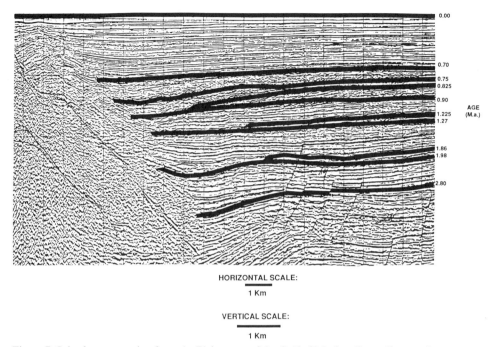

Figure 7. Seismic cross section from the Pleistocene of the Gulf of Mexico. Heavy lines mark sequence boundaries (courtesy TGS Geophysical Company).

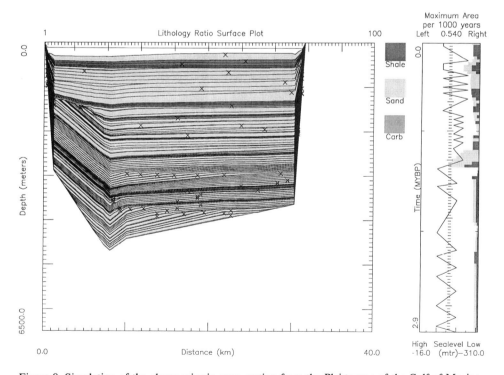

Figure 8. Simulation of the above seismic cross section from the Pleistocene of the Gulf of Mexico, shown in Figure 2. The diagram to the right shows the sea-level curve and the area of clastics (in km²/1,000 years) deposited per time step. See Figure 5 for explanation.

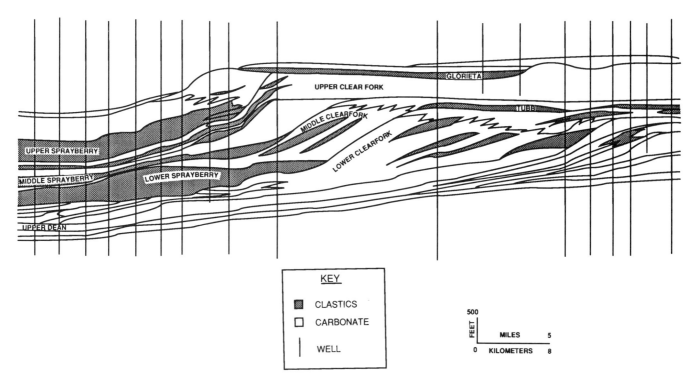

Figure 9. Well cross section from the Permian basin of west Texas of the Clearfork Basin after Sarg (1986).

level fell, clastics were introduced into the basin as a low-stand systems tract. Then, as sea level began to rise again, carbonate production turned on while clastics turned off, thus producing a prograding and aggrading high-stand carbonate depositional systems tract. Sea level rose and fell twice and rose again to produce the geometries preserved (Fig. 10). The input for this simulation first included the sea-level curve seen in Figure 10. To test the tectonic model, we then turned off this variation in sea level, but used its sea-level–derived subsidence behavior for this margin as a function of time (Fig. 11). The subsidence is derived by converting sea-level positions to rates, then scaling the resulting rates according to position across the basin. The result shows a good match between the carbonate margin and low-stand clastics of the simulation and the stratigraphic and seismic sections, suggesting that these geometries might have been produced without varying eustasy at all. The major differences between the two simulation runs are that we did not include a general first-order crustal subsidence, which would have made the two geometries identical.

South Carolina

In two other simulation runs, we tested to see if tectonic behavior would recreate the geometries instead of sea level for the Danian of the South Carolina coastline (Muthig and others, 1990), where carbonates and clastics interfinger with one another (Fig. 12). In one simulation run we used the Haq and others (1987) sea-level curve (Fig. 13), and in the next run (Fig. 14), we took this same sea-level curve and used its sea-level–derived subsidence behavior as input for tectonic behavior (Fig. 15). We used two different crustal subsidence behaviors across the line of section. One had greater amplitude, but the same frequency of events, in a more seaward position where we thought the crust subsided rapidly; and the second one was in a more landward (i.e., inland) position with slower crustal subsidence and less frequency. The timing of the events was determined from the Haq and others' (1987) curve. And the resulting two simulation runs are remarkably similar to one another, suggesting that the geometries we see in this mixed carbonate/clastic terrain could be a product of tectonics alone, or a mix of sea-level and tectonics. Our conclusion is that this sedimentary sequence is not the product of tectonics alone, because it is highly unlikely that the tectonic movement was such that the Earth's crust was moving up and down with such rapidity that it produced this type of sedimentary accommodation (Fig. 15). Instead, we feel that there was a eustatic signal coupled with tectonics that was driving the stratigraphy that we see in the Danian of South Carolina. Nevertheless, the amplitude of the sea-level events cannot be determined, but the frequency of their occurrence can.

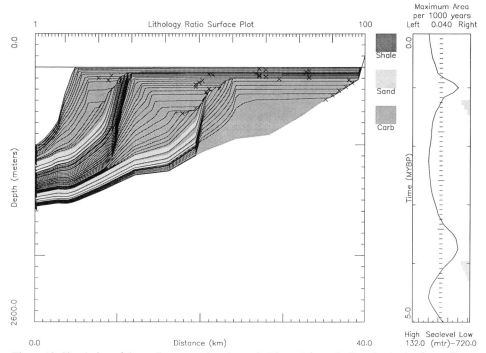

Figure 10. Simulation of the well cross section shown in Figure 9 from the Permian basin of west Texas of the Clearfork basin after Sarg (1986) using our own sea-level curve. In the sediment geometry rates plot, the darkened fill is of percent of carbonate and the lighter fill is percent of sand deposited for each time step. The diagram to the right shows the sea-level curve and the area of sands (in $km^2/1,000$ years) deposited per time step. See Figure 5 for explanation.

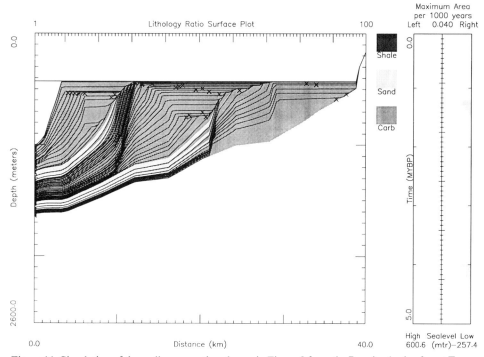

Figure 11. Simulation of the well cross section shown in Figure 9 from the Permian basin of west Texas of the Clearfork basin after Sarg (1986) using a subsidence history derived from the sea-level curve. In the sediment geometry rates plot, the darkened fill is of percent of carbonate and the lighter fill is percent of sand deposited for each time step. The diagram to the right shows the sea level curve does not vary and the area of sands (in $km^2/1,000$ years) deposited per time step. See Figure 5 for explanation.

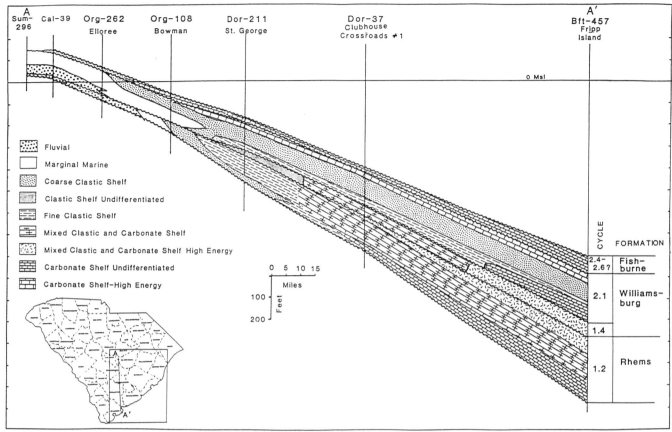

Figure 12. Well cross section of the Danian section from the coast of South Carolina after Muthig and others (1990).

CONCLUSIONS

We can show that eustatic signals can be recognized as worldwide events. The amplitude of the events cannot be determined, but if we assume a eustatic sea-level behavior, then tectonic behavior can be predicted or vice versa. The last two simulation results highlight the importance of taking care in selecting the sea-level model to be used in the simulation. At the same time, it is critical that, once a sea-level model has been selected, no matter what that model, it must be used consistently from basin to basin. Such models can be used to make extremely accurate predictions of sedimentary geometry. This is because sea level is only part of the accommodation for sedimentary fill, which also depends upon the residual of tectonics. The results of such simulations are reviewed in this chapter; they are remark-able in their accuracy. The amplitudes exhibited by sea-level events of Haq and others (1987) are undoubtedly model-dependent, and they may be very wrong or only partly wrong. We feel that with the advent of microcomputers, we are on the edge of a new age in stratigraphic modeling, which will enable us to make great advances in our understanding of the sedimentary section.

ACKNOWLEDGMENTS

We should like to acknowledge the financial support of Texaco Research Company, the Japanese National Oil Corporation, Mobil Exploration, and CONOCO. We appreciate the critical reviews of the manuscript by A. Simo and M. E. Johnson.

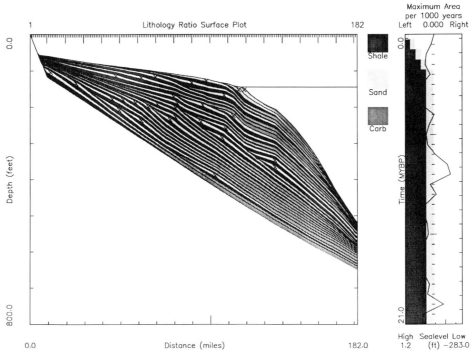

Figure 13. Simulation of the well cross section shown in Figure 12 of the Danian section from the coast of South Carolina after Muthig and others (1990) using the Haq and others (1987) eustatic curves. In the sediment geometry rates plot, the darkened fill is of percent of carbonate and the lighter fill is percent of sand deposited for each time step. The diagram to the right shows the sea-level curve and the area of sands (in km^2/1,000 years) deposited per time step. See Figure 5 for explanation.

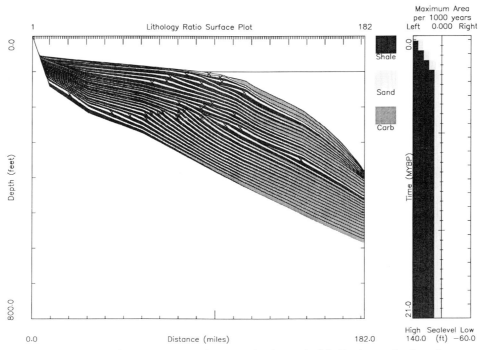

Figure 14. Simulation of the well cross section shown in Figure 12 of the Danian section from the coast of South Carolina after Muthig and others (1990) using a subsidence history derived from the Haq and others (1987) eustatic curves. In the sediment geometry rates plot, the darkened fill is of percent of carbonate and the lighter fill is percent of sand deposited for each time step. The diagram to the right shows the sea-level curve does not vary and the area of sands (in km^2/1,000 years) deposited per time step. See Figure 5 for explanation.

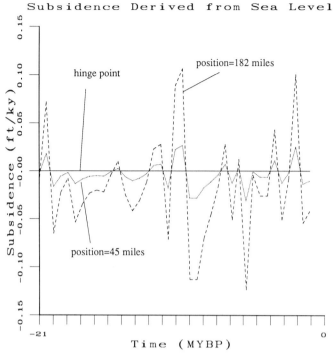

Figure 15. Subsidence history derived from the Haq and others (1987) eustatic curves used in the South Carolina simulation. The horizontal solid line represents the hinge point at the left (landward) side of the simulation. The dotted curve represents the rate of subsidence at a position 72 km (45 mi) basinward of the left side, while the dashed curve represents the rate of subsidence at a position 293 km (182 mi) basinward (i.e., the extreme right side) of the left side.

REFERENCES CITED

Barrell, J., 1917, Rhythms and the measurements of geologic time: Geological Society of America Bulletin, v. 28, p. 745–904.

Burton, R., Kendall, C.G.St.C., and Lerche, I., 1987, Out of our depth: On the impossibility of fathoming eustasy from the stratigraphic record: Earth Science Reviews, v. 24, p. 237–277.

Cloetingh, S., Tankard, A. J., Welsink, H. J., and Jenkins, W.A.M., 1989, Vail's coastal onlap curves and their correlation with tectonic events, offshore eastern Canada, *in* Tankard, A. J., and Balkwill, H. R., eds., Extensional tectonics and stratigraphy of the North Atlantic margins: American Association of Petroleum Geologists Memoir 46, p. 283–294.

Cogley, J. G., 1981, Late Phanerozoic extent of dry land: Nature, v. 291, p. 56–58.

Eberli, G. P., and Ginsburg, R. N., 1987, Segmentation and coalescence of Cenozoic carbonate platforms, northwestern Great Bahama Bank: Geology, v. 15, p. 75–79.

——, 1989, Cenozoic progradation of northwestern Great Bahama Bank, A record of lateral platform growth and sea-level fluctuations, *in* Wilson, J. L., Crevello, P., and Read, F., eds., Controls on carbonate platform and basin development: Society of Economic Paleontologists and Mineralogists Special Publication 44, p. 339–351.

Eberli, G. P., and 6 others, 1990, Simulation of the response of carbonate sequences to eustatic sea-level changes (Tertiary, northwest Great Bahama Bank): American Association of Petroleum Geologists Bulletin, v. 74, p. 647.

Guidish, T. M., Lerche, I., Kendall, C.G.St.C., and O'Brien, J. J., 1984, Relation-ship between eustatic sea-level changes and basement subsidence: American Association of Petroleum Geologists Bulletin, v. 68, p. 164–177.

Gutenberg, B., 1941. Changes in sea-level, post glacial uplift, and mobility of the earth's interior: Bulletin of the Geological Society of America, v. 52, p. 721–772.

Haq, B., Hardenbol, J., and Vail, P. R., 1987, Chronology of fluctuating sea-levels since the Triassic (250 million years to present): Science, no. 235, p. 1156–1167.

Hardenbol, J., Vail, P. R., and Ferrer, J., 1981, Interpreting paleoenvironments, subsidence history, and sea-level changes of passive margins from seismic and biostratigraphy: Oceanology Acta, Proceedings, 26th International Geology Congress Geology of Continental Margins, Symposium, Paris, 7–17, 1980, p. 33–44.

Harris, P. M., Frost, S. H., Seiglie, G. A., and Schneidermann, N., 1984, Regional unconformities and depositional cycles, Cretaceous of Arabian Peninsula, *in* Schlee, J. S., ed., Inter-regional unconformities and hydrocarbon accumulations: American Association of Petroleum Geologists Memoir, no. 36, p. 67–80.

Harrison, C.G.A., Brass, G. W., Saltzman, E., Sloan, J., II, Southam, J., and Whitman, J. M., 1981, Sea-level variations, global sedimentation rates and the hypsographic curve: Earth and Planetary Science Letters, v. 54, p. 1–16.

Jervey, M. T., 1988, Quantitative geological modelling of siliciclastic rock sequences and their seismic expression, *in* Wilgus, C. K., Hastings, B., Kendall, C.G.St.C., Posamentier, H., Ross, C., and Van Wagoner, J. C., eds., Sea-level changes–An integrated approach: Society of Economic Paleontologists and Mineralogists Publication 42, p. 47–70.

Kendall, C.G.St.C., and Lowrie, A., 1990, Simulation modeling of stratigraphic sequences along the Louisiana offshore: Gulf Coast Association of Geological Societies, Transactions, v. 40, p. 355–362.

Kendall, C.G.St.C., Bowen, B., Alsharhan, A., Cheong, D., and Stoudt, D., 1991, Eustatic controls on carbonate facies in reservoirs, and seals associated with Mesozoic hydrocarbon fields of the Arabian Gulf and the Gulf of Mexico: Marine Geology, v. 102, p. 215–238.

Muthig, M. G., Calquhoun, D. J., and Kendall, C.G.St.C., 1990, Sequence stratigraphy of the Black Mingo Group (lower Tertiary) in South Carolina [expanded abs.]: Bald Island Conference, 2nd, Hilton Head, South Carolina, Nov. 6–11.

Posamentier, H. W., Jervey, M. T., and Vail, P. R., 1988, Eustatic controls on clastic deposition 1—Conceptual framework, *in* Wilgus, C. K., Hastings, B. S., Kendall, C.G.St.C., Posamentier, H. W., Ross, C. A., and Van Wagoner, J. C., eds., Sea-level changes—An integrated approach: Society of Economic Paleontologists and Mineralogists Special Publication 42, p. 109–125.

Ross, W. C., and Ross, J.R.P., 1988, Late Paleozoic transgressive-regressive deposition, *in* Wilgus, C. K., Hastings, B. S., Kendall, C.G.St.C., Posamentier, H. W., Ross, C. A., and Van Wagoner, J. C., eds., Sea-level changes—An integrated approach: Society of Economic Paleontologists and Mineralogists Special Publication 42, p. 227–248.

Sarg, J. F., 1986, Second day–Facies and stratigraphy of the upper San Andres Basin margin and lower Grayburg inner shelf, *in* Moore, G., and Wilde, G. L., eds., Lower-Middle Guadelupian facies, stratigraphy, and reservoir geometries, San Andres/Grayburg Formations, Guadalupe Mountains, New Mexico and Texas: Society of Economic Paleontologists and Mineralogists, Permian Basin Section, Publication 86-25, p. 83–94.

——, 1988, Carbonate sequence stratigraphy, *in* Wilgus, C. K., Hastings, B. S., Kendall, C.G.St.C., Posamentier, H. W., Ross, C. A., and Van Wagoner, J. C., eds., Sea-level changes—An integrated approach: Society of Economic Paleontologists and Mineralogists Special Publication 42, p. 155–181.

Strobel, J., Cannon, R., Kendall, C.G.St.C., Biswas, G., and Bezdek, J., 1989, Interactive (SEDPAK) simulation of clastic and carbonate sediments in shelf to basin settings: Computers and Geoscience, v. 15, p. 1279–1290.

Vail, P., 1988, Seismic stratigraphy interpretation using sequence stratigraphy, Pt. 1: Seismic stratigraphy interpretation procedure, *in* Bally, A. W., ed., Atlas of seismic stratigraphy: Techniques papers and method oriented papers: American Association of Petroleum Geologists Studies in Geology, no. 27, v. 1, p. 1–10.

Vail, P. R. and 7 others, 1977, Seismic stratigraphy and global changes of sea-level, *in* Seismic stratigraphy—Applications to hydrocarbon exploration: American Association of Petroleum Geologists Memoir, No. 26, p. 49–212.

Vail, P. R., Hardenbol, J., and Todd, R. G., 1984, Jurassic unconformities, chronostratigraphy and sea-level changes from seismic and biostratigraphy, *in* Schlee, J. S., ed., Interregional unconformities and hydrocarbon accumulation: American Association of Petroleum Geologists Memoir, no. 36, p. 347–363.

Van Hinte, J. E., 1976a, A Jurassic time scale: American Association of Petroleum Geologists Bulletin, v. 60, p. 489–497.

——, 1976b, A Cretaceous time scale: American Association of Petroleum Geologists Bulletin, v. 60, p. 498–516.

Vella, P., 1961, Terms for real and apparent height changes of sea-level and parts of the lithosphere: Transactions of the Royal Society of New Zealand, v. 1, p. 101–109.

Wanless, H. R., and Shepard, F. P., 1936, Sea-level and climatic changes related to late Paleozoic cycles: Geological Society of America Bulletin, v. 47, p. 1177–1206.

Watts, A. B., and Steckler, M. S., 1979, Subsidence and eustasy at the continental margin of eastern North America, *in* Deep Drilling Results in the Atlantic Ocean, Ewing Series, v. 3, p. 218–234.

Wells, A. J., 1960, Cyclic sedimentation: A review: Geological Magazine, v. 97, p. 389–403.

MANUSCRIPT ACCEPTED BY THE SOCIETY JANUARY 14, 1992

Index

[Italic page numbers indicate major references]

Typeset by WESType Publishing Services, Inc., Boulder, Colorado
Printed in U.S.A. by Malloy Lithographing, Inc., Ann Arbor, Michigan